A NET IN WATER

A NET IN WATER

A Selection from the Journals of
MARY CASEY

edited by
Judith M. Lang and Louise de Bruin

First published in Great Britain by
THE POWYS PRESS
Hamilton's, Kilmersdon,
near Bath, Somerset, BA3 5TE

*The Powys Press is an imprint
of The Powys Society*

© 1994
Gerard Casey

300 copies have been printed.
Of these, 26 copies, lettered A–Z, have
been cloth-bound for presentation.

ISBN 1 874559 10 4

set in Monotype Plantin by Stephen Powys Marks
Printed in Great Britain by Antony Rowe Ltd, Chippenham, Wiltshire

'being moistened with life,
　　　　like a net in water'

Plotinus, *Ennead* IV.3.9

Editors' note

Mary Casey kept her journal almost daily between 1963 and 1980. In preparing this selection our aim has been to give the reader a representative choice of the original material, which fills ten large, mainly hardback, exercise books. Most entries are given in their entirety. Punctuation has been changed occasionally, and misspellings have been corrected.

* An asterisk indicates that there is an endnote on pages 223–229.

Preliminary

Mary Casey was born on 8 October in 1915. Her mother Lucy Amelia was the youngest of the eleven children of the Revd Charles Francis Powys, Vicar of Montacute in Somerset, and his wife Mary Cowper Johnson. In 1911 Lucy married R. G. H. (Hounsell) Penny, a friend of her brother Will. Mary was their only child. She passed her childhood and youth in Hampshire, at Horsebridge Mill on the river Test, which was owned and run by her father, until in poor health he retired to Shootash Hill near Romsey in 1938.

Mary married Gerard Casey in 1945, the year of her father's death. The following year they went out to Kenya, where her husband was already farming with her uncle and godfather, Will Powys. By the end of 1947 the Caseys were established on their own farm, The Beale.

The Beale stood on the slopes of Mount Kenya, between two of her uncle's larger farms. In 1956 they acquired another farm lower down at Ndere, beyond an area of forest reserve, where they built a cottage, known as Spring Cottage (or Springs Cottage). They had about 5,000 sheep at The Beale, and about 2,000 head of cattle on the more spacious ground at Ndere. In the late 1950s Gerard suffered from severe encephalitis, an illness that recurred at intervals for over ten years and necessitated a reduction in his activities. Part of the Beale farm was leased in 1964, the rest – including the Beale house – in 1969. By 1971 the farm had been sold to the Kenyan Government on behalf of the African Land Settlement Scheme. Gerard continued at Ndere; in time turning the farm there into a co-operative. He handed over its general management to Mbui Manyara (Mlefu), his headman for many years, but remained one of the directors until the mid-1980s.

From 1963 – the year this selection from Mary's journals begins – the Caseys began to spend longer periods in England, at first staying with Mary's mother in Mappowder, Dorset. Later they were able to buy the cottage next door. Mary's love for England, and her close relationship with her mother, drew her to Mappowder more and more, until she found herself torn between Kenya and Dorset. It is evident from her journals that this tension was never resolved, even after she finally decided to remain in England.

Mary Casey received most of her education at home; of delicate health, she attended school hardly at all, except for a two-year period at a girls' school in Weymouth. With her mother and other members of the Powys family she shared a lasting love of nature and literature. She read widely in both ancient and modern literature from many cultures, East and West, teaching herself a number of languages – from German and French to Greek, Chinese and Hebrew – in order to read the original texts. Her attachment to the Powys family was strong. As a young woman she discovered in the wife of her uncle Llewelyn, Alyse Gregory, in particular, a close affinity of spirit, which she later movingly expressed in some of her finest poems.

Her passionate need for intellectual understanding culminated in her intense response to the thought of the Neoplatonic philosopher Plotinus. Between 1966 and 1969 she wrote a 'visionary recital' of his life, *The Kingfisher's Wing*, which was published posthumously by Rigby and Lewis in 1987. But it was her friendship with the poet Valentine Ackland that touched the springs of her poetic genius; only after meeting Valentine in 1966 did Mary Casey begin in earnest to write poetry. During her lifetime very few of her poems appeared in print. Since her death three volumes of these have been published: *Full Circle* and *Christophorus* (Enitharmon Press, 1981), and *The Clear Shadow* (Rigby and Lewis, 1992).

In keeping her journal faithfully for most of her life (this selection ends shortly before her death in January 1980) Mary Casey was pleased to claim companionship with many other diarists, known and unknown – including other members of the Powys family – who have recognised the value of this art. She borrowed from Walter Scott the term 'ephemeris' for her daily capture of an essence of passing time. 'As with some of my Victorian prototypes, I come here to refresh my mind,' she wrote in 1970; and earlier in the same year: 'One of the things about writing a journal is the discovery of oneself in the mere choice of what to write each day. Mind skims through the hours without, the timeless moods passions wonders within, as with a magic wand ... which touches now the minute of watching in the muddy track an emerald dove, walking and pecking unalarmed – the greenness flashing.' 'Within' and 'without'; as her pen met its shadow on the page the words written gave expression to a conjunction in her mind of inner and outer experience.

The flowering oat grass a shimmering net; the entelecheia of the created world, of the thoughts that intersect it, retreat from, embrace, penetrate, shake, vivify it and receive invisible life from it, this I would win with pen-point, set fairly on a ruled page ...

(24 February 1964)

Albrecht Dürer T.L.S. 3.12.71.
but all his work, written, engraved,
cut into wood, painted and drawn
— came, as he himself said, from
"the gathered secret treasure of
the heart."

Even for individual intuitions
outward expression is necessary,
as a Sacrament in which the
minister and recipient are one   123

All aesthetic experience is feeling
arising out of the realization of
contrast under identity   101

<u>Religion in the Making</u>.

art is a mode of
Contemplation

Flyleaf of the Journal starting July 1971

1963

2 January, Kenya   Welcome to my heart were two letters from Mother after the interval of Christmas. Through the sunny afternoon the three men working on the grass roof on the car shed talked interminably, one on high against the sky in more than sky-blue shorts, lashed together the grass already tied in small bundles by those below and passed up to him in a kind of faggot, secured by a cord. For some reason the shed looks like a Japanese erection: its not steep pitch, a rustic ladder leaning on it, and two tall leggy trees flanking either side, mere sticks with a tuft of foliage on the top. The gloom under the fringed eaves gives a sense of coolness to the little garden bright with flowers.

3 January   This evening we went to Sirakoi,* all the cattle are there now, nearly a thousand, with twelve Kipsigis to watch them night and day. The place above the Duggle-Bear Drift is beautiful with graceful thorn trees as well as those round flattish bushes of thorn which become so swiftly impenetrable if you wander into ground they forbid. The lime-green trunks and branches of the *mareras* were gilded by the last sunlight of the day as Guy's cattle moved along the slope on the other side of the stream. The last bland moonflower-scented night of our New Year stay at the cottage of grass and cedar.

5 January   Snow has come to Dorset and I feel anxious for Mother in the cold weather. First she wrote of two inches, then seven; today's letter told of drifts ten to twelve feet high between Mappowder and Buckland. Now the newspaper says Dorset has had yet more snow, since Mother's latest letter was sent. She describes so well the perfect silence of the village with no traffic and the air hushed after the blizzard.

16 January   Katie's* death on Friday 11th is the news I found at Timau this morning. It was eleven days since I had heard from Mother; there were two letters, and the first told of her walk from Mappowder to Buckland through deep snow, the last as it proved of her many pilgrimages to Katie for the past two years. After a heart attack Katie had a slight stroke and Mother was warned by the doctor she would not live more than a day or two. One can only think of it as a liberation after so long-drawn-out a season of decay. Now come the swift visions and memories through all the years of our friendship: the clearest, Katie waving her stick exultant.

17 January   Under the rug I lay listening to the wind, the inland wind that blows, one would say by the sound, across the sea. I thought of Katie so much in the day, seeing especially the red earthenware basin and ewer she used for so many years for her morning and evening washing. Now she lies buried in the chalky soil of East Chaldon which must always seem more than any other Theodore's* village, where he wrote his books and lived with his melancholy.

19 January   When someone dies who has known you from childhood, you lose, it may seem, not only their living presence, their affection and the reciprocities you had with them, and could have, in just that way, with no other fellow being, but also that part of yourself that was the you they received and valued.

20 January   A heavy shower this Sunday afternoon was followed by a really wet evening, to put a stop to all shearing tomorrow. Gerard and I helped to drive in the ewes and lambs and then came home soaked through and thankful to jump into our hot bath. I have the weariness tonight that is always the companion of sorrow, a different thing from ordinary physical or even nervous exhaustion, an indefinable all-pervasive malaise that is part of the mystery of death when it is someone you love who is gone.

21 January   More rain and no shearing at all. Gerard and I went to Timau and found delayed Christmas mail, and the unwelcome news that England is again deep in snow. There was a letter from Mother written on the day of Katie's funeral. She saw good Mrs. Lucas* in bed in Chaldon. Neither Francis* nor Isobel* were well enough to be at the funeral, but their children Stephen and Anne were there. Mother was very tired and worn by the bitter cold continually to be endured. But Kathleen* was looking after her in every way in Katie's house. She was going to return to Mappowder and her frostbound home on Saturday morning. O, I do hope she will be safe.

25 January   Violent storms of rain with dazzling clouds and sunshine between gave me the sense of living high in heaven among the rainbows and tempests and looking down like Zeus on forest and plain and the works of men. There is no Katie now to share the endless joy of weather watching: I see her a white seagull flying over High Chaldon and out to the Atlantic Ocean.

27 January Meister Eckhart reminds me in his preaching of what I have read of Zen, that we can do nothing, and that to do nothing, to close the five parts of knowledge, is better than any action whatsoever. All, it seems to me, that can follow from this is to let the mind at all times dwell upon this nothingness, to recollect that though unattainable it is the way of peace, to believe in it through grace. This inward concentration of the soul or contemplation in stillness is not, is far other than, the idleness I was taught to shun and which has made it a point of conscience with me to be occupied with mind or hands all the day long: with things which I consider as 'useful or intellectual'. What might be one's state after true contemplation I can guess by the bliss I know now and again when I wake in the early morning after a sleep of utter oblivion. I think nothing can compare with the happiness of nerves thus fully refreshed and in the most sensitive yet secure harmony. Swiftly with waxing day the mood passes but the fulfilment is not altogether lost.

2 February Rowland George Hounsell Penny.* How the names so carefully chosen and given to the child at his baptism form themselves into all that belongs to him for his own life and for the life that is left in those who have known him. Think of Katie's fine names: Catharine Edith Philippa Powys; saying them over just now it came to me as if I hadn't known before that she was no more. Catullus is in the book of the Loeb Classics that I am reading and I found him in the Encyclopaedia with that excitement that at certain times seems to arise from a mysterious mingling of one's own intangible invisible essence or aura with the same imperishable and timeless fragrance of another mind, or the art that is its immortality, that triumphs through and by the *nox est perpetua una dormienda.** Though whether I shall be able to read his lyrics I cannot say. Gerard was kept at home by pain this evening and I walked with the dogs.

18 February Copies of Katie's will and wishes came this morning, the latter in her own handwriting photographed. It did move me to see her writing and read her own words both so characteristic and inimitable. I felt a touch of some of what Mother must have gone through. There was also in the mail a long letter from Redwood* very welcome to us, and a printed poem, an addition to *While the Fates Allow*. After a heavy thunder shower in the evening I walked alone and as I returned I left the track to avoid fast-flowing flood water and my tread disturbed a tiny bird which flew away in the gloaming a few inches above the ground. Bending down I could just discern the roofed grass-built nest of a cisticola, with lining of some white down.

21 February 'Let us bless the Lord.' The words as he uttered them at the Compline services that first summer at Mappowder are always on Theodore's* lips when I think of him, and I hear the very tone of his voice. Reading Meister Eckhart I like to think the book was in his hands also and I watch for his marks, the lines by which he put a very short sharp pencil mark, and the sign which indicated where his reading came to an end for the day.

26 February From the time we left the Beale on Sunday morning in mist and rain at 6 to our return here at noon today, all went well. Francis was very good at his baptism and Rose* looked charming with the little dark-eyed boy in her arms. Will* drove us back to El Pinguan and after tea we walked down with him to the formidable River Narok with its bulrushes and awe-inspiring granite masses, to see the great hydraulic scheme. A dam is being made across the river to provide a steady flow of water to a turbine which will lift a supply to the house and farm. We crawled and scrambled among the rocks to see some carved by nature into arches over the stream. All next day we spent with W.E.P. going over his 44,000 acres seeing cattle, sheep, dams, bore-holes. At the last just before sunset we went down into the Pinguan Valley to Theodore's* grave. Will is building a shearing shed of vast dimensions in a plain with boundless horizons. Elizabeth* and her friend Mrs. Carew went away during the day so we had tea alone with Will at about 7 when we came in, and a quiet evening. Charles* was driving out of the Timau Store as we were turning in, just back from South Africa and in high spirits at being home again. He'd bought six rams. Gerard and I saw the new moon at Pinguan.

4 March This day we went to Wamba. The mountain was most beautiful with blue shadows, and a violet bloom as the usual afternoon thunderstorm brewed up. The thorn trees with slender trunks and airy roof of foliage of emerald green looked enchanting against it in the storm-light. When we returned to Archer's Post the fat corporal told us our stolen cattle had been found near Isiolo. We raced there and out along the road to the Pump House only to find they were Somali cattle stolen the same day and recovered by their owners. Also on that unlucky day 130 Meru cattle were stolen, also as were ours by Samburu, and we kept encountering weary Meru who'd been following the traces of their beasts for scores of miles. Thunder pealed and rain streamed down half veiling and rendering more majestic and mysterious the desolate hills. As soon as we arrived at the cottage in the dusk with the rain-washed air loud with robins' singing we learnt a calf had just had its back broken by a leopard. And three sheep were missing at the Beale.

30 March The custom of the cows is to return slowly towards the house in the evening. Today they came in crowded together with Lucian the bull and the aged white ox Bogo early in the afternoon. They all stood without grazing, only the cows with small calves suckled them. Late after them and blaring came up a tawny cow with troubled mien. I feared for her calf. And indeed sometime after word came that it had been discovered in the glades of the forest killed by a leopard. In fact the leopard was seen lying in the grass close-by by the man who found the dead calf. The cattle remained near to the house for the rest of the afternoon, grazing by the veranda while we drank our tea, and a small flock of yellow wagtails moved lightly between their hoofs.

2 April Gilfrid's* men had a dance last night, the sounds penetrated my sleep before I woke at 11 to listen to chant and chorus punctuated by hand-clapping and stamping; pure African rhythm, primitive, touching a nerve unknown in one's everyday life. The sultry night lit by a young moon, the braying of an ass and the lowing of cattle mixed with the ruthless throbbing and sudden percussion of the games of these night-skinned children of the earth.

3 April I went for a long walk this morning to Eland Hill and beyond. When towards noon I arrived at the river I thought nothing could be more perfect than the cold water, the white falls over black rocks, the feel of it on my feet and arms, and the sound. I felt as I imagined a water nymph might, restored to her native element after an intolerable drought. When I saw Gerard again at tea-time he was full of the news of Southern Rhodesia, the bitterness of Sir Roy Welensky, the interference of America and the suggestion it should be handed over to the United Nations. The Republic of South Africa and the possibility of war, of Britain supporting the Africans against the European government of the country, all this occupied our minds; together with an article Gerard had read, while he was waiting at the court for the Samburu who of course never came so the day was wasted, by Julian Huxley in praise of evolution, or what his brother Aldous called Brave New World, that is the world liberated from God.

6 April I read last night the pamphlet on my uncles* by R. C. Churchill, reading it almost straight through with the kind of attention one gives to contemporary writing and which is quite different from the way the mind embarks on the classics. I thought the critic was sensitive and his essay well prepared, but I missed something of John, his poetry and philosophy. Gerard, who read it this morning by the stream in the forest, wondered why the historical novels were not touched on, and said he thought *Owen Glendower* one of the best. But he said he had an idea modern critics couldn't read them at all. He thought the real Theodore eluded Mr. Churchill.

14 April   Easter Day. Jupiter had risen clear above the horizon this morning. Gerard and I went to church at Timau. Someone came into the pew behind us and I heard a fine rubbing of palms of the hands on thighs. It was Charles making his Powys gesture.

22 April   Mother's Wedding Day 1911. How strange it all is, and it is the memory of the individual which at a certain level gives life its significance. Mnemosyne to whom John prayed, the mother of the Muses, and who now has all but forsaken him, is the reality of one's own life; and is hardest to think of as being no more. There is in Cowper's letters no theology or metaphysics, which might have helped him in his darkness, but only the shadow of his idea that he was utterly condemned by God, or now and again a rare gleam that perhaps after all he was not an utter outcast. His was of course the Age of Reason: all is carefully ordered. An exclamation like this I read today is unique: 'O, I could spend whole days and moonlight nights in feeding upon a lovely prospect. My eyes drink the rivers as they flow.'

18 May   Two letters from Mother today gave me more news of Phyllis.* She is in Llandudno hospital and by now must have had an operation for a tumour in her side. J.C.P.* is in the Blaenau hospital. Isobel went there and arranged for him to go into hospital; she wrote that he did not know her but seemed to miss Phyllis. We have had two days of brilliant sunshine. Most of the men have gone to vote, the ones Gerard took to Timau early this morning have not come back. Only Mugambi* is here, he has given up his vote to look after us. After three days they all vote again, and a third time next weekend.

20 May   By candlelight I say good night to this Monday. Gerard and I had a happy evening with Will and Elizabeth with good conversation and fine candles burning on the supper table in silver candelabra. Then we saddled our ponies and rode home by starlight. The black cuckoo mourned in the trees by the spring when we came to the cottage and a hyena was whooping. But when we came here in the afternoon the sun was bright and between the medley of flowers of every colour countless swallows wove to and fro.

5 June I copied out another Chinese poem, a snow scene, incomparable and untranslatable, four lines of five characters each, though now and again I feel for English words, trying one and another. Clouds darkened the day; the evening was fine with a chill wind and sorrowful wet grass and plaintive pipit pipings at dusk.

8 June The last night at the Beale. Gerard and I have had a quiet day walking in the forest and on Windy Hill, as the clouds came and went and the sun shone, with Foam, Slate, Karoi, Moss.* Yes, a happy day between the rising of Venus and the four stars of the Cross.

11 June, Mappowder Barnaby bright all day and no night. A perfect summer day with sun and voices of thrush and blackbird and cuckoo. We came to Mother's cottage in the afternoon. The door was open under the clematis, and I found Mother sitting in the garden, all unthinking we had arrived, because the plane was delayed and I had sent her a telegram from Entebbe saying we shouldn't be with her for another two days. That time of waiting, all one night, at Entebbe, the day by the lake, the wild goose-chase to Kampala, are all forgotten now. Mother, Gerard and I walked on Theodore's field and in the freshly mown hay.

12 June The south-east wind had an edge tonight but our walk in the fields and woods was one of enchantment, so deep were the coverts of leaves, the meads with grass and flowers. In the highest corner of a grassy slope newly mown by the edge of Crooked Oak two blackcaps were singing, and a chiff-chaff, and as we waited and listened while far away on the muffled side of Nettlecombe a cuckoo called, a nightingale gave some fragments of that music that one recognises by the way it strikes the heart.

14 June, Corwen Under a cloud-bound sky Gerard drove Mother and me into Wales. The most romantic part of the journey was following the valley of the Dee from Llangollen to Corwen, the heavy-laden trees and the precipitous hillsides veiled by haze and sunlight lighting on green sprays and green pastures between the river and mountain where sheep grazed. With Mother we walked for over two hours on the Gawr, delighting in the flowers and the many birds. All round the earth and stone defences of the ancient camp we walked among springing bracken and sheep and looking down on the fields and river, across to the town and the Berwyns and Pen-y-Pigyn. The cracked bell chimes.

15 June, Maentwrog At the inn called The Grapes with a chill rain or mist coming up the estuary of the Afon on the south wind from Harlech of the many sand dunes. The day-time hours were like Kenya with clear sunshine and strong keen winds, but in this long slow-fading summer gloaming, we all have a sense of sorrow and deprivation after seeing Uncle Jack.* He has gone far away into a world of his own where he makes signs and gestures with white lean powerless yet fearfully eloquent hands and the tones of his voice, now articulate, now wordless, so well remembered come as if from beyond the tomb. Phyllis, recovering from her operation, was with him in his room in the Blaenau Hospital, she indeed looks better than when we saw her last. Blaenau was *en fête*, bunting across the street, swinging-boats, band playing martial airs, balloons let go by the variegated crowd, floating up over the blue roofs of slate across the gray slate tips, across the stern mountain face to vanish in the sunny azure skies. Before the hospital, the green vale of the Afon with thickets and clustering groups of trees ran down between mountains towards the sea; white gulls flew back and forth, black daws fluttered over the hospital roof.

18 June When we came to Mother's cottage at 3.30 this afternoon we found a note from Mrs. Vallence* on the table to say Uncle Jack died after a heart attack yesterday evening. We are all going to rest for a few hours and then start at midnight to return to Blaenau Ffestiniog. Mother has to sign something before he can be cremated. I pray she will not be too tired. Poor Phyllis.

19 June Our night drive went well, there was still light in the west when we started at 11.15, and the first trace of dawn showed soon after 2 a.m. We were at Blaenau at 7. The matron received Mother into the hospital and gave her a hot bath. Phyllis was prostrate with sorrow and we did not see her. But Gerard and I went to Colwyn Bay to arrange about the cremation tomorrow. We are staying tonight in a funny old Victorian hotel called The Queen's, right under the gray mountain and slate tips. We met Gamel Woolsey* at the station and drove her to 1, Waterloo* where she is spending the night. I did feel sad standing in Phyllis's room but I like to think Gamel is sleeping there.

20 June Among the little white and gray houses under the mountain are the painted toys of last week's carnival, and caravans blue and red and yellow, and washing of gypsy colours hung out, all forlornly gay at the foot of a Gibraltar-like rock with mist-crowned peak. We followed Uncle Jack's coffin to Colwyn Bay, Mother, Gerard and I and Gamel, and Gerard helped to carry the coffin into the building where all was to be consumed. Phyllis was better today, we all spent some time with her and she talked freely. To Gerard and me she offered Uncle Jack's Greek books; we have taken his Homer, Homeric Lexicon, New Testament and *Prometheus Bound*. In the upstairs room we looked into one or two of the many volumes of his diaries, so closely written all over the pages in every direction. The last of these red-bound books was for 1961, the entries grew briefer, the writing larger; the last was for 28 May, except for a final shaky one on October 28, verses he'd scrawled before on several other pages

> I am the god Thor
> This is my hammer main
> Against which of sorcerers and demons
> None can prevail.

This is from memory and not right. Mother is sleeping in our room tonight. Mists close down over Blaenau.

21 June Home at last, the drive of about 250 miles safely accomplished, the songs of thrush and blackbird sounding musically on the chill and murky air. There are robins too and hedge-sparrows, but no wrens, all or almost all were slain by the great cold of last winter, and I miss so much the tiny creatures and their joyous song. Gerard is staying here now another week before he goes to Ireland. One happy thing of this last visit to Blaenau is having made friends with Gamel whom I have heard of for many years and who is so charming and intelligent.

26 June Uncle Jack's ashes came by post this morning, we had planned to go to Dorchester on the bus so we took them with us and there hired a taxi to carry us to that beach beyond Abbotsbury where it is our custom to go on each of our sessions at Mappowder. The whole day has been fine, even warm now and then, and though there was haze there was faint sunshine on the sea as the high waves came crashing over on to the shingle, spread in immaculate foam and withdrew sucking back the noisy pebbles. Where the stones were already wet and dark Gerard spread the ash, then we three stood still and silent looking upon the sea until one of the arching waves was shed over them and sank back carrying with it the last earthly vestiges of John Cowper Powys. Βῆ δ' ἀκέων παρὰ θῖνα πολυφλοίσβοιο θαλάσσης.*

27 June The joy of this morning was the song of a wren in an oak tree when Gerard and I were walking back after calling on Louis.* I heard the song several times and saw the tiny bird with upturned tail among the oak leaves. A pair of goldfinches is often in Mother's garden. We all three walked in the evening to the gate into the common by those favourite wood-shielded meadows. Chiff-chaff were calling. Mother and I went into Mrs. Garrett's cottage where she has lived for half a century. She is eighty-four and can no longer go to Dorchester, to her sorrow. But she is full of lively talk. ('I said to her, Violet,* you don't want to go and live in no copse'), and showed us photographs of her granddaughter's wedding, and more remarkable, one of her mother.

6 July Cousin Marion,* the Poor Clare, who since her youth has been in this closed order, wrote to sympathise with Mother after J.C.P.'s death. I thought he would have liked her words: 'I was wild with excitement for a week before when I knew he was coming to stay.' I see now from the window a red round sun as on a frosty winter afternoon, hail to the sun which from early morning till 6 this evening was lost in a most gloomy and impenetrable cloud canopy from which almost ceaseless rain fell. At that hour Mother and I went out to walk on the wet roads, we rescued a slow-worm we found motionless with raised head in the road not far from Theodore's house. Then we saw a rainbow.

17 July Valentine Ackland,* that accomplished lady to whom Katie was so singularly devoted, called today to collect a few books from the house at Buckland. She has some mysterious and perilous disease which may involve a tricky operation, she is seeing her doctor in London in a few days and may then know something more definite. She brought to show Mother an embossed gilded casket (late eighteenth-century she said) which at a touch opened and revealed a tiny iridescent feathered bird which turning this way and that with quivering wings and opening bill seemed to sing. The clearest of musical bird-notes rose from the bird-adorned casket until on a sudden the singer vanished and the lid closed with a snap.

6 August Gerard walked in Melcombe Park alone yesterday discovering the ways; he saw a deer. Today we all three went there with a little picnic. Doves cooed in the shadowy depths of the wood, and I kept thinking of 'all that forest ground called Thessaly'. Instead of a deer I saw a pair of vipers close to me in the rough grassy track but both twining away. I had just thought, 'There may be adders I must walk in front of Mother.' Further on at a gate we saw a pair of skins hanging up of two snakes that had been killed. At the foot of Nettlecombe Tout (as Bosworth* has it) we sat on an oak trunk to eat our biscuits and apples. Doves are still brooding eggs in their rickety stick cribs.

13 August, Queen's, Nairobi　Llewelyn's* birthday. Before noon on Sunday we left Mother and her home, where we had been so happy, on a day of piercing storm sunshine and purple shadows – and the young cuckoo was in the garden all the morning – for London. On Monday morning Gerard and I went out from London to Sible Hedingham to see Redwood at Lamb Cottage. He was in bed recovering from an attack of bronchitis, but what makes Gwyneth* more anxious for him is that his heart is not good now. Between this and his blindness he is often sad so Gerard was very glad we went to see him. On our return to London we bought Schuon's new book *Understanding Islam*, translated by Matheson, at Foyles, and then went off to Gatwick. The flight was well accomplished.

16 August, The Beale　Peals of thunder and fearsome lightning signalled our departure from Nairobi and very soon we drove into sheets of rain. The drive was slow, the rain began again at Nyeri and continued most of the way home, it is strange to have so much in August. Gerard brought me a letter from Mother today to my comfort.

17 August　To see again the stars, shining bright in high heaven. Orion and great Jupiter and the waning moon. And in a little while the mountain showed, clear but very dark. How complex are my woes, folding over one another, interleaved and ever menacing from incalculable depths below the common plane: I gaze and then like Zeus turn away my shining eyes.

19 August　I would like, were it possible, to enter in my journal something more of my contemplative moods and of my, shall I say, intuition of metaphysics, in place of vignettes of each day, some scene that has pleased me, some forest perspective or a bird song that has made my soul vibrant with anguish and joy. But I know I can only reach towards the former as it were slantwise and by way of an expectant waiting upon the latter. And it is not otherwise with prayer.

21 August　Tony* found me weeding in the kitchen garden this morning. He said first that Elizabeth was very seriously ill in Nanyuki hospital, that Rose was with her, and a specialist coming from Nairobi in the afternoon. Gerard didn't see him though I thought they might meet on the road. Gerard and I talked of The Pasternak Affair in our evening walk. For all Thomas Merton's sincerity and zeal and devotion to solitude I have a kind of distaste for the flavour of some of his writing.

22 August　After dark tonight good old Twarochio* drove down here with a note from Will, a brief note in shaky writing, to say we must cancel our meeting with him planned for tomorrow evening because Elizabeth was in hospital and he was staying 'around Nanyuki till she is better'. Gerard and I rode to Ndere to telephone the hospital this morning. The sister said there was very slight improvement. Will was staying at the hospital and the children at the Silverbeck hotel. So the cloud that is not at all unknown is over me again, my heart is weighted, my mind torpid. The note for Gerard with its affection was very moving, and so also was Twarochio's troubled face in the light of the lamp I carried out.

23 August The passion-fruit leaves on their trellis, the window frame, even the couch in Gertrude's* painting that Will kept a little time and then gave to us, caught some happy reflection and new lightness of tone from the late afternoon sunshine as I went into the big room, and something about the green of those leaves woke hope in my heart for Elizabeth. Rose, when Gerard spoke to her this morning on the telephone, was most sad and anxious for her mother, saying she had septicaemia as well as the original pneumonia.

29 August Zeus loudly thundered as we were starting to go to Elizabeth's funeral and a blue-black cloud was before us until we ran into its rain. Hills and mountain, all the landscape, was mist-veiled and exquisite with the fugitive lights of stormy weather. It was not until we were on our way home that a gleam of sun touched the dark ploughed lands and fields of ripe barley. Will all in black with his policeman's cape on his shoulders, his silver hair and ruddy face was the dominating figure in the large gathering in the cemetery where the service was held. His profile was all the time perfectly still and his look far away. Elizabeth's sons Charles and Gilfrid, her sons-in-law David* and Tony, carried the coffin. It was interesting to see that look of intentness and even satisfaction at *dealing with matter* showing through the set in sadness expressions of the young men when the time came to move out the supporting pieces of timber on which the polished coffin with silver handles was resting over the deep dug grave, and to lower it by means of a massive cable down into the ground. There had been no strangers, no black hearse. Here she comes, Gerard muttered, as though she still lived. And there was Charles alone driving the cream-coloured car which even so was not long enough, the two doors at the back could not shut and had to be tied together against the end of his mother's coffin. When Richard Carles* had read his last prayer to the damp windy air, and the service for the Burial of the Dead was over, I felt reluctant to leave that quiet place of grass-covered graves marked for the most part with simple stones. A few men, as the crowd moved away, went singly to the newly-dug grave and looked into it with bleak faces. I spoke to no one. Only Dorothy* came up to me in silence and gave me a kiss. We all went this evening to see Charles and Jennifer* at Kisima.* Jennifer, dressed in green and nearing the end of her pregnancy, welcomed us, and Charles presently came back from Nanyuki. He looked very well and very huge with shining eyes. 'Gilfrid's coming to supper,' he said joyfully, 'I must see the cook.' He said Gilfrid had given up his post as game warden and was going to live with Will at Pinguan. Mother's letter today told me that Phyllis was going to stay with her, driven all the way by the invaluable Mr. Davies.*

4 September Mother's letter of 1 September by my side, how thankful I am to have it. Phyllis was with her when she had the news of Elizabeth's death; together they went to Montacute and to see Alyse.* This evening we rode on Ndere with John,* all the farm is dry again, the uncropped grass the hue of ripe barley. Four giraffe surveyed us, making various patterns on the azure sky. I sank into the deepest sleep last night and woke at 5 to see again the stars feeling I had known the most perfect fulfilment: perhaps after being with Rose, with whom in some way all tensions cease.

7 September To learn to have regard for certain exquisite privileges, to take nothing for granted, is something that comes only with growing old and preparing for the end and has part, it may be, in that becoming again as a little child. The wind with great bluster, wrestling as it seemed with itself, veered from east of west this afternoon and blew then from the west till dark. The first night for so long since I've had all my books at my side – and now a cold binds faculties and senses, is a weariness on head and limbs.

9 October A happy moment late in the afternoon when the sun shone after a sparkling shower; all was transformed, all colours heightened: the feathers of sunbird of dove of starling; red flowers and blades of grass. I dreamed last night, after reading Jung while Gerard played chess, of a long timber bridge of rotting planks and crumbling posts over a measureless depth of dark green water. I crossed over it once in safety though holes opened under my feet and the boards broke. But as soon as I reached the opposite bank it was necessary for some reason to return, to re-cross the perilous bridge. When I was about half way over it gave way and I sank unalarmed into the waiting water.

11 October The dogs killed a jackal this evening. When Gerard went to make sure it was dead he found it had a snare round its throat, it was weak from starvation and we were glad they had put an end to it. The suffering of animals is something to be reckoned with in thought, it always seems to strike right to the core of my love of life.

27 October The strangest sight this evening when we decided at sunset to leave the blaze of the grass fire to its own devices was a group of ostriches far off across the black plain moving this way and that as if in distress. It could only be that they quitted their nest before the blast of the fire and after it had swept on returned to the site of their nest, with no doubt many eggs, laid by several hens, and found nothing but destruction. The fire was advancing on a front of many miles when we left, but slowly as the wind forsook it. However there is a fine glow staining the white clouds to the north as though it is burning back in the direction whence it arose. Swallows from England hawked for flies keeping just ahead of the flames, and at one point through the smother and glare a few white storks appeared standing without motion as though they were like the Phoenix.

24 November In vain the mother ran slowly as if allowing the dogs to believe they would catch her, in vain the fawn lay still in his bright coat on a bank of red earth. I went on grieved at heart with his last bleats in my ears. Sad over the fawn I did not write at all last night. Late this afternoon a cow came up the fence with deep lowing calling her calf. This cow was suckling two calves, an orphan one as well as her own, and we learnt at night both are gone, they must be dead, killed perhaps by a leopard in the forest.

25 November Gerard found the two calves sleeping together early this morning when the jade dew was on the grass. It is exciting at this time before sunrise when this virid grass seems to reflect its greenness upon the lucent sky, or else you are tempted to think the piercing heavenly green enhances the colour of the grass. High in the clear air buzzards mew their aubade.

2 December What strikes me most in *The Mystical Theology of the Eastern Church** is the mediaeval sense of the nearness of heaven, a real perceptible heaven, and so far there hasn't been a word of eternal damnation, as well as of intimate awareness of the Communion of Saints. My puritan nature is less happy with the mystical fervour of Orthodox worship, and the Trinity being considered as it were before the metaphysical Truth, the Godhead, does not allow of a pure metaphysical approach. On the other hand there is little of morals in this book which so limit religion and deprive it of its highest significance. With the emphasis on grace and the Holy Spirit I am in full sympathy.

6 December It is interesting to see what one can make oneself do in one's worst, most contradictory moods; set hands to their task, content the heart, even keep attention and ὑπομονή * before the mind. But, surprised by another human being, there is first anger, afterwards pride and despair. Unlike yesterday this afternoon brought a torrent of rain, the flood-dragon whelming all, changing the very substance, as it seemed, of earth and herb; rocks turned gargoyles, tangled roots in their dynamic motionlessness having features malign. We walked in less violent rain to the lambing camp, helped to drive in the ewes laden with wool and water and young. New born lambs chilled and helpless bleated feebly. Gerard and I returned in the darkness, with now and then a blinding flash of lightning, wet through.

22 December Will came to tea, the first time I think he has come to the Beale since Elizabeth's death. I felt a certain anxiety for him, thinking he didn't look quite as well as when he went to England. He didn't say much about Mother, and Mappowder, but spoke of being on Portland Bill with her and Phyllis, and of seeing the Goya and Corot exhibitions.

29 December 'I have not and never have had any reserve with people I value, least of all with you, ... but that is not enough – I am aware of a want of spontaneousness ...' So wrote John Stuart Mill to Carlyle who had urged him to write to him 'with abandon'. I am, I have a notion, rather the other way round: I can write at a certain level, or on certain subjects, with at least a sense of spontaneousness, but I have innumerable underlying and deep reserves. The sky-scape today has reached the height of furious and stormy grandeur, clouds wilder than imagination, and the colours of heaven between them the purest most exquisite water-colours. At certain times the light changed almost with every breath I drew.

1964

11 January Most of the day Gerard was sorting out cattle, about 170 big calves have been weaned. In the evening we rode round Lizard Hill enjoying the greenness and the shadows among the hills as the sun sank behind them. Eland ran under the thorn trees, there were two giraffe near them, and we saw herds of impala. On the way home Venus was on our right, the mountain before us. The hill grew dark. I made a translation of the poem by Mêng Hao-Jan called 'Leaving Wang Wei', a moving poem, these brief ones are the best.

14 January Halcyon weather, each green grass blade pricking up vivid and pointed with the sinking sun behind it, the ungrazed oat grass with a dark bloom on it after the sun has gone down; coming upon it suddenly with west at one's back it is like the wine-dark sea. The sunshine through the long afternoon is a still flood of golden light in air agitated by wind, the stillness as perceptible as the commotion, intellect and emotion.

15 January I was just in my bath tonight when voices broke out and I knew there was a scare of some kind. Thieves had come to a sheep boma we'd passed a little while before in the gloaming, the sheep tranquil, blue smoke rising from the shepherd's hut. Gerard was out in the Land Rover for an hour searching, but the thieves carrying our luckless ewes on their shoulders had already vanished in the forest. And so there will be motherless lambs.

16 January A quiet day with an evening ride towards the mountains; a multitude of storks flew down after sunset, the sky will seem a desert when they have gone. Then appeared the new moon two days old, with Saturn and Venus below, and the gold and flame of sunset.

18 January This evening Karoi was pierced in the throat by a white-tusked boar which the dogs were baiting at the mouth of its hole. We were walking through the wilderness and I had a sudden panic before as they ran about in the thick bush chasing the pigs. My mind was on the revolution in Zanzibar and I said, 'I cannot stand violence and bloodshed.' Soon Karoi was crying desperately with blood streaming out of his throat. Gerard carried him most of the way home when the bleeding stopped. I read the strange account of the Pope being mobbed.

19 January I saw Mercury in the rose glow of sunrise. In the evening Jupiter, moon, Venus, Saturn; flowers of gold down the western sky before nightfall. Karoi lives though weak and bloodless. I heard him drink the milk I left by him in the night and felt hopeful then.

21 January The manifestation of human disequilibrium, as Schuon calls it, in Tanganyika has been much in our thoughts today; the revolt of the army, the chasing away of its officers, the vanishing of Nyerere, the arrival in Dar-es-Salaam of Okello who brought about the overthrow of the government in Zanzibar. What can one do but try to lead one's own life, as far as may be *en rapport* with the immanent equilibrium, and to pray.

23 January   Shearing started this morning. The evening was curious with a dense haze between us and even the nearest hills like dust that fills the valley after much traffic has passed in the driest season. At the same time there was a high wind.

24 January   Still the haze which even became rain for a few moments and gives the hills a most sad look when the sun has set. With my quiet occupations in the house and the garden, my books and writing, the hours pass and again it is night and time for dreams.

25 January   Conversation of St. Paul. How many books of how many different themes have I opened and read in today, until with books I am all but satisfied. We returned this evening in that mysterious light when the sun has set and daylight lapses into moonlight, and you wonder if your shadow from the afterglow in the west has changed into the shade cast by the moon, with tawny halo aloft in heaven's high bower.

27 January   Letters from Mother and Gertrude,* the latter from Cairo all about the city and the desert, and new books from Heffers: *The Philosophy of Plotinus* by Dean Inge, Chrétien de Troyes and a small sky-blue volume of the poems of Emily Dickinson. We went out last night in moonlight and dew-drenched grass with the mountain snows shining above us.

29 January   Moss disappeared yesterday morning and we haven't seen her again. By moonlight Gerard and I set off this morning to ride across the Beale to count some sheep and cattle. Dawn in the east was followed by a sanguine sunrise, all the small clouds tipped with fire and the unseen sun shooting up golden rays. I was sewing up bales all the afternoon; the wether fleeces are magnificent, white and clean-looking. In the gloaming I walked on Windy Hill while Gerard talked to John. Now they are playing chess.

30 January   I began reading the introduction to the small book of poems, in Cambridge blue covers, we have given ourselves by Emily Dickinson whose forefathers went to New England in the seventeenth century from Cambridgeshire. I read as far as a perfect poem on Hope. Gerard stopped the shearing rather earlier this evening and we rode to see the sheep and shepherds. Bonnie went like the wind.

31 January   The last day of the double-faced month has been, one way and another, an unsatisfactory one. A day of stresses and troubled undercurrents in our rustic life. Two or three wild dogs disappeared into the bush as we were coming up the forest track at dusk. Interplay of intimacy and secrecy is one of the qualities of the Chinese poems that endear them to my heart. The poet may take you by the hand and point to what you would not have seen, your foot moves by his, yet the mysterious is enhanced.

1 February Further sadness for Redwood is with me, as Mother says he is not improving and may live only a few weeks longer. I feel at such times I would like once more to be in touch with someone I have known well and who is soon to depart, to speak and to hear their voice again. There it is, he has had a long life: let Schuon's four things that matter sustain his mind — the instant, death, encounter with God, eternity.

2 February R.G.H.P. 1945. Charles's little Patricia was christened at Timau church. Will was there and Gilfrid with him. A thief came in the night to the shorn sheep soon after moonrise (11.15). The night watchman said, 'Who are you?' when he saw him beginning to climb over the fence into the fold. The man replied '*Mumeru*.'* 'What are you doing here?' 'Looking for sheep.' 'Wait.' The thief ran away. The Kipsigis called and blew his whistle. Gerard and four other men went out but caught nothing. The moonlight was brilliant, the wind high and cold as ice. For some time I watched the ponies and cattle.

3 February It is interesting how the patient repetitious counsel offered to monks and hesychasts in the *Philokalia*, the same theme of prayer, sobriety, strict asceticism in food and sleep and conversation, avoidance of anger and irritability, laying aside of all cares, and constant remembrance of God, how these pious often uninspired admonishments and directions for obedience to the hegemonos can yet, read day by day, communicate to the soul a sense of tranquillity, a belief in the virtues of the lives of these self-absorbed (in a sense) and devoted men that is a reserve of benevolence for all.

11 February Shrove Tuesday. Football, cock-fighting and bull-baiting were much indulged in in Shrovetide according to *Chambers Twentieth Century Dictionary*; then, I suppose, one confessed and was shriven and was ready for expiation and the great fast of Lent. Gerard rode Dan for the first time this perfect evening, he went very well. When he came in I cooked pancakes for our supper. Mother set off today to stay in London.

12 February Gerard and I rode to Ndere this Ash Wednesday morning on Danny and Bonnie. Thunder brewed up in the afternoon with fierce black cloud over an opalescent sky. I walked alone after tea while Gerard went to Meru to buy maize from Konge.* Poor Konge is in doubt and confusion and is suffering from sleeplessness. He says a man has returned from Europe who has been to all the schools – '*a mtu ya scienci*'* – who is telling the Meru there is no God, science has proved it. Then also he is disturbed by the rocket going to the moon.

14 February   My Valentine was a letter from Mother, and there came also from her a review of *Weymouth Sands* with a fine photograph of J.C.P. near the end of his life. Phyllis, Mother says, is to embark for her voyage to South America on the 18th. On his way to Nanyuki this morning Gerard met Will.

17 February   Another letter from Mother, already describing her journey and her first days in London, how I eat up every word. I read this morning the last poems in the little blue book of Emily Dickinson's – especially pleased with the bat. How these exigient 'in-scape' sharp-edged poems that give much in short lines and unworn words make me feel my writing to be a sprawl, without point and image curiously concentrated by inward pain. Well, one is one's nature, I am too careless, too impatient to be a finely dedicated hermit, though I fancy I do recognise now and then an affinity with this priestess of death.

21 February   The forest ways are being opened up again. Gerard and I walked in the morning down as far as the beautiful pools in their basins of rock, the water at noon, where it lies still, is a perfect glaucous colour. Light and colour ... my consciousness so absorbs them, that is one reason why I am distressed if I do not wake and rise at dawn when the dark, the creeping gray twilight, when my senses are at once purified and sensitised by sleep, communicate grace to my spirit.

24 February   The flowering oat grass a shimmering net; the entelecheia of the created world, of the thoughts that intersect it, retreat from, embrace, penetrate, shake, vivify it and receive invisible life from it, this I would win with pen-point, set fairly on a ruled page, find in a poem, a breath, the game the mind plays with death. Is suffering, and the extreme of egocentricity, necessary to intensify to the fire of poetry a woman's mind?

27 February   The bright moon shines all night long; Jupiter is now passing Venus about a degree to the north. Poetry, *Plotinus, Le Chevalier de la Charrette*,* these I return to from thinking of all that is wrong, and find some succour in the idea that it is right to let the soul dwell where belief is approached by way of experience refined, of thought, of art. One must devote oneself to what one can.

3 March Thunder, lightning, rain all night long. Charles was so excited by the tempestuous night and the *house shaking* under the volleying thunder when I saw him at the Ngare Ndare this evening that he looked like Katie. I had forgotten till he spoke how the house had vibrated, but at his word I remembered how half sleeping, half awake, I had thought – Zeus bowed assent and great Olympus quaked. Charles, Jennifer and Patricia;* Rose, Tony, Michael and Francis* were just leaving after their birthday tea with Will when Gerard and I arrived, so we saw them and had an hour or two with him alone, which was as I liked best. He was excited, a little flushed, full of good stories in his old vein; and going off to Malindi in the morning. I began to read *Weymouth Sands* last night, and could not, and Will said the same, or rather that he could read history but something made up, like *Weymouth Sands*, didn't feel right here – and he looked at his stomach. He was thrilled by *The Blue Nile* and Napoleon sailing fifty miles up the great river. We sat side by side on his bed, grandfather's and grandmother's bed, looking at the book.

5 March The more I read of Inge's *Plotinus* the more I find myself in sympathy with the beliefs and thought of the two men, the scholarly dean and the pagan philosopher who attacked the gnostics and taught by *gnosis*, that which all men have and few use, that is perhaps use consciously.

6 March At breakfast Gerard said he would like to go to Cornwall 'to look round' as soon as we arrive in England, before he goes to Ireland. We went on talking of the duchy and read it up in the Encyclopaedia. Together with Northumberland it is a part of England I have always wanted to know and have never visited.

7 March 'In the knowledge and love of God – in knowledge of whom standeth our eternal life.' Knowledge 'contains' love, can love be without knowledge? So I would say to my mysterious author of *The Cloud of Unknowing* who so firmly insists that it is by love and not by knowledge that his dark Cloud is pierced. Otherwise I like his tone, his mild manner, his keeping close to the spirit of what he would say and not resembling the *Philokalia* which in retrospect seems so much devoted to what ye shall not eat and drink, until rationing meat and drink and sleep threatens to become an end in itself. But he belies himself in this love when he speaks of *reading, thinking, praying*; or lesson, meditation, orisons. It, the way of the bhakti, may be the way of mysticism but it is not really the way of the painstaking author of *The Cloud* – who approaches it unknowing by gnosis.

8 March This morning we went riding up to the moorlands where it is so long since we've been. The new farmer Wilson is doing great works, fencing and ploughing. Galloping up to a fence Bonnie fell and threw me over her head, landing on my nose in the grass, I was not hurt.

10 March The more I read *The Cloud* the more fond I grow of the writer, thinking often how T.F.P. would like his shrewd remarks. As: 'God will work sometimes by himself and then wilt thou think it merry to let him alone.' And his advice 'to try to look as it were over the shoulders' of the things that pass between you and God, or else 'to cower down under them as a caitiff and a coward overcome in battle.'

27 March Good Friday. The moon all but full in the yet blue sky as we rode home from the highest corner of the Beale. After more rain all was wondrous clear, cornlands, recession of cone-shaped hills, later the mountain peaks. Colours and cloud shadows on those sky-bearing ridges, on the face of Mount Hickson, were sublime.

28 March A note came from the K.F.A. to say our two seats are booked on the aircraft flying on 14 June, so our lots must have leaped out. Dean Inge quotes the well-chosen sayings from the writings of Walter Hilton and Julian of Norwich, but the Spanish mystics are another matter. I think I shall feel more at home in the last two essays or lectures rather, on Nature Mysticism and Symbolism which are subjects near to my heart.

29 March Easter Sunday, all sunshine. We saw a herd of buffalo from the veranda in the light of the moon and the dawn. I went to church in Timau, Will brought a blind African with him; Rose sat next to me, her infant is due to be born in a week's time. I posted a letter to Mother to tell her we have our seats. Who wrote, 'He pits his wits against the Almighty'? The words came into my head one night when Gerard was restless and without sleep.

13 April *Le voyage de l'âme* of St. Teresa* continues to preoccupy me, and I began this morning the introduction to Allison Peers's translation of her works. ('The sunlight, so potent and blazing a draft of light, the tremendous gusty wind, must surely impregnate my pale page.') Some of her sentences scorning all needless words are as vivid as Chinese, as close to the earth and the boundless, as allusive and open to the free interpretation of each individual soul.

14 April   I have a letter from Mother with a primrose, three *TLS* from her also, one containing an excellent appraisal of Sir Thomas Wyat's* poetry. We saw the new moon last evening, the slightest silver crescent, Venus high above. The Muslim saying: 'Only the dead know the importance of life', because they know God and God is life, ἐν αὐτῷ ζωὴ ἦν.* Whence comes the certainty that death is the 'encounter with God'.

26 April   The first day of the week, the full moon, a solitary day for me with two long walks and two conversations, one with Marethi who gave me a discourse on religion, one with Manyara, the old shepherd, who told me his daughter Salome could speak and write English. A third brief meeting in the twilight with the tall old Kipsigis night watchman who was a porter in the First World War. He wanders round a little while with his bow and arrows and then I am sure sleeps as soundly as I do.

27 April   The days and nights around the full moon are fine and clear, and full of light and winds as of ocean for purity and vigour. Walking over the Beale where now grass is scarce and short there are far more sheep than acres (which is one of the things that wakes me and dances in my nerves at night) I consider, with rainbow and stormcloud and gazelles for company, the Spanish mystics; the dark night of the soul; water and dryness; ecstasy and union. One and another of them is declared to be a brilliant theologian, but this, together with intellectual power, is not to my mind in the extracts quoted where thought seems lost in feeling and a kind of naïvety.

11 May   We finished today our reading together of *Prometheus Bound*: this, I think, is my fourth reading of this greatest and most elemental tragedy of Aeschylus. The sky, firmament, aether, welkin, heaven, empyrean (what does that mean?) this evening was in as wild and threatening a state as it is in the last lines of the tragedy with dark clouds swirled in masses, sun-obliterating, curtains of rain gliding between the hills revealed how what one regards often as a simple barrier is composed of ranges rising one beyond the other after the manner of waves.

12 May   Charles arrived at breakfast time with nine rams. He talked a little while and I felt how devoted he was to Kenya, to country, soil, birds, animals, above all to Kisima and his farming life. Then at 5 p.m.

came his father in happiest mood that perfect sunny time. I went up to the red gate with him and he quickly made a sketch and watercolour of the panorama of mountains and plains, all divine blue with deep cloud shadows and one exalted castle of a snowy cloud in the sky. His big sketch book was missing and I found in an *Illustrated London News*, of which there was a pile on the floor of the car, an advertisement page with a clear white space on which he made his picture. He gave me a most affectionate farewell.

15 May   This day next month where shall I be? The finest of fine weather. Smoke rising from the charcoal pyres drifting up the hollows of the hills marked out the long diagonals of the ridges this evening when we went down to Ndere. Cows and calves came past the house, all the herds have foot-and-mouth now.

16 May   We read that scene today when Demeter sits by the wayside at Eleusis near the Maiden Well and the four girls come to her with their pitchers of bronze. How immemorial and eternally symbolic are these meetings by wells that recur in classical and biblical literature, and always they come upon the spirit with the freshness of living and life-giving water.

18 May   The bulls sleeping just outside make breathings like hippopotamuses; one woke me last night with his bellowing roar. When he fell silent again I listened to the young swallows twittering in their nest above my head. Six swallows were flying round and round inside the cottage in the afternoon. We rode to the Beale in the morning; later two men came who are interested in leasing it to grow crops, the part above the main road, or in buying the whole farm. I thought much this evening of A.R.P.*

4 June   Ten days, and we should be in the air, but Gerard's passport is not yet in order, the tickets have not been given to us. We may in fact have to go to Nairobi a day or two before the aircraft is due to depart to visit the Income Tax people. All letters and telephone calls seem vain. Where, I have lately been wondering, does an aesthetic sense come from? Not certainly, as R. G. Collingwood says, *from* a sunset or a beautiful landscape, these are before many eyes that neither see nor delight in them. Yet having it myself I question it not at all, it is a birthright, the solace and serenity that come from nature and a certain kind of intellectualised emotional response to it.

5 June   This morning while I was gardening Martin Becker came to talk to Gerard about buying the Beale. He will come again on Sunday, the day after tomorrow, with Gibson* his partner. The idea is they should take all the farm except the house and Windy Hill Paddock, and perhaps buy the sheep also. The night is now from the setting of Venus to the rising of Jupiter.

6 June   Sleep is the condition of concentration, I read today; without this intense oblivion, this passing without earthy alloy into the Absolute, man cannot long live. In sleep the dissipated, enfeebled forces of mind as well as of body are restored by becoming one with the light shining in darkness. So in the approaches of sleep, and for a brief interval after it has withdrawn, the consciousness in stillness is most able to be illumined.

9 June   St. Teresa's 'Seventh Mansions' is by far the best part of *The Interior Castle*, here she really does in her writing touch the truth. Much of what goes before, as well as her 'Life' exaggerates to my mind the importance of *favours* as she calls them, repeats and repeats again the forms they take, the effects they have, her response to them. She herself did not seek them but they do seem to have been sought and desired by her nuns, almost to be regarded by Teresa as necessary experiences on the way to the Seventh Mansions. I think *favours* of this visionary or audible kind have no place in a metaphysical approach to truth and even to a mystic are rather a distraction than a support. They came to Teresa herself unsought and overwhelmingly, but rather, I fancy, confused than purified her faith in Christ.

11 June   St. Barnabas. Barnaby Bright All day and no Night. Which is true enough, since we mean to rise at 3 a.m. Quietly this afternoon I read the final sections and conclusion of the *Bhagavadgita*, and was restored from the weariness that goes with packing and impending departure. The treasures of the house – paintings, books, glass, china – have all in this golden evening sunlight their haloes of memories, now one now another calls my eye. The car broke down and had a puncture when Gerard went to Timau this morning, after spending most of the day yesterday being serviced. You cannot now stop accelerating so we shall have a lively trip to Nairobi. But I have another letter from Mother. Yes, this light is rare to me because I am not often in the house at this hour.

13 June   New moon in the limpid pure mountain air was our farewell to the Beale. Now at Limuru this Saturday morning the world is cloud-enfolded and everything dark and chill as Hades. The cows plunge to their milking through seas of mud. Gerard quickly had the passport fixed and we met Becker and Gibson at the lawyers to talk over the agreement about the Beale. We shall see them there again this morning and probably sign it so they can start their ploughing at once.

16 June, London   The surprise of the flight was a descent to Nice in a fresh morning wind from the east after rain in the night. After the aircraft and cramped windowless night it was a liberation to feel this air and walk up and down on the Côte d'Azur with a sea of protean hues, the mountains beyond mountains running inland and a white lighthouse pillar where they ended in water. After the Magnificat I heard the notes of a blackbird in Westminster Abbey, and saw the tiny dark form of it flying in the height of the roof close to the fan vaulting. Will it ever escape? I spoke on the telephone to Mother and she said there was a blackbird singing on Theodore's tombstone when she passed.

17 June, Padstow   Mother was at Exeter station as we had planned, how at those moments you see only one among all the rest. Side by side in the train we talked and looked out of the window for the second three hours of the journey in full contentment, in all the childhood security and tranquillity that belongs to travelling in a slow train. This line is to be closed in October and the many little country stations where it stopped were shabby and unpainted. The cuckoo calls and calls at Padstow and white seagulls float by across the yellow spits of the estuary, across the green fields which slant across the window. The distances are far and the elevated horizon meets a gray western sky. I close my eyes, when I look again mist has possessed all.

Evening of the same day: O, we have had a happy day, with gentle walking; taking a bus to Tintagel we walked to the church, ancient cruciform, with square tower, Norman windows and Saxon arch over the north door ... standing alone on the cliffs. We walked on over the thymy grass to look upon King Arthur's sea-girt castle. In the evening we walked on the quay here, and to the church set in tall umbrageous trees, very large and well-cared for. The gray day withdrew hour by hour as into an infinite twilight recession.

19 June   Our long day yesterday criss-crossing the duchy and ending at Land's End proved to Mother and me one thing, that north Cornwall is the part we like by far the best of what we have seen so far, the country round Padstow with its fine prospects and golden sand spits pleases us by far the best; the whole climate of the place as well as the friendliness of the people. I am beginning to learn the characteristic Cornish features. Small birds are rare, and I have seen only one butterfly over the abundance of downland flowers on those ultimate cliffs. A family of pied wagtails runs over the bowling-green here, and in my walk before breakfast a wren was singing in an ivy tod at the end of the lane.

22 June   Mappowder at last and such a chattering of Mother and Mary: we came by taxi from Yeovil through may-scented lanes; blackbirds and thrushes sing, tall pink lupins in the garden and Canterbury bells and sweet williams. Louis telephoned to greet Mother. I took Vera* the heath from Dartmoor. The longest day. O, this is a peerless blackbird, surpassing the two at Plymouth that sang this morning at the western end of the Hoe. Swifts scream. The air has an inland stillness and syringa sweetness. This returning to England summer by summer, to the country where men in their gardens speak King Alfred's English, is like the Golden Age.

23 June   An essay in the *TLS* on keeping a diary was of interest to me, explaining why to those who are solitary it is a particular satisfaction. For example, the writer says: '... it implies a lively consciousness of time, and language asserts time as no other medium of communication can ... the specific character of the diary is that it records events from a close perspective and that its unity is established more by the unwitting discriminations of the temperament than by the foregone conclusions of a conscious purpose; that it is written for the writer ... when Elizabeth Fry rejoices that "it leads the mind to look inwards" she is properly concerned not only to discover what she is, but to alter herself by contemplation ... through Rousseau the diary became the avowed means of asserting what he called in the *Reveries* "the feeling of one's own existence".'

24 June   Mother telephoned Alyse a few minutes ago and I listened to her voice and was wafted to Chydyok, to youth, on its intonations. Even now the sun of this day of high summer of leafy June is vanishing into pearly haze, leaving only the merest hint of crimson. I went into the church in the afternoon.

25 June   Through the enchanted wood-bound mead where in the clay soil flowers of marsh and down grow together, Mother and I walked, finding traces of badger and deer, listening to the warblers, chiff-chaff on all sides, willow-wren, whitethroat, blackcap. Then into a cut hayfield that runs up to Crooked Oak, and there, stealthy among the swathes, now showing red coats, prick-ears, white-tipped tails, now hidden in the grass, were the foxes, the little foxes that spoil the grapes.

This sight of a pair of fox-cubs, aware of us and unafraid, was a singular delight to Mother and me, until from Cockcrow, the wood on our left, there was a small sharp call. Heeding the vixen's warning the two ran different ways, into a patch of long grass, into Crooked Oak. A jay began giving the alarm in the treetops of Cockcrow.

28 June   Early church with Dr. Jackson.* The day was marked by clouds and changing winds with only a few moments of sunshine, always it seemed night was approaching. Mother and I wrote letters and walked. St. Teresa begins to hover again in the borderland of my mind, but I feel more at home with the genius of my present companions Colet, Erasmus, Sir Thomas More who sang in Latin to his motherless children, 'If I beat you at all, it was with the tail of a peacock.'

30 June   Early this morning I saw Mrs. Tiggy Winkle at the end of Mother's garden. I was attracted by a small sound which was made by the hedgehog pulling off bits of green grass. With these in her mouth she waddled to the rubbish heap and disappeared. She returned quickly for more grass, then to collect fallen leaves. The impatient way she grabbed the grass and picked up the leaves one after another in her mouth was in contrast with her laborious walk, her short skinny back legs could scarcely carry her up a bank of a few inches when her mouth was full. But her face with pointed snout looked alert. Clouds cover the sky now at the day's end but the sun was tireless until about 7 from the first moment of my waking. Mother and I walked by field and wood to my favourite hill, Nettlecombe, following a badger path up the last slope and resting in a flowery bed of hawk-weed, golden as dandelions; lilac orchids and bird's-foot trefoil. The unending hyperborean twilight gives me a mysterious passionless rapture and often at this time I hear calls of flying plover.

1 July   Sunshine with scarcely a cloud. Africa outshone. And this day Mother and I have spent for the most part alone together. It is interesting to read in the account of *Utopia* of so many wise reforms suggested by Sir Thomas More in 1515 and still waiting to be carried out.

2 July   Owls invaded the village at about 2 a.m. this morning and their hisses and hoarse exchanges of tu-whit, tu-whit went on for an hour or two. I saw one on the roof of the house opposite in the faint moonlight and another I think fed it. There must have been one on this roof or in the garden. In the silent night of the country, the calm air, their voices are startling. The attempts to train the mind to concentrate by learning languages and reading only certain books, a kind of discipline of the intelligence, is I think a preparation for pure intellection, for that intuitive understanding which begins to be approached when learning grows less day by day.

5 July   Dr. Jackson, after his sermon on belief in the divinity of Christ this evening, told me (in church and still wearing his surplice) that he was going to London on Tuesday for an examination at Bart's. He hoped to return on Friday but ... 'they may want to keep me'. At eighty-four he looks well and vigorous as ever, but he said in a letter to me he'd had certain 'monitory and minatory symptoms'. I cycled to Buckland this morning and went into Katie's garden.

6 July   Mother and I went to Stalbridge this morning to see Mrs. Mahuzies.* All crippled, twisted, bowed, her head bent to one side 'like a poppy' she welcomed us into her kitchen where she was preparing dishes in a charming blue apron. Returning to Sturminster we had our meal of cheese and biscuits on the river bank with yellow waterlilies raised up among level floating leaves and a host of house martins skimming the water. I cycled to Buckland this morning to pick peas in Katie's garden and was very much aware of her so that I would not have been surprised to see her ghost. When I spoke of this to Mother she knew at once, saying, 'Yes, she haunts that garden, she is much more there than in the house.' A wild wind from the south today sets bush and tree awhirl, clouds travel gray upon gray.

12 July   Dr. Jackson has come back. 'They did pull me about, and were doubtful, but I told the sister I must go home.' Sunshine so welcome at the end of the day, but the thrush sang as blithely in the clouded morning as it does now. I watched a tree-creeper running up alder stems as I stood with Mother by the stream on the way to Buckland. Dr. Jackson took a brief evensong with no sermon.

13 July   A sheer summer day, nonpareil, high-flying swallows, sun in a golden stream warming me as according to my custom I drank my tea in the garden, at 6.30; and there was a chiff-chaff in the Chinese willow. We walked in the evening in that flowery mead with impenetrable Cockcrow on its northern march, the flowers purple and gold, the roundness of Nettlecombe blue and unattainable, mysterious as the ramparts of consciousness. A solitary mallard was on the pond and after she had flown away we watched a hare feeding and gambolling in the green aftermath. No words, not a Greek poem, not Shakespeare can tell these tranquil days ... together.

14 July   'Only pure metaphysics and pure prayer are absolute and therefore universal.' And it is pure prayer that I do not know how to attain, this essence of inwardness and silent revelation of the truth. To know this gift is ours, to prepare, to attend, and then suffer from intrusive trivialities or come only to a formal disremembered repetition. But it is possible to acknowledge 'the gift of impersonal contemplation such as will allow "God to think in us".'

15 July Rain there was at night, but the whole day was warm, fine, sun-filled. We walked past what is left of Short Wood and saw the queer flower elecampane that according to Johns* the French make a *vin* from. There is a field of charlock in full flower near the road, so sharp in scent and in colour and carrying me straight into childhood. Mother persuaded Vera to come into the garden and we sat under the young acacia tree from Norfolk. Vera, always cheerful in her solitary gnome-like existence, confessed to Mother tonight something of her sufferings, the sedatives and sleeping pills she takes at nightfall and at 2 a.m. give her grotesque dreams and small respite from her head-noises. I was in church for a time this morning, it could not have been more serene, more still and fair with the sense of holiness and light.

16 July A.R.P. The sun has not yet gone down but for almost the first time on this long day has moved into clouds that are fiery below and shining above. I had a particularly good reading this morning of St. Paul and later of Schuon on the same theme: of seeing God everywhere. 'To see God everywhere is essentially this: to see that we are not, that He alone is.' And at this, to the music of the thrush, the Sun shines forth, dazzling my sight so that my pen is as if dipped in blood.

25 July The leader of the Kenya Trade Union declares all British farmers must be out of the country by 28 August, their farms to be given to Africans to be run communally. In the garden in the plenitude of sunshine Mother has been reading aloud from Katie's diary written sixty years ago when she was seventeen and eighteen: the free life of a young child, walks, tree-climbing, adventures with Willie in the Easter holidays, walks before breakfast and after, before lunch and after ... even till nightfall. The whole vivid, immediate, the best descriptions of a hailstorm or mist and dew. And it was only this very morning that Mother showed me the small green diary she gave Katie for 1963 and I read the entries for the first few days of the year, on each one the direction from which the wind blew was recorded, on the last, the 5th January I think, there was written shakily: 'Eyes very bad, and breathing'.

26 July With a hint of autumn in the morning swallows began to gather, to sing and preen on the wires against the foggy sky. The day presently grew hot and sultry dulling the wits, but at length a cool wind came from the west, perhaps a distant thunderstorm had cleared the air, and we walked all three in green pastures by flowery stream, hedgerows and long-shadowing trees. Mother continued to read from Katie's artless diary when all the world was young. I confess I have never felt more reluctant to go back to Africa.

31 July Kneeling at the window of Mother's room I have watched the first autumn sunset of soft brilliant hues, shedding a spiritual brightness upon the cool night, a rare consolation, reaching widely across the sky on either side of the elm tree we call Theodore's. Last night at this time the rooks roosting in Short Wood began a great chorus, cawing that went on for a quarter of an hour or more. For our walk tonight we went through the familiar fields and the slope so pleasing covered with rye grass, gray-green, rippling under the breath of the west wind. Here came thirty and two milch cows to their evening pasture. I had a special letter from Alyse today. Now I shall go to be with Mother.

2 August, Kenya London, meeting with Gwyneth, flight all with various delays accomplished. Rain was falling when we arrived at Nairobi and here at Theresa's* house it is damp and chill after three wet days, November-like. The parting with Mother only yesterday morning is already as though afar save for the grief like a rending of the spirit. London was all in sunshine and so hot the aircraft could not take its full load of fuel and had to come down at Khartoum for more. A dinghy race made the Thames gay with blue sails all over the sullen water, 218 of the small craft were turning and heeling in a stiff breeze. Theresa is not very well and has given up the idea of nursing. My heart rather sinks at Kenya.

3 August, The Beale Rain at the Beale, how often we have returned home in rain. A large area above the main road has been ploughed and there are preparations for building a granary close to the road. Arriving early in the afternoon we could unpack and take a walk over the isabelline hard-grazed landscape. The ewes and lambs have been moved to just where they should not be. So the affairs begin again and also the attic evenings with the hissing lamp, the leaves turned of our books. There waits the 'passional mysticism' of St. Teresa.

13 August Ll.P.* Rain at dawn instead of cold and scintillant stars. It is interesting how Africa has now become a desert to me, all unreal, I move as in a dream, or as a ghost that flits through familiar but desolate regions. To the best of my power I hold my peace, perform those little tasks of the day, set before me (as I may) a poetic vision, remember my reading and symbolism. My cup runneth over ...

14 August As I read and re-read *Beowulf* I grow more aware of how the whole tone of the poem changes in the last part to a minor key in keeping with the age and death of the hero. The might of the young man, his spirit and his adventuring give a force to every line in the battles with Grendel and his mother. Even the ship bearing the dead out to sea is a symbol of high quest, of leaving behind the sure and known ground.

15 August A day or so ago I was feeling a kind of sorrow for Africa because, if you please, I no longer felt the same rapport with this known part of it, tonight under the monotonous gray of heaven I was again at home in the bleak landscape, with a hyena whooping, a pair of black duck flying down the valley to the forest with soft secretive quacking, a bush-buck's bark.

16 August One reason, it may be, for my devotion to the twilight is because then Earth is neither dominated by the sun nor obscured by her own shadow so that she may be influenced by radiance from the utmost regions of the cosmos. The ardours of the day, the dark which brings death and healing, are both in abeyance, the planet is in these hushed hours freed from her own particular diurnal and nocturnal burdens, and I might almost say from consciousness of her freight of humanity.

31 August Shearing started this morning, Gerard is pleased with the lambs' wool. So things change: from morn till night Sherard* was burning grass on Ngusiru where we left a little grazing. Clouds of stained smoke drove along through the sunny afternoon and later there was the red glow of the fires devouring grass we'd asked him to let us rent for our sheep.

9 September I am, I fancy, more *edenic* than idealistic: all that pertains to earth experienced as a paradise wakens in me the most intimate response and hidden reciprocity; all the unhuman qualities, and the nature of things, finding realisation in the poetic vision of mankind. The essence of things from their creation, this world of Eden, is that their forms and utterance have always the wonder that belongs to the first time, and so there is no oppression of time and nothing grows old.

14 September   I had a vivid dream last night of a flock of blue birds flying up from water. One was caught and a ring put on its leg, at first after this it failed to fly but presently rose up and took wing.

22 September   The sense of something soft in the toe of my boot made me hurriedly draw back my foot this morning. I turned the boot over and shook, out fell a large toad and set off over the moonlit boards. I was glad I hadn't hurt the creature which thought it had found such a snug hole.

23 September   As when a child begins to read it has only a few books, well-known, that it can indeed read, so now I have only a few books I can read; most of those dearly loved, read and re-read in the past, I cannot open now, their titles, the look of their covers which once roused a thousand delights say nothing now. That is one reason why I have this month begun to learn Hebrew, though with the utmost slowness, for it is to be no task. Yes, almost any book now that does not touch what is of supreme importance I do not take willingly into my hands.

25 September   Kibrono, the old night watchman, was telling Gerard it was the custom on moonlight nights in the First World War to go about on Kilimanjaro; the bright night, he said, reminded him of his time on the mountain long ago, and that he could see it clearly in his mind.

28 September   Walking to see Will last evening Gerard and I saw him setting forth to meet us, a sheepskin cap of Phrygian shape on his head and a shepherd's crook in his hand. We walked with him I suppose between two and three miles round his maize fields, through the cows and calves, back across the river to the piece of ploughland where Elizabeth spoke of the wild duck. As time passed he grew ever more genial until in the firelit room he was telling stories in his most amusing vein. Gilfrid's daughter was born on the 19th, one year after and one day before Charles's. Yesterday morning (Sunday) we met Charles in the forest thief-hunting. Soon after we left him Gerard and I came on, right in the path, the head skin bones horns of quite a large eland and the bush-roofed lair where they who slew and ate him had slept.

3 October   A quiet day darkly overcast: it is interesting how after all these years in Africa, nearly twenty, I feel so strongly now I do not want to stay here any more, though I am not exactly homesick for England. It is perhaps the effect of the end of an epoch working on me unawares. Like Llewelyn I should like to go to Palestine before I die.

4 October   We lost our way several times in the forest today, for a time we went round in circles in impenetrable bush and heard buffalo going off in a bed of tall thin plants about ten feet high with white flowers wavering at their tops like cabbage butterflies. The glades where once was game are now utterly eaten out by Tim's* stock. Already sheep are sick, after dipping, their legs rotting, several had to have their throats cut. I rebelled in my heart at living in Africa.

22 October   As in a Homeric simile a lion leaped into one of the cattle bomas on Ndere at night. The men shone their torches and saw it swishing its tail. It growled at them and would not retreat from their shouts. Then the cattle stampeded and all broke out of their pen. So the lion missed his kill, none was missing when the herdsmen collected them again in the morning. I made marmalade. Gerard inoculated sheep which are going to Ndere.

4 November   Charles visited us this evening after dark when we had lately come in from burning grass on the middle plain. It was a pleasure to see him and reminded me of Elizabeth's rare appearances at the same time of day. I read Collingwood's summing-up of his own philosophy towards the end of *Speculum Mentis* this morning with much admiration; from this reading my mind recovered its tone.

13 November   A trogon was on a branch of a tree beside the way as we came down through the forest, rarely they appear and it is with something like a sense of awe one sees the rose-red and green with sheen as the bird flies into some deeper shade of the sunless groves where it lodges. I had my tea alone in the cottage and walked alone in the gray evening pondering many things.

19 November   Moon round and yellow with Jupiter close I saw in the west this early morn: but no rain. Gerard and I spent the evening burning old old old grass on Windy Hill till night came on and the flames grew bright. I like to see those fragments of flame torn from the rest of the fire that leap free and vanish.

14 December   Gerard and I went to church at the Good Shepherd this morning. Rose sat by me. On the way home we called to see Will. He was by the fire with Francis in the room with him, and the new copy of poems by J.C.P. published by Macdonald in his hands. Rose came in with Martin* in her arms, and we sat on the floor while Michael blew peacock bubbles which Francis broke and Martin tried to pick up. I had a feeling Will was not so strong, his voice faltered now and then and had a quaver in it.

15 December   We walked over some of the corn this evening. O, it is sad to think of so much good grain wasted, the green blades bravely risen, defeated by drought. My own mood was charged with sorrow, although the day had been so quiet.

16 December   Often, more often than I can say, my heart would fly home as an arrow. A day of mist, parting and drifting towards evening alone until the sunless light grew clearer in moonshine. A pair of heron, thin with heads sunk in their shoulders, stood motionless in the dead cedar tree. From Windy Hill glided down four Abdim's storks to circle about the tree and then on planing wings to vanish in cloud.

17 December   The diamond-studded hammock cobwebs stretched everywhere through the grass last evening were unseen in the sunshine of this day. The heron and the storks were gone also. We have ceased to look for rain. I finished the second blue chair cover this morning. As usual, my best, that is most tranquil, hour was between 5 and 6, stars, waxing light, bird song.

18 December   Gerard bought today in Nanyuki a second-hand Peugeot motorcar but it is not yet here. We took, to Sarwan Singh to mend, Aunt Kate's* chair, first taking off the new cover. It has had, ever since it came to us from Norwich, a castor that fell off whenever the chair was moved or used. This good Sikh said at once it wouldn't defeat him to restore the hollow leg. Gerard bought from him a Scotch cart with iron wheels which had been standing outside his shop for a year. The tale or fable of Tobias and the angel absorbed me this afternoon.

20 December   Morning in a cloud and evening of utmost clarity, to far mountains rarely seen through blue and rose the eye sped. Ndere is parti-coloured green and gray, there has been enough rain for that. Choice, and all one does in one's own way and time, these are pure luxuries. Mind is thought, says Collingwood, so – no thought, no mind? Instinct and emotion. But does too much thought cause loss of all spontaneous response?

21 December   A long evening on Ndere under a dramatic sky, and rain-storms here and there along the hills; clouds, black and silver-lipped, white, gold and glowing, distant lightning, all the visible presences of tempest. A huge blackness overhung the Beale with a narrow margin bright as light between cloud mass and escarpment. 'Abstractions are only second-order objects made by the mind out of its immediate first-order objects as naturally and as unconsciously as bees make honey out of flowers.'

22 December   A thunderstorm tonight caught us so that we walked home through mire and pools and water-filled ruts; with darkness the rain ceased so we walked on, Gerard, Mlefu* and I, with bright flashes of lightning now and then to show the way. Wading across the last streamlet I saw a pair of glow-worms among the fragrant watermint I grabbed with my hands. There is much sound sense as well as startling and provoking thought in *The New Leviathan*,* a definition of duty which makes it almost ἀνάγκη:* 'a man's duty on a given occasion is the act which for him is both possible and necessary; the act which at that moment character and circumstance combine to make it inevitable, if he has a free will, that he should freely will to do.'

Christmas Eve   Early this morning when a deep dew overlaid all and I was in the garden a note was given me in Will's handwriting, very tremulous, which said, 'Charles has had a gun accident putting his gun into the safe. He is dead.' I told Gerard as he was returning from his walk. We went first to see Rose and Tony. Rose said: 'Charles would like some heather, could you go and get some from the moorlands?' At Kisima I saw Will for a moment sitting in the twilight room with his dead son. He was reading the book of Tobit. Charles was on the bed covered by a blanket, his two feet in gray woollen socks exposed at the end. Gerard and I drove up to the moorlands and picked giant heather, sage, St. John's wort, yellow daisies, and other shrubby things. Lower down men were ploughing with many white storks standing on the freshly turned earth. We took our farewell of Charles near the Beacon Hill and Katie's Wood. In the afternoon he was buried in Nanyuki cemetery. Gilfrid drove his brother from the hospital and I sat by him. Gerard was one of the bearers. Two fleeces and the heather were put into the grave. Gilfrid did not know how to leave it. After the crowd moved away and Will and Rose and Jennifer had gone I looked back to see him crouching by it. Again he went back, and again. Charles above all men deserved the epithet of Homer's heroes: ἀμύνων.*

Christmas Day   Gerard and I went to the Church of the Good Shepherd at 8. Will was there, very white but steady and when at noon we went to Rose's house he said he felt better, that yesterday's shock had make him forget his pain though he still felt it, as it were, afar. To some temperaments tragedy is a challenge, they rally to meet it. With Will and small Michael we walked round the paddock or small field in front of the house looking for mushrooms. Gerard and I walked on the Beale in the rainy evening. The cool wind blowing on my face helped me out of doors, and wandering airs that come in through the window at night.

26 December   Last night I read the poem in the new book of J.C.P.'s Mother has given us called 'To Lulu',* and thought of Gilfrid. The exceeding sadness of many of these verses and especially of certain lines here and there among them matched my mood.

29 December   Night and day to me he cries – but that is not true, rather night and day it is a silent, close presence whose eyes I meet, and which sometimes gives place to a vision of boyhood or youth, the tones of the voice with words heard or unheard, certain exchanges of fun that could not be shared with another.

1965

2 January   Mother's letter written on Christmas Day when she had heard the news of Charles came to me today. And there was more Christmas mail which we looked at in the rainy evening until we went out to walk in the gloaming. My thoughts just now are at an end, I feel as though my skull lies white and empty in the soaking grass, with the soft blind blades pressing up, urgently growing about it.

3 January   Rose and her father arrived at the cottage at tea-time with a black cloud which soon brought a fierce rainstorm upon us with lightning and thunder. They were so happy together it was good to see them. Will told Gerard for the first time the whole story of that night's calamity. They left, the rain ceased, a triple rainbow overarched the cottage, all wet tree stems and boughs shone with a silvery lustre.

4 January   An inch of rain while we were away at the cottage has made all greener; nearly 60 lambs have been born. The new moon, first of the year, appeared to us this evening, two days old. Already the Scorpion is in sight in the east in the mornings, Venus and Mercury were beside it today. Many storks flying high with whistling wings glided to the forest.

5 January   Eve of Epiphany. Sometimes it seems as though on the tide of sorrow the mind is borne to where there are no poles, where all things cease. And after this rest in nothingness it returns rejoicing with exceeding great joy, like the wise men when they beheld the star. Or if not with joy, with the sunless windless calm after all storms.

7 January   Venus and Mercury less than a degree apart in the glow before sunrise, hoar-frost in patches on the grass, thicker in the valley, edging with crystalline fringe blade and leaf, crisp to step upon; eight buffalo in David's* glade wondering how to escape from the vermin-proof fence – this before breakfast. Later as we sat eating it on the veranda a large leopard, tawny as a lion in the early sunshine, came strolling, quite at ease, into the field before us. He looked more than once in our direction as he slowly crossed the field towards the ponies – the rams so often there were not today – but they didn't heed him knowing perhaps he was well fed and in play. As a cat he flattened himself in the grass and again moved forward on his long legs. We called some of the men to see him. This strange leopard was in the field about five minutes, never once hurrying, pausing now and then to sit up on his haunches like a dog, to look about him. Finally he went right to the bottom of the field, out, and along the outside of David's fence.

8 January   Yesterday's leopard killed two of David's sheep last night. He was not there today, although earlier the dogs had chased him on Windy Hill.

9 January   Nanyuki Show today to which we pay no heed. I found satisfaction in my reading of Thucydides this afternoon, and wrote a little. Pray without ceasing, says St. Paul, this is hard, but I try to be what St. Teresa calls 'recollected' and to wait upon 'the prayer of quiet', that it may be fulfilled.

20 January   Sometimes the mysteriousness of the cosmos and of life seems to be to me beyond all fathoming, my mind, which is thought, simply halts before it, before it all, or before a single aspect; then again for a moment the whole sensible world as it is in my thought of it becomes not transparent, but as it were thin or diaphanous, as though reality were so close in the next breath I should know, have in an instant perfect *connaissance*. Rain at sunrise and again in the afternoon after a long cloudy morning. Gerard and I went riding on Ndere. Walking in the evening twilight he saw something bright among the unending thorn bush, a red flower or incredible scarlet fruit? Approaching we found a pair of pomegranate trees with handsome dark green leaves and a few bright blossoms, a trio of fruit smooth, hard, gay as flames. We picked one and I carried it home, a symbol in my hand, and not unmindful of Persephone.

20 February   Sun rising, while we tailed lambs; setting, while we rested by the Rhino Dam, with no cloud. Only the smoke of fires burning in this quarter and that turned to copper both western sky and sun.

Taking things for granted – that is what makes for weariness, boredom, lack of originality, yet it is what one all the time does, has to do. Still one can know, carry in a cell of the mind, that not a miracle is more strange than how things are by nature, than words, than the knowledge of God.

1 March Saint John of the Cross writes well on *spiritual* gluttony. When I'd read his words, I quickly closed the book for fear of indulging too much my own failing which lies (I thought as I read) in the direction of intellectual gluttony. This saint is, as Gerard said, a good psychologist.

10 March Perhaps it may be the barrenness of Africa that turns me, however little I may do, to write. All the things I like to do I put in the infinitive for they have (I fancy) a touch of the infinite about them: to think, to pray, to read, to write, to walk. And, which is all these, in stillness, to contemplate. Early this morn I had a vivid dream of Bedouin, dancing in the desert with their black tents near-by. The jingling, the beating of the tambour, the half-bent figures, are still with me. The dream sent me to look up dance in Doughty.*

11 March A bundle of newspapers was waiting for us at the cottage, left by Will, and on a slip of paper under the string that bound them was written: Fare Thee Well. In my infinitives I forgot 'to sleep' – the first and last, for without it in this life none of the others could be. In sleep the 'individual soul' receives the light of the 'human Intellect'.

12 March Moonlight, waiting for Gerard. In my walk I saw a bushbaby flying in the gloaming from branch to branch; and earlier a gaggle of geese, nine in all. The afternoon I spent on a couch of soft sand between a low bank and a clump of rushes with green leaves in circles like spokes. My clock has stopped so I do not know how late it is, now and again I go out to look at the stars and moon, to see if I can see Cherry* coming home.

18 March I finished the second book of Lucretius, and how it does end on a note of pagan pessimism, but I have found much that has pleased me well in this book. The dramatic history of Thucydides is now at its Syracusean climax, the final defeat of the Athenians in Sicily has begun; judging by the thick notes on the inter-leaves this part was the one most closely studied by the undergraduates.

19 March Thunder, lightning, gales ... The late afternoon was suddenly humbled under a black cloud and twining mists, all sunshine fled. A flight of swallows skimmed over the grass as though fleeing before the tempest. Now the day has yielded to black night and howling wind.

20 March I read a good chapter (XIII, Book III) in *The Ascent of Carmel** this afternoon on the poor in spirit. We were out late this evening, after discovering a lost ewe and lamb, and walked all the way home by starlight, about three miles, the stars a trifle hazy but lending enough light. Two glow-worms at different points shone in the grass, not scattering unbeholden their aerial hue.

21 March Two sunsets of great glory and long lasting, with those ice-crystal clouds curved as wings, thus the rain clouds have taken leave for the present. When the sun shone level with the bronze plain, blue swallows swiftly passed over. A beautiful sandpiper with white tail and musical calls flew up from the marshy ground and joined a snipe that rose also with its impatient cry.

24 March Many loud peals of thunder this evening but the storm clouds went away over the mountain. A sick colobus monkey came feebly close to Gerard when he was in the forest. The dogs did not worry it and it climbed into a bush and sat only a few feet above the ground. He found the expression in the little creature's eyes very moving. How illness masters us all and changes our wild ways and treetop flights.

27 March Hidden in my shady nook by the river I heard three loud cries, chak, chak, chak, and a black bird flew by upstream. Peeping round a yellow acacia thorn trunk I saw it, perched on a root in sombre gloom under overhanging bushes with the black water below. The large bird, even a trifle clumsy, remained for about two minutes on its root so that I could examine its straight fierce beak, black breast and feet with a trace of red where its short legs left the body; back and tail were black, faintly speckled with white and there were touches of white round its neck. It was, I learnt on my return to the cottage, a female giant kingfisher, a very anomaly of the kingfisher kind with no jewel-bright plumes and about 15 inches long, to which be added three more of bill.

10 April Slight rain in the night and early morn, a sweet fragrance rose from the damped grass, birds sang, but soon all was dry again. Welcome letter from Mother telling me of her days with Will. One also from Gertrude, the first this year. She, like Rose, told of the unusual temperatures in England for the end of March, 75 °F and

76 °F, strange to have warmth and bare trees. I like St. John of the Cross's use of the symbol of Jacob's ladder.

11 April The morning show of thundrous clouds over sea of gold before the sun rose soon passed and there was no more sign of coming rain. Gerard and I rode all the morning. Now I want to praise the gift of stillness, greater than the gift of tears, for it is the outer mark of contemplation and a soul composed, and rarer, for who does not fidget and fret especially when most he should study to be quiet and inwardly at rest, as when he is being led beside the still waters which restore the soul. 'This repose and quiet of this spiritual house the soul comes to attain habitually and perfectly (insofar as the condition of this life allows) by means of the acts of the substantial touches of Divine Union.'

13 April Never since those Victorian tales with a moral of my childhood have I cared for allegories, while with the good but 'real' stories, like Mrs. Molesworth's, I was so happy that her name alone brings me a reflection of joy and satisfaction. And I feel just the same now about *The Spiritual Canticle* of St. John of the Cross, there is altogether too much sensual imagery oppressing wisdom and discernment; and it is always more possible to write well of sorrow and suffering than of glory and rapture. For all the high praise given to *The Canticle* and its explanations, I would say it is better to know God in silence. It is the difference between jnana and bhakti.

20 April 'Behold, bless ye the Lord, all ye servants of the Lord, which by night stand in the house of the Lord. Lift up your hands in the sanctuary, and bless the Lord. The Lord who madest heaven and earth bless thee out of Zion.' This psalm I can see now in my mind's eye copied out in pencil in shaky writing on a scrap of paper. When I was about seven and Mother was going to take me to stay at Cromer, the most important part of my packing-up preparations was the copying out of this psalm, which I had already learnt by heart, in case it must be that on so long a journey I should forget the words. This evening I have just read this childhood chosen song in Hebrew, with an English translation below.

15 May Full moon; wind soughing; into the sunny afternoon slanted a sprinkling of raindrops. After sunset a mist was born in the mid-region of the forest and came journeying up here across the west – the sky of aquamarine. I read yesterday a few pages of 'The Little Mermaid' in the Hans Andersen book Will bought for his grandsons and lent us, remembering it was one of my favourite of the tales as the

'Forsaken Merman' is among Matthew Arnold's poems: it has not lost its magic.

7 June Too tired last night to write a word. I am much better this evening at the cottage. Arriving with a number of letters to comfort me over the shingles, I read them under my bush that creaks like the tackle of a sailing ship and felt restored. There were two from Mother and even some medicine she sent me by air mail. O Mother Mother. One was from Alyse's house and Alyse wrote too and said how seeing Mother gave her new life.

10 June Only a few hours after we returned to the Beale word came that there was foot-and-mouth on Ndere, already confirmed by the vet and only three weeks after the farm was cleared from quarantine. A handsome young cheetah ran past us in the evening walk very near with all its spots and tawny pelt plain to see. The dogs put it up a cedar tree. We could see the topmost boughs shaking while they barked below.

28 June Parisian postcard blue gold white: ivy wall, river, Notre Dame – a real picture from France, with Gallic cocks on the stamps, Mother has sent me. And she and Phyllis sailed up the river in a boat by that ivy wall. O what fun to have it, to see it now propped against the Chinese books which lately I have not opened very much. Jupiter rose into my vision this morn in the little east window in the big room.

23 July Watching the glow growing in the east and remembering certain words as I waited for day, that was a happy moment. Another was writing to Mother, another reading my first Hebrew passage about Jacob sleeping and dreaming and seeing the ladder.

25 July Prayer is being in silence in the living consciousness. Something like this came to me as I watched the bright dawn. St. Teresa's 'prayer of quiet' it may be, but one has to make one's own approach to what is known to all times. 'To live is to despair or to pray.'

26 July Often now it seems to me I have lost what I used to regard as myself, that customary complex of likes and dislikes, responses and retreats, affections and doubts. I am merely a human being as any other, part of the process of coming into and going out of existence; or is this merely another act of imagination?

27 July This strangeness or detachment is an approach to the universal, as in the plays of Shakespeare. But there must not be with it disintegration or acceptance of the dissolving character, even in having being only incompletely, a momentary catch, as it were, in the filaments of the generations before and after. In youth one may be a pelagian, later this passes, one can do nothing with oneself.

29 July True prayer is universal for each one, how then can any say the prayer of another because of difference of creed or tradition is unavailing? Priests who are ministers of the universal, those who guide all to the highest, forget or deny this at their peril; and they forget or deny when they condemn anyone who is directing his mind and strength to worship the truth.

31 July In one of the back numbers of *Tomorrow* I read an essay by Kathleen Raine on poetry and symbols and tradition which interested me as containing thoughts in agreement with my own. There was a brief note from Marie Canavaggia* and another review in French of the *Autobiography*.

1 August The threat of starvation is much in my mind now, for cattle and all creatures that eat grass, for birds, for ants that move now ever more slowly over the dry ground or over our clothes, in search of food or moisture, when we rest on the grass. Death is hard to bear, when the life-giving earth ceases to succour the ten thousand things.

3 August Each day I type a few pages of my book *The Agate Lamp** not without enjoyment of the story but considering the vocabulary meagre. I lack familiarity with strong and out-of-the-way words, for one must know, that is be intimate with, words in various contexts before one can use them naturally and surely; they must, when there is need for them, spring to the mind, point the sentence, sharpen the image, and this they won't do if they are hunted for.

4 August, Nairobi Whistle of an engine which always pleases me to hear, but walking in the blue-lit street just now I heard a prisoner in his cell call out, then bang on the door, the kicks on the door grew louder as we walked away.

5 August In the afternoon Gerard and I drove to Olorgesailie,* an exciting drive, facing at first the Ngong Hills with their emerald slopes and blue smoke rising from their folds, then descending to the floor of the Rift Valley down to 3,300 feet, to the site of the stone hand-axes chipped 100,000 to 200,000 years ago on the shores of a lake that lay between the volcanic and romantic mountains of Olorgesailie and Ol Esakut: the cacti planted round the site grow natural axes of just the same shape as the innumerable stone ones which are on the whole larger and flatter than those on Ndere. We had a good view of four elephants. This visit set us talking for an hour after dinner of evolution and metaphysics.

6 August   Returning from Nairobi when we were about 9 miles from Nanyuki the car skidded in dust and corrugations, crossed the road, went back to the near side, struck the verge and turned completely over, landing on its wheels again. We were unhurt though the whole windscreen was torn out. Gerard started the engine and began to drive slowly on, presently stopping a passing car to send word to the garage. Within less than two miles of the town the mechanics came out to meet us, and one of them soon drove us home. There was a letter from Mother at Timau.

7 August   Christopher Gibson came this morning when I was in the middle of baking a sponge cake. He had a very happy time in England with Anna, but it is all rather sad here with his crop ruined by drought. His lease expires at the end of October and he will not be able to pay any more rent. Gerard has agreed to extend it for six months, if he cannot pay for it at the end of that time Christopher will withdraw completely and his house and store built on the farm will be his payment. He is so pleased with the way his men have worked and built the dwelling at Marji ya Mturackwa which was to have been his and Anna's house.

10 August   A flock of round and woolly ewes lies close to us tonight at the cottage, the moon as round shines upon them. The cattle we saw in our walk are thin, life is a hardship for them now. Day by day it grows drier and one or another lies down and tries no more. Old toothless cows fall by the furrow and cannot rise. Only the cicadas are unsuffering and sing to the moon.

23 August   Life without St. Paul, his Epistles, would be unthinkable I decided, when I discovered that Margaret* knew only the passages set for the Sunday epistle. I'm tempted to say his writing has been the strongest moral influence in my life and I have read and re-read continuously his writings from childhood. The power and character of his words and phrases impress themselves immediately and indelibly on a child's mind.

17 September   Sheep dipping the last two mornings, and tomorrow the Company meeting in Nanyuki. Bogo, the most old white ox with mighty horns, mild air and stately gait, who has long been toothless but maintained his bulk in full roundness is worn now by the drought, his white hide is soiled, his massive horns too great a burden for his gaunt head, very stiff and slow is his walk now, but still he often keeps his place at the head of the herd.

3 October Swifts have come into my sky in the last day or two. Already have died 30,000 cattle of the Samburu, 10,000 of the Derobo. I remember how once Elizabeth wrote daily in the farm diary *drouth*. Gerard and his mother left for Nairobi this morning. Christopher came in for a little while, otherwise I have been alone reading the *Upanishads*.

11 October A sense of having reached the ultimate is with me as I walk over the gray land into the teeth of a raging barren wind, but it is no more ultimate than the despair of certain moods that lay hold of me. Still, it is a harsh and cruel time and cannot but bring a certain weariness of spirit.

16 October Alarm at tea-time yesterday of cattle thieves making off with three oxen from among the milking cows. Everyone went to the forest and probably because the cattle themselves objected all escaped. The horses joined in the excitement, trotting up to the rails, staring out over the forest, even neighing. One ox had a bad spear-thrust and the bell was gone from the neck of another.

17 October Rain on the roof tonight after a day of gloomy dark, sunless and rainless both. I think of it falling on the bones of all creatures the drought slew that will not eat the grass springing anew. Ho, everyone that thirsteth … My ears drink the sound. We saw last night four great ground-hornbills, birds always associated with rain.

27 October Stillness, conscious or unconscious, is an exterior mark of thought and prayer of a dedicated life. One may also walk, but that is rather a concession to restlessness. But quickness and activity belong to the everyday life, this stillness is not idleness but concentration and devotion. There is no need to express anything, that is opinions, emotions.

30 October All dawn this morning looking to the east I saw a comet, the head not far above the horizon, the tail, somewhat like the beam of a searchlight, reaching I imagine between a quarter and a third of the way to the zenith. The impression of this luminous train in the crystal sky before sunrise has been with me all day.

2 November All Souls' Day. Twentieth anniversary of my wedding. Gerard and I went to see W.E.P. this evening and did not find him, but saw Tony who landed for a moment on his way home from Nairobi and flew off again. He said he'd read the comet was first reported by two Japanese astronomers who saw it quite separately from one another and who had both also, oddly enough, discovered two other comets. It is a new one and will not return for 500 or 1,000 years. By the gate on our way we met Will so we did have a little talk with him in the gloaming.

3 November Will came to tea and we went out with him afterwards to look for a black walking-stick given him by an African, which he'd lost the day before. Gerard found it. I thought Will was sad, almost admitting he felt old and was unwilling to go far from home. He said Sharman told him this was the largest comet ever to whizz round the sun in man's time. All the morning Gerard and I were riding; in the afternoon I was by the river.

25 November Waiting on my bed for Gerard and the lamp I considered in the quiet dark, with the miniature crusader in Mappowder church before me, the theme and subject of my next writing. I decided I could not continue with the crusades following further the characters I knew, especially Isabella and Amalric. I remembered how some time ago in one of my dawn sessions of sweet silent thought, I decided my next romance must be more metaphysical; now suddenly in this intense obscure stillness I knew that I should study and write of Plotinus. Mother sent me a letter from Streatley; she said David* was there, and how thinking of this age-fellow made me recall the pale rather thick-set small boy in a peaked cap which his mother was always telling him to touch to women we met in the village in our nursery walks, how angrily he would not, and how Angela* and I enjoyed our exemption from this point of etiquette which at that time nearly reconciled us to being girls.

26 November I used to think I was real and all others unreal, now it is the other way round, every human being alive has a distinct individuality and I, the writer of this, am a shadowy spectator, something embodied in the present of all who have been before me, whose being causes mine to be what it is. The stamp on Rosemary's* letter from Sierra Leone represents just such a lily as I found on Ndere on Sunday, on this gay stamp the flower is called simply 'climbing lily'.

6 December How I justify my reading to myself if not to the world is, and I began this afternoon to read the first book of the *Georgics* for perhaps the twentieth time, by the idea that the classics read for sheer devotion gain as well as give life. I also mixed Christmas puddings and made the butter, and Gerard and I had a good walk, cloudy and sprinkled with rain, with a fine scene at the last of the cows on a bank above us black upon a luminous gulf in the west.

8 December   Vivid dreams of the last two nights still appear before me: as always water – a deep deep well near a castle that stood on the very end of a narrow headland running out to sea – with some sense of drama and swift messengers. Last night I was pursued by a straight-horned ox, the massive horns jutting out from his head on either side six feet or more, and he had also a gray mane lying in long strands on his neck. He was, I knew, Behemah, and I plunged into a river like the Uaso Nyiro, down into opaque water. One horn just harmlessly touched me in this refuge. Then a herdsman shouted to me from the far side. I was saved.

19 December   Gerard and I rode to visit Will this morning. He was in the studio making small paintings of the mountain for Christmas presents. A long list of names and presents lay on his desk. Still he seemed not unwilling to be interrupted and kept us for lunch. Afterwards he showed us in a little notebook the verses he had chosen for Charles's grave from *Pilgrim's Progress*, the two verses beginning: 'No lion can him fright'. When Gerard was saddling the ponies he asked me to find for him in Grandfather's Bible the text Jennifer had chosen, John xv.13. From the silence after he read I knew the words were a revelation and even something like a death-blow to him. And so it happened that as we had found him sad and turning over things in his heart and mind so we left him (after a cheerful time) in a stern mood. All the passionate and psychological elements of a Greek tragedy are here. It struck me last night how two men with the same name are at the beginning and end of the life of Jesus.

20 December   A pyramid of green serpent-skinned fruit flanked by oranges, lemons, red apples, all between the silver candlesticks; still life in no need of verb. Gerard went down to the dipping and met H. and W.* there. He sold them all the best steers and the worst milk cows simply because of the long drought. Many of the cows are so poor he asked nothing for them, only glad to have them taken away.

22 December   Gerard's mother came back here yesterday, St. Thomas's Day, with his father. This morning I began reading again Inge's *Plotinus* with much satisfaction.

24 December   With my mind on Charles and on death I have been polishing the silver.

Christmas Day We all went to church at Timau, Gerard asked Mr. Le Page to call for a minute's silence in remembrance of Charles Powys. The name sounded brave in the church. His father sat between Rose and Gilfrid. I came home alone while Gerard took his parents to the Catholic church in Nanyuki. When he returned we went along the forest path by the stream.

29 December Three letters today, Mother, Alyse, Mrs. Theophilus.* Mother told me Alyse was weak and dizzy, and this letter of hers is as a farewell and so perfectly Alysian. It was odd how in Gilfrid's house with its quiet books, arched opening between two rooms and light of a Dutch interior I had a vision of Alyse passing through with a little shawl over her shoulders, and her purposeful tread, quite at home but not regarding me.

31 December Farewell to the year with my mind on Mother, Alyse, Plotinus, and the hope of England in the Spring. There is a stillness of thought and it may be St. Teresa's prayer of quiet.

1966

9 January A crimson feather lay on the path in the forest, of liquid brilliance so that yellow leaves were discernible through it. I carried it home to set in the corner of the mirror frame where once my father set a tiny photo of me, the mirror into which looking once he said 'I suppose 'twill kill me' of his bronchitis, and the words I could not believe were yet a knell.

13 January Alexandria, after my reading of the last day or two, is much in my mind; that great city with its majestic buildings and temples, the ruins of some visible even now at low tide below the sea; the Gate of the Moon, the mole a distance of three-quarters of a mile from the city to Pharos; the harbour Eunostos, Fair Return, and the inner harbour the Box, Kibotos. Old Kibrono was knocked over by a buffalo today near Gertrude's tree. Its hoof struck his thigh, and it was swinging round its horns to attack when he thrust the tip of his bow into its nostril.

14 January In the afternoon, to clarify my mind after reading 'Sounding the Sixties – the U.S.A.' and a review of *The Strings are False* by Louis MacNeice in another paper sent me by Mother because he was at Sherborne Prep under L.C.P.,* after a few moments of reverie in which certain impressions formed themselves, intense and isolated, I write. 'Sounding the Sixties' caused me to want to start work at once on Plotinus, however feeble and ignorant I may be, so I have something to live in reading that I like. I smile over this. Then the look of that Irish-born poet confirmed the sense that is strong with me now – that we never belong to ourselves, even when we think we are being most rigorous with what we regard as our own nature, most fastidious in choice or taste. But partakers of the past, in mind as in body, however we bend to the future, still only in the reflections that every flow receives. Mother's letter today has set flowing again that sparkling water which dances through the days from the meeting of minds.

19 January The cruel drought and Plotinus, a vision of his towering interlocking structure of thought, are with me as presences when I wake in the night, and Plotinus became unreal, perhaps because of his disregard of evil. Yet by day I return to him as to reality or to what gives substance to the mirage of myriad being. Why is Pharos a day's journey from Egypt in the *Odyssey*, was it further then than the three-quarters of a mile of the Alexandrian mole?

19 February A pair of black-winged plovers has joined the crowned ones in the field in front of the house, and the usual red-legged ones are a trifle doubtful of the new-comers. I finished *The Philosophy of Plotinus* this morning, to my sorrow, so valuable and thoughtful a study it is; and the most consoling and exciting to my mind.

25 February As the cuckoo clock called 4 the rain, which has threatened all day, began a tentative pattering on the shingles. And the great ocean roar of wind charging through the gum strees sank down to a sough. The cloud cap under which I have moved, and tried to use as a thinking-cap, has come right to earth now, a fog against the window. The drought has broken, the rain-starved corn all unharvested.

27 February At last at the cottage. Aged Musa said a man came one night with intent to break in. Karoi gave the alarm, he waited in the shadows until the man came close and then shot an arrow. The would-be thief groaned, staggered, and then ran away. We went to see Will and found him entertaining four people to tea. They soon left, but O Will is ill with this bad influenza, with a frequent deep cough and the tickles of his allergy tormenting him. For all his feebleness he would walk with us through his banana plantation. And he told tales of lion and leopard cornered and speared in true Homeric vein.

6 March 'Our spiritual life is a vision and a creation'; I read this morning the introduction to the *Upanishads* by Juan Mascaro and filled my soul with silence. Then I went out and lay in the sun under singing cypress trees and thought until I fell into a glowing dark wholly without words and the wild wind waves in the trees ceased. In this soundless stillness and inner deep there was a small flutter of wings close to me. My eyes opened to see the bird, a babes-in-the-wood robin, come near with bright eye. The wind-singing began again.

14 March The fine judicial essay on George Fox by Gerald Bullett contains a memorable passage by Hooker and a quotation by Smith, the Cambridge Platonist, which sets forth something that has been much in my mind lately: 'That is not the best and truest knowledge of God which is wrought out by the labour and sweat of the brain, but that which is kindled within us by a heavenly warmth in our hearts.' And in a follower of Plotinus this is not simply emotional. But I have thought I probably identify faith too closely with the activity of the mind. The brain, for all that, must think, and what better activity can it have – trying to employ the utmost powers of its reason in seeking God? The will to use reason in this way comes from the heavenly warmth in the heart which I should call gnosis. Last evening we spent happily with Will driving out over his farm, seeing sheep and cattle. He made sketches of the mountain. We came in to a blazing fire, to books, letters and pleasant talk. The evening of this day, as of old, Gerard and I were on Ndere, we went to the Derobo Beacon and Gerard counted sheep. All the stock is now in this corner of the farm where the tail of a rainstorm has brought out of the dead grass here and there a green blade. Thanks to this the cattle look a shade better than they did last week.

15 March Gerard's birthday, and the day on which it has been long said that the drought would end. Certainly this night resounds with ceaseless thunder on all sides so as to be almost terrifying and lightning is continuous, as if the whole world were being bombarded. I cannot remember such storms, echoes and reverberations. And now as I write out of the high-thundering sky-god Zeus rain begins to fall on the thatch.

16 March Yes, that thunder, peal running into peal, went on for two hours, and when at last it died away the terrible roar of the river in spate sounded instead. The rain below was $1\frac{1}{4}''$ and here on our return I measured 2.19. The early morning at the cottage after the rain was exquisite, the eastern sky, the shapes of the trees, the singing birds.

Christopher in mid-harvest has withdrawn his combine and covered it with a tarpaulin.

17 March It seems to me that all these philosophers pass over and disregard, one and all with the exception of Uncle Jack, suffering, cruelty, pain, torture: evil itself is not a thing to be overcome as if it were not, by any love mysticism. Certain Christians on the other hand glory in the wrath of God and the torments suffered by men *because* they have sinned. And the agony of animals? My faith in Christianity springs most of all from my hope that through Christ no suffering is meaningless or unregarded. It is inherent in life, it must be while life is, and through Christ it may be just possible to believe it is one of the ways by which evil is to be conquered. But it must be faced to the full, to say God is Love is not enough, nor is any talk of being a sinner, of penances and denials and austerities. If it can be transcended in Spirit, love must also be transcended, a quality with an opposite cannot be One.

18 March 'We notice in this mysticism of Clement a total absence of suffering or of purifying trials, it resembles in this Neo-platonism, and in particular the mysticism of Plotinus', say the writers of *The History of the Primitive Church*. No doubt in the third century pain was as little regarded as it is in the east today. I suppose one might say insistence on suffering and on the importance of dodging it, or relieving it, is an idea that has steadily increased with the passing of the centuries since Christ. But it is in the later mystics that the lack of recognition of it disturbs me; not the virtuous self-inflicted suffering, but the ignoring of the suffering of the world.

19 March I was interested to read in the *TLS* the essay on Mircea Eliade, a Rumanian philosopher and historian of religions whose books are being translated into English: his theses of all men's need for religion, that whether they know it or not they live by the myths in the depths of their nature, that the earliest religious myths of human beings cannot be known from primitive religions because they spring from a far more remote age of human time.

20 March Resting on the roots of the giant fig tree I finished *The English Mystics*, and read how Gerald Bullett dealt with the One of Plotinus, which he also calls the Good, although it must be beyond our good and evil. It goes with, I think, 'There is none good but God', which means that in all else there is both good and evil, but whether it is true metaphysics I cannot say: 'while what is beyond good cannot conceivably be evil, what is beyond evil cannot be conceived otherwise than as in some sense good. The goodness of that which is beyond the categories is a goodness which, lacking the counterpart of evil, has real but not logical being.' And so I did not see Will who called in the afternoon, but Gerard and I walked down the river later and found him in his studio painting one of his innumerable pictures of the mountain. His spine is troubling him and he is wearing a corset, still for all he went for quite a walk with us.

21 March A happy time again near the spring with paradise fly-catchers both red and white and the *Phaedo* in translation, although it was only some time after I left off reading I was aware of the spirit of it and heard in my head the authentic voice of Socrates. Thunderstorms on the horizon when we went out nearly to Sirakoi after tea, and saw on the way what we'd not seen before, a kori bustard displaying his plumage, very odd indeed he looked standing motionless in the midst of a flat bare fire-eaten plain.

24 March It was my luck today to see a most interesting bird that rose up suddenly beside me from the little stream in the forest so that for a moment I saw it well, striking bright orange legs dangling as it went up, brownish back and white below. It flew away through the trees with no cry. To find this beautiful and unusual bird took me some time looking through the book, but at last, when we had almost given up, I lighted on it by seeing a plate which showed those orange legs: finfoot. The bird book notes that this aquatic bird has been seen to take a butterfly.

25 March Another bird adventure befell me this evening, as I was walking over rocky ground I perceived just in time a sitting bird below my descending foot. So scared it was, as it flew out it caught one of its two eggs with a foot and sent it two feet or more from the one below me, so it came to rest against a stone. Nightjars' eggs are laid on the ground without even the slightest scrape. The egg that rolled away was not harmed. I restored it to the side of its fellow and prayed the bird would come back. Failing to secure a room in the Montague Hotel I asked Hotel Bookings to find us one, and they have – in that grim brick late Victorian Gothic one in Russell Square. I can't help a regret for the Georgian Montague with a small back garden where a blackbird sang last time we stayed there in the Spring.

3 April In morning sunshine with my eye taken by the snowy mountain I take leave of my journal until England, dedicating it, my pen, my books and papers, and all the quiet hours in my room at the Beale to the Muses, with the hope that all they have given me may be a joy also to others.

6 April, Mappowder Home, Mother, Mappowder church; a long fine sunny spring day, all the birds and flowers, fields green, trees and hedges bare, brown, outlines on the sky. Last evening Gerard and I went to the service in Westminster Abbey.

7 April At 3.45 the bantam cock crowed, two hours later the birds began to sing. The day was perfectly sunless and murky. Isobel's son, Tordis and their children came to tea, they are staying in her house for Easter.* Afterwards we three walked down the lane to the field, Mother showed me one or two cowslips and I picked palm for her to smell. She made one of her tiny bunches, as no one else could ever do.

Good Friday Willow-warbler in a bare hedgerow bush and larks singing between gate-bars as in autumn. After the ninth hour the sky cleared, the sun shone, Mother and I walked together to the field I call Lark Rise. I have seen bluebells. I have begun to read *Reality and Man* by Simeon Frank.. Kathleen Ryall came and planted potatoes for Mother. Gerard pulled the bell for Dr. Jackson this morning. O, I read a perfect piece of descriptive country writing: J.C.P. describing Phudd Bottom,* in the *Philobiblion*, an American university magazine.

9 April A happy day, wind changing from north-east as we walked before breakfast, high moving clouds. Gerard and I went to Dorchester and saw Louis in hospital: he did not look bad and only seemed to wander slightly in his head – but whether he really knew us or not I don't know. He was sitting in a chair by his bed, and fully dressed. The bus ride we enjoyed very much, looking at the country. All evening we walked with Mother in the fields, rain-soaked puddly fields with gateways deep in mud; we were in high spirits. Skylarks, no curlews.

13 April Sunless, colder, north wind, talk of snow on high land, *no trace of sun all day*. I bought new boots in Dorchester and they somehow hurt my ankle, so it is very swollen and painful, while I was exulting in the shivering meads that they didn't hurt my toes at all. We picked cowslips and marsh marigolds, these very few and dwarfed, not like the golden massy kingcups at Horsebridge.

14 April Snow covered Mr. Moore's roof when I woke this morning before 6, and the flakes continued to float down till after noon. The depth was about four inches, Rosemary telephoning from Somerset said six. The roads are clear, but roofs, hedges, fields, trees still covered tonight. Again no gleam of sun and the faithful north wind. The country and the favourite fields under snow is a strange sight to me. A farm man told Gerard he'd seen two swallows yesterday: 'they'd best go back.'

15 April Fourth day of obscurity ever deepening as the hours came and went until in the early evening a stealthy rain slid straight down through the windless air already murky with moisture. Even this, so low is the temperature, scarcely wears away the snow and many patches of white overlay the loved greenery. Gerard has read all day long. He has now before him the monumental *History of Christianity* Mother has given to him. I read in the *TLS*, 'inwardness always leads to transcendence': which could have been a comment on S. L. Frank. I think he writes too much, tends to over-analysis, passages of illumination or original insight are rare in *Reality and Man*.

23 April Thrush singing in the top of the bramley tree so bravely at sunrise and sunset. April weather at last, showers, sunshine, rainbow when we picked wood anemones near Heaven's Gate. From Sherborne westward trees and hedges are far ahead of these.

26 April Cuckoo this morning, when I was in the garden repeating the 130th psalm, called to the east and another replied further away to the west. I had a letter from W.E.P. and his back is not good. He tells of rain. A cold east wind blew this evening when we all three walked in other fields, to find one with many cowslips.

30 April Not one cloud in heaven this fair day, each hour could have been told by a sundial. Four times this morning I heard the curlew's bubbling cry and saw the bird crossing in flight a green meadow. This spring call, with the peewits in February, the skylark's and wood-wren's songs and certain notes of the thrush, is most thrilling, makes chords vibrant that no other sounds touch.

2 May Summer. Mother and Kathleen* and I went to Chydyok* today, walking most of the way up from the village to Gertrude's home, locked, empty, but with a sense of welcome. On we went, seeing larks, corn buntings and a wheatear, to the cliffs. Sea and Portland were all but invisible in this dense fine-weather haze. I saw a fox run out of a gorse thicket and a little later a deer sprang up, the same kind as the one on Ball Hill, but this had quite fine horns. Returning to East Chaldon we went to Mrs. Lucas, ninety-two years old now, but keen and loving, sitting by her fire with temples hollow and skin transparent: 'but I be getting better'. Katie's grave with its wooden cross we visited next; and then Mrs. Cobb* at West Chaldon in her fine old house with the high hill rising up beside it like a wall. The meeting of valleys, lines of the downs, seagulls, Chydyok; a cuckoo called all the time we were there.

11 May New, renewing, renewal of life, that is prayer in this world grown ancient in its repetition and recoil upon itself. Repetition (and what one might call relative fulfilments) has in itself a quality of timelessness; but what is always perfectly new, as it were from the very beginning, pristine, is every single gesture towards inward prayer, of mind or of heart; a simple gathering of attention; a conscious cessation of consciousness. This is new and as life-giving as that imcomparable opening of the Book of Genesis, 'In the beginning God created ...' My adventure today was a watery experience and a failure. After Mother had gone off with Valentine (who like Sir Thomas Wyat cannot rest, and often cannot sleep) I set off in rain on my bicycle to see the Cerne Giant. I was out for three hours, the rain did not cease for one moment. I failed to find, in spite of his magnitude, my quarry with the club. Rain, cloud, driving mist, obscured the hills, I was too soaked to make a careful search. I had to walk down as well as up those steep hills because the brakes would not hold in all the wetness.

14 May All day the garden warbler has sung in my head, the passionate intense music of a bird newly arrived. The early sun lit it in the ash in Theodore's lane, of gray twigs and leaves infinitesimal giving no screen to the bird with tremulous throat. With scarcely a pause, as though indeed it could never cease, it sang; not moving about the tree but turning its head a little one way or the other. Rare is a moment so exquisite and I must remember, remember, remember: when the bloom of poetry is dashed away, another winged and gay cometh.

15 May By far the warmest day, the village is all decorated with lilac and apple blossom breathing sweetness. In the fields I went very slowly through the seventh and eighth hours of the day, resting by the corners of hedges, near bluebells and moss. And I saw in an ash with ivy festoons a pair of long-tailed tits, their small zree zree first calling me. The grass was very soft, the oaks of many colours, a gold by a green, others touched with red. The most persistent bird in copse and hedge and high bough singing chiff-chaff, the best cuckoo day, too.

16 May 'In May he calls all day ...' Bland, windless weather, woods and fields as in a trance; on returning from these spellbound pastures a wholly unknown dove startled Mother and me by the churchyard corner, a coo like a boy's call; high double coo, a pause, one lower and shorter. The first bursting out. Then the bird, a medium-sized pigeon (between ring and turtle) flew over the way.*

18 May I had a good reading of my selections of Plotinus this afternoon, but the other books I have been hoping to get from Francis* about him are all out of print. I should like to have another translation besides this of Taylor, although he is probably not bad. 'So may we also in heart and mind thither ascend and with him continually dwell.' Ascension Day Collect. 'The transcendency of the contemplative energy. True vigilance is a true elevation from, and not in conjunction with, the body.' (Plotinus)

3 June Full heat of summer: the first wild roses. Michael Hooper* called this morning, I was making bread. He had his wife and three daughters with him. 'That's a Kenya smell!' he said when the loaves came out of the oven. I like Michael, and I thought he looked white and tired, and as ever a little like Charles. He said he was homesick for Kenya all the time. Yet he lived there for so brief a spell. In the afternoon Mother's friend Glen Cavaliero came and sat with us in the garden for about two hours. He is ordained, but just now studying at Cambridge, aged nearly forty. Isobel came in and took him off to view her house. After that I visited Vera and persuaded her, keeping firm hold of her hand, to walk to Mother's garden for the first time this year. The news of the landing of U.S.A.'s *Surveyor* on the moon, a soft landing.

7 June Living oblivion of sleep, most blessed of all states, when consciousness rests still in reality. Though I did have one dream last night, of a mountain volcano, Kenya perhaps, overhanging a soundless sea. Down rolled rocks and crags hurtled through the air and trying to escape with others I found myself on a scree of whitish uncrossable shingle that crumbled away under my feet so that no flight was possible. I spoke for a minute or two with Sylvia Warner* as she sat in the motorcar at Mother's door. She did not look well, and the brown eyes that looked into mine were as appealing as those of Valentine's small poodle Fougère. Even, Sylvia had the same hair-fringed face. I liked her, the tone of her voice and her agreement with me over the mercy and the purification that is quiet sleep. Nocturnal sleep, that is; sleep in the day may rather dull the senses and brain and leave behind no lightsome mood.

11 June Barnaby Bright all day and no night, so I write in the sun of an un-ending summer day with a single thrush singing. The blackbirds still flute snatches, melodious snatches of spring song. Last night was a fierce thunderstorm, two hours of peals and volleys and dazzling lightnings, from 10 to 12, suffocating heat and almost no rain. *Sir Gawain** is a flawless poem, I read it last thing with a sense of all whims satisfied. The description of country and weather so keen amid magic and mediaeval glories, courage, romance. The braided belt, girdle of green and gold; poetry, I, as the knight did, take into church.

14 June The wish for a river came to me in the night so this day, when Mother had Kathleen,* I went with the bicycle, climbing first Bulbarrow and walking also down to Woolland, Okeford Fitzpaine, a detour to Fiddleford, then 'clotey Stour'. Hiding my machine in the deep grass I went to the riverside about 100 yards below the bridge where was a fir-willow-alder-maple group, the willow with many trunks forming a seat, a couch, a hidden lair for me where I could watch grayling feed as I fed, hear reed warblers. A tree-creeper came to spiral up the willow stem, alighting once a foot from my foot. I went presently up the footpath to the town, on my way home, to Sturminster Mill. I could hardly believe it when I heard the familiar noise of a mill merrily turning; sacks filling, a man within to greet me, a clear mill tail, a rush of white water over the weirs. There were many cotes on the wall and a crowd of pigeons on the roof. Sleek red Hereford steers grazed among buttercups across the stream, by the bridge meadow cranesbill. And it seemed all my life I had never left the eddying river and the smooth running mill.

19 June Owls and a wakeful night haunted by human mortality which, I fancy, is in the air in England where there are so many old old people. But the cloudy day brought a sense of grace and thankfulness. Oliver* brought his father to tea. Frail, thin, rarified, his abundant voice checked, Louis still has his gallantry and aplomb undiminished and commands his spidery legs to bear him. His complexion still the colouring J.C.P. so marvelled at. Amusingly Oliver said he'd seen me one day in Dorchester and was following to speak to me when I vanished from his view into a church and he gave up the pursuit: 'I couldn't follow you in there.'

30 June End of midsummer month to my grief. But for joy today came the great book I ordered from Heffers, *Plotinus*.* This complete translation I have given myself from Mother to mark the summer of 1966 in England, Dorset, Mappowder, Mother's house. A wonderful fine day – breakfast tea supper in the garden.

5 July 'Off centre' I heard said in the night, with a vision I cannot recall well enough to describe. But I knew the description was for me, and it may be also for Plotinus. Schuon says the position of man is absolutely central, so I might choose to interpret this by saying I do not wholly belong to humankind, and it is possible perhaps that certain aperçus may be granted me from the obliquity of my eyebeams at eternity. A calm sunless day, with soft showers: but I want to say also what a powerful and liberal introduction this unknown S. J., Paul Henry, gives to my volume of Plotinus. His intellectual grasp is fully worthy of his subject.

6 July Mother and I went to Dorchester by bus, and by walking very slowly she was able to go along the river path. A swan came floating downstream to meet us where the limpid water was black from overshadowing high-foliaged trees. We saw also a reed warbler. Now at the last hour of the day for almost the first time the sun is shining. Valentine wrote me a letter a few days ago which I value telling me something of her search for truth. She is extraordinarily self-controlled and expresses her responses and emotions in the most level and unemotional voice. I think she has the gift of discovering the best in people and also (like Athos) of taking care her own sorrows leave her turned into joys for others. To my joy the first time this visit there were two smartly painted caravans at that corner a mile or so out of the town, two well-groomed horses, and a troop of gipsy children.

7 July This day, which began with my reading *Twenty-eight Poems* by Valentine and making a poem myself,* has been a memorable one because I have seen Alyse again – after how many years I know not. Isobel drove me to Morebath through little lanes all the way: first I walked the church path and then went into the church and even found a flycatcher's nest on top of the stone post and under the lintel of a gateway leading into a farmyard. When I went up to Alyse's room, by her welcome I knew all would be well and indeed we had a happy and precious time – too brief – alone together. And she does look well. How all the almost thirty years of our friendship fell away and it was as if I was with her in the attic at Chydyok. The day was fine cool sunny all the time. Ham Hill clad in grasses tawny as its stone, the whole sweep of country below. East Coker church tower in pure gold and field vert.

10 July Sunny morning, wet and windy evening. I have felt sad today, but I read Valentine's two loose-leaf books of chosen quotations. Most of the writers of east and west are there, those who have been Gerard's and my companions all these years, and a few others I do not know. Her accent on the whole rather on morals than metaphysics but some are singularly well-chosen. I thought there was too much of Dom Chapman for my liking and I missed out Francis of Sales. I read more of J.C.P.'s essay on St. Paul aloud to Mother and exulted in the cosmic gale of language.

11 July   The fearsome power of the swifts is in my mind, I catch my breath, my heart misses a beat, as they whirl out of heaven to a little ledge of wood under the eaves close to my window where before them sparrows and starlings have been, a crevice, spiky with dead grass and with a long string dangling. They dive through the aether with demonic screams in ever lessening circles, shooting ever nearer, desperate it might seem that after sixteen hours on their curved wings they must seek a refuge, a humble support. The pair descends only to pierce heaven again in fury, to vanish far. At length they leave their wild liberty, yield with muted shrillings to night.

30 July   Tempests from the south-west, brilliant raindrops flung against the window-panes, black clouds, blaze of sunlight. A glorious evening with the wind west again, gold and blue gulfs in the storm-dark heaven. Best of all the prospects from the high ridges between here and Maiden Newton when Gerard and I drove to see Valentine, a most exciting drive whirling down into those narrow bottoms, racing over the hills in a gale as though in air. Then Valentine in her room, her garden house, by her river, Sylvia came also for some of the time. Gerard liked them both and was interested in their powerful emanations or 'radiance'. Sylvia was particularly kind to me, lent me a book for Mother – who stayed at home because she had a cold – and described to me a thunderstorm in autumn when green lightning transformed the grass to spring in that brief moment that is all.

28 August   I had a good reading this afternoon in the garden when everyone was out, Plotinus, Virgil, Euripides. Yesterday I took down my George Herbert and copied a few verses. Each year I think I read certain of his poems with more attention. Isobel drove Mother to Winterbourne Tomson and had tea in the garden with us.*
North-east wind today. Gertrude* tomorrow, I look forward to seeing her.

29 August   In Sherborne Abbey I kneeled by the tablet of Sir Thomas Wyat and gave him Valentine's thanks as she had asked me. Gertrude's train arrived punctually. The day began and ended with rain but there was sunshine on the gold stone of Sherborne, Gertrude's skin the same tint, and her hair.

31 August   Warmth, haze, west wind, a day-dream day. I went to Dorchester with Gertrude, showed her the portrait of Judge Jeffreys and saw her off on the London train, sped back along South Street to the King's Arms, saw Valentine as she rose to meet me and delivered myself to her for the rest of the day until 4 o'clock when she brought me back to Mother. I was taken to the river at Moreton where we saw a gray wagtail and a swan, then to her home by the same river. I miss Gertrude.

12 September   Mother and I came in from a walk in the beautiful fields in wind and clearest sunlight to find a tiny note from Isobel to say Louis died last night quietly in his sleep: the only thing left him to do, but we feel sad and the living Louis keeps coming before us, and the sound of his voice speaking out of another age of leisure and ease and love.

25 September   Early, when earth floated and mourned in a white fog that made trees shower tears, I opened the church door to find scarlet berries glow of deepest crimson, flowers low on the floor, green apples on ledges gleam and inward glow of brass. A quiet communion, vibrant with farewell. Then for the evening and Dr. Jackson's triumphant Festival of Farewell and Harvest the church was brimful, hymns shouted, his voice leading all resonant, no quaver of age. At the end he shook hands and spoke a word to each one: the last Rector of Mappowder. *Ave, ave, numquam vale.*

8 October   Fifty-first birthday. Lilac mist in light drifts where woods shelter the fields early. Soon sun warm, sun all day, wind east but indiscernible, unfelt, so sweet a heat. We went, Mother and I and Gerard, to Fiddleford Mill where the river is most beautiful under the wooded hills, broad calm reflective as a lake, dashing in white waves over the three tiers of weirs. The small stone mill rebuilt as the legend cut in its wall said, in 1566, was working with the perfect smoothness of nymph-fed water-power, grinding barley into a fine meal. Then we continued to Hammoon richest in mediaeval atmosphere and the ancient church above all endowed with the gift of bestowing peace, serenity, the grace of the prayer of silence. Cows and steers and mares and foals fed in a verdant meadow by the eddying streams of the beautiful river, we watched them for long, the dancing prancing curvetting foals, a slim-limbed bay filly and roan colt with fiery mane and tail. Home over Bulbarrow; Corfe Castle and Montacute Hill in the clear view. Tea in the garden. First portent of this happy day moon and Jupiter in a misty ring.

9 October No light heart tonight for farewell to Mappowder, Mother, the benison and consolation of the church, the closeness, the bare and wooded beauty of the three hills. The ash tree under whose meditative and medicinal boughs I have passed almost every early morn. Those scattered wild rose petals, then the ash which grows in perfect stature where the road just there is highest, a slight humpiness my feet find as I salute the tree and giver of reverie and remember the garden warbler's lyric singing. Now in the time of leaves falling glowing changing to dark or gold, silver or scarlet or no-colour, in the favourite month of October, in my most immemorial year, I must take leave of all these, with thanksgiving and praise.

12 October, Africa Gerard and I came home to the Beale last evening, drought or at least extreme dryness still rules. Foam had died, on 10 September, we did not know till our return. The other dogs are well. There was a fine cock crowing in the heart of the rose glow which suffused all the sky and then gave place to an emerald radiance.

9 December The 82 bales of wool went off the farm today in four lorry loads, to be shipped from Kilindini, on the *Uganda*, if all is well. Good luck to the voyage and sale. Weight about 32,000 lb. I had letters from Mother and Valentine, and presents from them both. And a perfect Christmas card from Nellie,* a really exquisite design with her two children, shepherds, angel, star, stable in outline.

12 December Gerard and I went round Ndere for the first time since our return. It was especially populated by storks stalking and performing their lofty gliding dances from earth to zenith. In the evening we called on Will and found him much better and happier. He'd been out again in his Land Rover, flown to Kisima for lunch with Rose, had a teaparty, and then walked with us to see his angora goats, which must have been nearly two miles there and back.

21 December Our first ride for certainly well over a year this morning: we went round Eland Hill on Bonnie and Cherry, the storks are still here. In the afternoon I went to meet Sally* and we walked back along the river path, though there is little river to be seen most of the way. She loved the lambs, the cottage, my Fig Tree seat. After tea we visited the three waterfalls. I was happy all the time with her and so was Gerard. When he drove her back he found Will had gone to bed and was looking more at ease there.

30 December   Noisy comforting hyraxes this dark night, for there was a rainstorm, perhaps over the plain where the oryx was, and Orion is cloud-hung and no moon risen, so the tree hyraxes creak and croak after their conversational fashion on the darkest nights and the brightest. Venus was clear tonight; we found with her influence a lamb lost in the thickets.

1967

7 January   First week of this year gone by ending with an even fiercer flame than last night; as the celestial transformation began a breeze set black leaves aquiver and the light resembled an eclipse. The incandescence with the silver planet in the midst continued for nearly an hour, drawing with night closer to the horizon until it seemed the reflection of a distant city given to the flames ... the flaming ramparts of the world of Lucretius could never have lit the cosmos with radiance more intense, nor have I known a more prolonged and thrilling irradiance within, shivering waves of nerve responses.

8 January   We went to church at Timau where Richard Carles read prayers. I had a vision last night as I do now and again. This was of a willow twig, a small brown leafless twig with tight pearl-gray buds, against a clear blue sky. This twig which I saw so plainly was myself. I knew this and felt myself it completely, when the buds fully opened, became gold soft honey-sweet catkins. It was a memorable sensation of seeing and being. Who could possibly tell beforehand, I thought in this state of golden grace, a dry brown sprig could be so transformed. And I remembered who it was that shed grace on me.

11 January   A low-water day with grieving for old age – and just low. I wrote Alyse. Mother says the cliffs above Chydyok are being ploughed up, I feel Katie's shade rage at this sacred turf being turned, complain as did the Greek in the epigram whose bones escaped the sea to be scraped by the ploughshare.

13 January   The feeling is always with me now that I am not anyone, no person at all, nothing real. Perhaps that is because I do not have bad pain now as I used. But pain also can destroy with its fierceness, destroy the sense of separateness. I read this afternoon about Pindar in the Encyclopaedia and I have sent for his poetry in the Loeb Classics, difficult though it is I am beginning to feel after all these years of Homer and the Tragedies I would like another writer.

23 January   All power I may have comes from that depth where grief and joy, pain and pleasure, longing and fulfilment, each tense straining pair of opposites, draw their life and wild music, there where they are one force; one source sets contraries aquiver. Since we live by the interaction of polar rays this knowledge is dangerous, a dark power, an abyss of nought over which mind swings and balances on those strings of extreme passion, of love and despair. Both broken, both at once cut, the abyss, how find there 'logos'. A letter from Alyse. Walking between the two bright planets at the same level above the horizon in east and west I was conscious of their clear influences softly darting into me from either side, meeting mingling in flesh blood bones of me.

28 January   My heart is heavy tonight because a letter from Valentine written on Tuesday told me Mother is ill again, in bed with a return of sickness. I was woken from a deep sleep last night soon after midnight by a lion roaring very near. I've never heard such roars before. I woke Gerard and we went out almost expecting to see it. There was a flood of moonlight. Bogo the ancient milk-white ox came stalking stiffly towards us, a noble sight. Bonnie and Cherrie grazed quietly. The Kipsigis night watchman who came to collect Bogo explained this was the roar of a full-fed lion and the cattle and horses knew this and so were unalarmed, even if he came among them.

14 February   Mother's letter written the day before Will's arrival brought me joy, for she wrote with spirit, and after the X-ray. But on the outside she added: The end has come to Dr. Jackson and so the shade of the undefeated brave old man haunts me tonight. Riding through the *ruai** all in flower the air totty with the smell of it we had moving all the way above us a company of strong-winged swifts northward bound drawn no doubt by the insects the blossom drew. Shall I hear them scream in Mappowder.

16 February   My father's birthday 1882.

    Chang Ngo (by Ling Shang Yin)

 The candle wavers by the glittering screen, deep the shadows,
 The long river flows softly on and on,
 Mist dims the stars of dawn
 While Chang Ngo can only regret she stole the mystic herb.
 Jade the ocean, clear the heavens, night night at heart.

No paraphrase can touch the desolate longing and the beauty of this, one of the most exquisite Chinese poems.

19 February   The sun a glaring tawny-eyed lion this evening set all the land luridly alight because of the smoke of a dread fire on the mountain which has blazed for the last two days. All up the Mackinder Valley the flames raged and last night danced on the ridges; set heaven above aglow. Reaching the area without vegetation immediately below the peaks the fire on this side ended today. But it is in the forest above Nanyuki now and an even more terrible dark and sanguine smoke banner was reared high and threatening tonight.

20 February   'We have caught the radiancy of Being …' I made a poem for this this afternoon in hot sun on the window-sill. Saying my prayers in the dark now (lion roaring) I felt a yearning for Dr. Jackson – especially thinking how every morning he visited the church setting the door wide to the font, saying collects before the altar. The fire has moved down and away from the mountain and is probably in the lower forest now … The lion again with a despairing strain through the deeps of the fierceness. I went downstairs but it was silent.

27 February   Late in the afternoon when I was writing to Valentine by the open window there was a whirr of wings over me and a small bird alighting on the top of my head and set through hair into scalp tiny sharp claws. For an instant the delicate being of feathers with faintest perceptible warmth and weight stayed, then fled again into sunlight too swift for sight to identify though I did just see its form, maybe a sunbird.

3 March   William Ernest Powys seventy-nine. A blessed rain fell all through the night, ceasing at dawn. The air all day was soft and gentling, at first fragrant with the refreshed leafage of the gum trees. This herb-like breath of eucalyptus kept coming to me in wakeful dream-sweet night and my fancy then took it for the savour of rain-drenched sage borne down from the mountain by the night wind. There was snow all along the ridge far below 'Dinas Brân' in the morning and the mountain was gloriously white, I admired it through the little glasses. I made a little poem of the bird visiting me the other day.

14 March   I was happy to have a letter from Mother; one from Will too, and he sent us the portrait of Tolstoy he has been painting from a photograph Mother sent Gerard and he gave W.E.P. It is a rugged face, a strangely questioning tormented eye, Gerard is very struck by it. The afternoon ended with a hailstorm, it was fun to see the dancing grains, the sheet of ice like pearl aslant the valley.

Palm Sunday   A good ride this evening to see the sheep and the cows with tiny calves. I had just put the soup on the table at lunch-time when a visitor arrived in the shape of a three to four feet long snake, coming in through the open door and going under the table, he was both uninimical and unalarmed, and Gerard and I had great difficulty in getting him out of the cottage after our meal as he simply did not want to go and would not even when he was beside the open door. And finally driven forth he sat in his coils with his head raised about a foot watching for a chance to shoot in again. Iganata said the snake was called *mararu*. It was near the kitchen yesterday.

1 April   My brain today has felt as if a chrysalis were within it ('the golden-coloured resting stage in the life cycle of a butterfly') and only this moment at day's end has the butterfly fully unfolded its painted wings and taken flight. Splendours of lightning tonight and a rain-mourning wind.

22 April   Mother's Wedding Day, that too a Saturday that long ago. Yesterday Gerard and I went into St. George's church in Nanyuki. An African was sitting on the step near the door. Smiling he opened it for us and returned to his work. When we left he was happily polishing the silver chalice. It interested me to see this sacred vessel in the open air, to see it flashing as if it held all the sun in its bright curve.

26 April   The rain-bird called at dusk in the Windy Hill valley as if he had followed us up. Tonight after rain there is a chorus of hyraxes in the forest: a stillness and starriness after a grand and furious pageant of clouds on the brink of night, shapes savage if not obscene at which I could have cried aloud in a kind of terror.

2 May   You are returning to the anonymity of the skeleton: this came to me in the middle of last night as an aural vision, and partly woken I fell to considering how much all that we think we know of a person is of the flesh ... and when that is gone ... And yet, how we cleave to one we love *bone to bone*, and how it is in blood and bone that we seem to experience most completely certain deep and passionate emotions.

9 May   Pure and gleaming sunlight over the floating land this early morning, birds calling with liquid notes. A small copper butterfly ablaze on a sedge in the delicate watery world fired the jade drops on the grass blades near it. This pristine brilliance heralded even heavier rain.

We splashed most of the time in our evening walk. But Gerard did succeed in reaching Timau first and returned with letters. Mother's for me held a cheque for £200. I thought I might invite Gertrude here for a visit with part of this present. I enjoyed my morning both before and after breakfast today, reading thinking writing.

11 May   Earth replete with rain – any more water shed must spread a smooth silky coat over the surface. The green and pointed blades of grass and grain diamonded bend with the burden of wetness and pierce no more the air that never calls them with the clear sunshine to stand erect as spears. From our rock and root seats on Windy Hill this evening we saw in a tiny window in the clouds a point of gold, the tip of the new moon's horn, like a star. The tiny curved vessel sailed through the obscure space and was gone in the gray mass. A hint of hope it may be of fine weather coming after these long rains. Some malaise assails my mind and hand tonight so I can scarcely write.

14 May   Off and on for three or four days I have felt ill, and especially queer in my head, a taste perhaps of what Gerard has gone through since his encephalitis. The grass is waist high now on Ndere, green and with a sheen of flower-heads, soaking to walk through too for there was a silver shower in the afternoon, and with dew it will be still more steeped in wetness. A rare gathering of shining ones in the west: moon with a halo, and almost between Castor and Pollux, Jupiter and Venus.

24 May   The delight at night, after their absence through the dry years, fireflies. Over tall grass and bush black before moonrise the small streaks of green light came and went. And it is interesting how this moving and in-and-out-flitting starlight is so much more dynamic and disturbing and exciting to the eye than the meditative, still and romantic lamp of glow-worms. We were out for seven hours on our ride and it was a happy one. The cattle are sleek the sheep fleecy. There was an alarm at Sirakoi, a shot fired in the air and a blowing of whistles and yells – but a false one. Everywhere grass green and sown with flowers. Sitting under a thorn I read the third *Eclogue* to the ewes.

3 June   Taking up my pen after typing business letters I thought the virtue for me of writing is that it takes me out of time into a sphere endowed with a certain detachment of intellect, as serious reading does, but in writing there is something about unison of brain eye and hand that gives the act a unique human completeness, that makes writing when it is an expression of mind and will for their own satisfaction a resource and a relief from one kind of tension by means of another, as to a different temperament playing a stringed instrument would be. Egypt and the shade of war darkens our minds. We go to see Will this evening and sleep tomorrow at the Norfolk. I see the lambs from the window, gold and fleecy in deep grass, too well fed to do more than nibble delicately at the flower-heads.

10 July, Mappowder   Gerard and I parted at Hazelbury at 8 this morning. I went on to the beautiful river at Sturminster and by the Halter Path to Stalbridge. This time I went into the church and visited the tomb of my great-grandparents. My best time was by the river at Sturminster for two midday hours. I had my picnic by the only clump of white waterlilies I saw in the whole yellow-bordered reach I walked. A rare thing it was to be so close to the gold-hearted flower afloat on the stream, to watch the mystic curve of the moon petals. And almost at once I heard the shrill voice of a kingfisher and the bird with blue back blazing in the sun flew low over my pure lilies.

13 July   This afternoon Valentine came to meet me in Cerne Abbas: we were together for an hour in the church of St. Mary where it was cool. The heat and haze were all powerful. 'Spain', she said, as we crossed the street to the car and Fougère. When she had gone I climbed the long steep mile of hill hardly aware of the green cliff-like slope, the little town below plunged in mist. All the time in Africa I had longed to be with her there. To the cool clear spring I went alone.

17 July   An assembly of gray clouds has slowly overspread the sky this evening for my farewell to Mappowder, and there is in my heart an old grayness curiously lit and sharpened by piercing sorrow as when I was putting away the cups and little plates of Mother's in her cupboard after tea, each piece agleam with an uninterpretable signal for the sun still shone then. Gwyneth came for tea and was charming. Before she came Mother and I were very happy under the bramleys talking and reading. I am thankful and blessed. Mother has just come and stood at my side in her blue nightdress with a shawl Phyllis gave her over her shoulders ...

18 August, The Beale   Summer still in England, the month's name reminds me and it seems now to me years since I was there with ash trees and peewits and all I love. A very Plotinus' 'There'. The problem is to write a silent, a contemplative diary – for write one I must while I can, that at least is one thing certain. There was thunder again today and the moon rides among clouds. Shakespeare in Edith Sitwell's *Notebook** is fine ...

19 August   Thirty thieves, I was told, have been sleeping in the forest. I went to Nanyuki, happily there were letters for me from Mother and Valentine. Mother had been nursing Vera who was ill with bronchitis and sitting up at night with her. Is 'thinking' and reading the Bible, and philosophy, only a way of avoiding thinking (being aware) of suffering, a constant attempt to bring light into darkness that can never comprehend it ... not I but Christ in me. That One who alone can say with truth ἐγώ εἰμι.*

20 August   Mighty lion roaring last night when I put out the lamp and lit the candle in Daddy's brass candlestick. The day was quiet but for thunder, a sheer solitary day for me in my house of wood and stone. I wrote and read and walked and returned to read and write. At the beginning of the evening walk I was given a prize, a brown-green silver-sheen swansdown-edged feather from the wing of an ibis (Hadada) and the green plume went with me over the hills.

30 August   'What is everlasting life, what do the parsons mean when they speak of it,' Will said quite suddenly in the midst of our luncheon in his house today, when we'd been talking of the usual things. And I said: 'all life is one. The principle of life is eternal.' But he said at once, 'I don't understand you. Once I'm dead and under the ground it's all over.' We had such a happy time together for this visit of mine of one night to him which felt as if it were long, for ever, to us both. He is so much better and more active and hungry, and yet so feeble too. It is hard for him to endure the kind of pretence of what he used to do in a day. My bed was near an east window and many times I opened my eyes on the stars, on the rising waning moon at 3 a.m. in Taurus. Tony came the night before. I was glad to see him, and hear his talk of the splendid leopard he saw with huge head and shining whiskers in the torchlight – all else lost in the long grass. Will and I drank our early tea soon after 5. I watched the stars again, become few and vanish in the red sky of dawn into sunrise. Then we set off, and had a breakfast picnic alone together under a flowering – small but sweetly flowering – tree beyond the Barana. Now at home again at 6 p.m. tea in the attic, silver rain and rainbow.

2 September   Now to the company of sorrow I come and cry; she will not speak again, I shall not hear or see or know – I was going to say, or feel her love for me – but on that false word her presence made me pause. Love is for ever. The letters today from Mother and from Valentine tell me Alyse is dead. She was found on the morning of the 28th dead in her bed. I have found to read a few of the latest letters she wrote me. 'There are some things one never gets used to.' (Tony*)

3 September I walked before breakfast for Alyse for that above all things long ago she loved. The mountain and ridge running west were lightly veiled with snow, for sorrow, a brief white mourning. The day went something heavily and I walked reluctantly to tea with Christopher, and rested under a cedar by the spring till he came. But really I enjoyed my two hours with him, the tea, seeing all he is doing near the forest, and the expanse of corn above the main road, in the keen air of the mountain: glorious grain.

6 September Mother sent me today the two letters of farewell Alyse left for her. I will copy them and send them back. 'I fear I have so little left to give anyone ...' Gerard returned about 1.30 today with Christopher who had gone down a day late. He is well and we talked all the afternoon. I found a beautiful feather from the tail of an augur bustard when we started on our walk, rufous red, black-tipped, white at the base and with white quill.

8 September Gerard has started a cold and was lying down most of the day, though he did walk ... I felt disheartened to see him looking so unwell again. I live at Chydyok with Alyse. One thing about knowing eternity – in Plotinus' sense of 'identifying Eternity with the Intellectual World since the Intellectual Substance and Eternity have the one scope and content' – is that, at least when one is not in pain, one suddenly finds one has no need any more of that virtue called patience: for one is not 'nearer' Eternity in one state or condition or mood, act or thought, than in any other one, though doubtless some are more comfortable and others are necessary for the Life that thinks – contemplates – the Eternal.

9 September There was such a natural Mother letter for me today telling me, with other things and in a way no one else would, of Alyse's cremation. I went to meet the sunrise on Windy Hill feeling returning strength and as I looked first into the white gold blaze of the eye of the sun I knew my spirit was free and the free spirit of Alyse was one with mine and is so for ever.

4 October Wind hurls itself upon the house tonight and there is fire in the forest, men burning a firebreak along the cut-line let the flames escape into the forest. At the cottage I looked through again *Avicenna and the Visionary Recital* and afterwards considering the whole of it – all the writing of Henri Corbin – I thought it wise and with the beauty of adornment but weak metaphysically and without a heart, a living soul, Christ. All he says in comparing the thought of east and west, and drawing parallels, is of interest, but Corbin himself runs into difficulties among his angels and archangels and says best in one place that really they are 'the same' as what we know as abstract intellectual qualities.

7 October 'Each one of us is in a position to recognize that his own essence is a *gift*, and that he has no existence at all through himself ... an essential unity which cannot but be apparent to a thought which has acquired for itself a certain degree of inner concentration.' (Gabriel Marcel, *The Mystery of Being*, II: 'Faith and Reality') I read the Conclusion to this in the bow window in evening sunlight after a long day riding, for we started at 9 and returned by 4, staying for an hour, an interval of falling rain, at the cottage. We rode with azure sky on the one hand and blue-black clouds full of thunder lightning and rain on the other. The colouring was strange and wild and on Eland Hill talking to the shepherd the wind was a hurricane which blew me over and tore away Gerard's words unheard. The three ponies Michael* went out with were stampeded by lion in the night, he was out searching, but suddenly on our way home we saw them.

8 October The day, my fifty-second birthday, has belonged to Charles, and I think of him in this 'definition of generosity' – '*a light whose joy is in giving light and in being light*'. I thought of how I saw him alive for the last time in the church at Timau, where we went today for the dedication of the plaque in his memory. In the box at the store I found a present from Will, a water-colour of Mount Kenya he showed me last Sunday and which delighted me so much by its grace and Chinese metaphysical quality. I want to have it framed. We saw Snow there unwell and brought him back with us. Early this morning sitting on the bare dry ground in his tree plantation where a nursery of infant cedars is coming up, Gerard wrote a poem for me of himself and his meditation in his morning walks towards the mountain and towards the north.

9 October Walking along the hillside in a rain-bearing gale Gerard and I spoke of the dangers of denying the creative spirit in the deepest nature of a man, for whatever reason or motive. This too is a sin against the Holy Ghost and leads to an impoverishment of all powers, to aridity. Liberality to oneself as well as to all others ... Now an agitated rain is beginning to strike the roof.

21 October Thinking is more important than living, spoke the 'exuberant god' within me. And after considering this and how thoughtfully one can do the necessary living, in some way at once intense and carefree (because life is like the morning dew) I inquired: prayer. Thought in its fullness is composed of the stillness of prayer. For praying is an entering into the infinite, at the point which is conscious life. In a sense consciousness is the dark which does not comprehend life. Yesterday was Kenyatta Day and Gerard and I spent the afternoon with Will. He drove to a knoll of rugged rocks above the Durdle Door and made a water-colour sitting on a campstool facing north. A rare tree met me in a sudden flash of storm-bright sunshine as I came over the brow of a precipitous craggy steep with sunset and fresh green new leaves. Splendour of silver-rimmed clouds, black shadows on gray scrub harsh hillsides. The mountain engulfed in a welter of wild cloudiness, suddenly reft apart by the peaks. I found a dead dikdik with pencil-thin limbs folded as though it slept. This was near a natural salt-lick, and on the way home a pair of wild dogs stood in the road there watching us ...

2 December In the diamond-clear afternoon Will came, and stayed a whole four hours, a thing unknown before and a happy visit: after tea on the veranda we walked to see the ewes and lambs white in bright green grass. We walked by the new river of clear water crested through the rushes, and admired the eland through the fence. Then there was a fire on the hearth, six candles alight and soup for him and Gerard. The Land Rover returned and he went off gleeful over the adventure of going down through the forest by night; and taking with him two books of my father's by Walter Raymond. In my dawn walk with all the bright stars and Venus and Jupiter I heard a faint quacking and a pair of black duck flew low across the amber sky towards the east, a fair omen; and always they make me think of Elizabeth.

4 December, Mappowder A whole day of sunshine, and I am safely here, and I have been for a walk with stars, and an owl hooting, and Mother is well and darling; only my heart is full of concern for Gerard who was in a wild mood of mockery and despair at the airport last night – O I am too sleepy for another word: why can't he know however helpless feeble suffering we are ἡμεῖς δὲ νοῦν Χριστοῦ ἔχομεν.* I am thankful to be here, but my heart grieves for Gerard.

5 December I made the Ndere oranges I brought with me into marmalade and baked bread this morning. Kathleen came and was here all the sunless day. And Valentine came for a very few minutes in the morning looking I fear not well. I gave her the fern I picked in the forest the last morning and a sprig of podo and cedar; and showed her pictures of Kenya birds. Now the day is over and I have Alyse's watch and clock as well as my own ticking away, and her autobiography *The Day is Gone* beside me on the table. I have never read it. Winter jasmine in my room in a tiny vase Mother put, and a primrose and a daisy.

6 December   Wind and rain when I woke but the cock crowed. Then the wind went to the west, the day was clear with high light, towering storm clouds, silver rain ... and a dazzling double rainbow over Bulbarrow while Mother and I were with Mrs. Jackson. I visited the Crusader this morning and read the lessons for the day in the Bible on the lectern. When I came back to the house there was a letter from Gerard, so quick and as if he were himself again, full of love so I was comforted. And a letter from Valentine, she enjoyed the marmalade I gave her and said she thought it one of the most *poetic* tastes she had ever known. A fine whistling wind tonight.

8 December   Great Cold. In a blackness I made my tea, drank it by candlelight sitting on Alyse's red carpet, read a Chinese candle poem, opened the back door to whiteness. Large flakes fell on my shoulders. I walked in a gray-white light on a virgin road to the top gate. The rooks in the treetops of Short Wood were making a queer kind of low disturbed sound not like cawing before beginning their day their battle for food. Later Mother and I found one black and glossy dead on the roadside. All day the temperature dropped, the snow froze crisp, and on the roads became a deadly glaze so that I feared to walk after dark as I did last night. 'What is grace ... but a personal relationship between God and man in Christ.'

10 December   'Truth is a curlew that gives its clear call, the light flashes, a feather drops at our feet, and it has flown away.' I put out the light when I read these last words of *The Day is Gone* in homage to the book and to think of Alyse. It is a two-dimensional *tour de force* perfectly sustained, lively and intriguing and bending my spirit – from my love of the author rather than from the virtue of the book, but it does not 'come alive', is likely enough not meant to. In the little room, lit by the moon and the gay glass globes burning in a holly tree on the other side of the road, I lay shivering in the icy night, the keenest so far, remembering Alyse, knowing I would miss her tones as I might Li Po's kettle of wine, at his party of three, the moon, himself and his moon-made shadow. It is certainly her best book, surpassing the novels and *Wheels on Gravel* for wit and philosophy. 'To find strength and inspiration in the fruits of our own minds is our only firm stake against disaster.' But how can we be sure our own minds will not turn against us, be not only fruitless, barren, but even menacing, our utter undoing? 'For those of us however who have drunk, as from a living fountain draughts of new, strong life from the written word ...' As the last page was under my eyes an owl began to hoot. Owl, moonshine on crisped snow, a piercing white night, wild beating heart salutes the spirit of Alyse.

30 December This last day of the last week of the year brought a rare photograph of Alyse in youth in Naples in a mock marriage-dress given her by a millionaire's daughter, her eyes as ever evasive under the floating veil, an odd little square casket-like door with stout hinges and immovable bar forever closed in the wall by her side ...

31 December Keen wind but pure white light and sunshine. Holy Communion with Mother, the church gold with sun. Valentine came to see us in the afternoon and talked staying more than an hour and a half, telling us of Cornwall and the sea. She brought me her last letter from Alyse and copied for me part of an earlier one writ in July. Last night Mother showed me Alyse's wedding ring which came to her from the Powys family. There was hid in it a tiny key which she had shown not long before to a boy who visited her. But its niche in the ring is empty. The key is lost. I went with Valentine as far as the Nag's Head and came home in the sharp hoar rook-cawing gloaming liking to look in at Mother's lit room through the uncurtained window.

1968

1 January Night. Gale of high force from the north-west, wild, wild, wild. I have pinned into my jersey the tiny brilliant brooch Alyse left me, a topaz in a ring of diamonds. Pain of the spirit, I thought as I prayed, can be light, the purest luminosity, white as winter sunlight, and in this light all things are seen new. Mother and I walked today to the house between the two hills that used to be the Fox Inn, the air was balmy and sunshiny, all the little leaves on the bank alert. I pressed my face into that which smelt of itself and of primroses. The black retriever dog went all the way with us.

10 January Yellow moon woke me shining on my face, illuminating the frost foliage so that the icy panes seemed a crisped barrier between earth and infinite sky. Excited, I remembered the poem of four lines by Li Po in which he mistook moonshine on his bed for hoar-frost on the winter ground. Here now were both as I had not seen them since long ago I learnt the poem. I began to say it to myself looking at the gibbous moon, and it continued to say itself delicately in my mind for the rest of the night, as if the characters were scratched in rime on my sad mind:

> The bright moon shines about my bed
> I see the earth with hoar-frost spread
> To see the moon I lift my head
> It falls   my thoughts all homewards sped.

11 January   No great frost after all but layers of ice here and there on the road with water flowing underneath when I went to Buckland. I saw Francis* and he showed me the alterations he is having made to Katie's house. Then I called on Miss Spicer and rode home. The little parcel from Valentine that came before I left I opened, and it was ginger. I ate one nugget and it tasted exquisitely hot and exotic after my cold ride.

12 January   Dry, dim sunshine all day, and all things cold. A few days ago I sought an oracle in *Behold, This Dreamer** and was given 'The lion glares through the dun forest', this morning a letter from Gerard tells me of numbers of animals killed by lion since his return. The collie dog Karoi at the cottage was killed challenging a lion which went on and killed and ate my old white pony Rime, the companion of so many long rides about the farm. Mother and I walked together in the east wind; and listened to a Mozart quintet with clarinet, feeling the shadow of our parting sadly on our spirits, thankful for this quiet day without any visitors ... strangers and pilgrims. Moon all night.

13 January   New snow when I awoke this morning and made footprints in it all the way up to the Rook Gate seeing here and there beside me rabbit tracks. But the wind was south, rain soon came and washed it away. Edith* and Rosemary were here in the morning, Edith shakier, her eyes more dim, but undefeated by the grievous afflictions the burden of daily living under old age from which there is but one release. I read aloud from *Scenes of Clerical Life*. I found, liked and copied out a poem by W. J. Turner. 'Fortunate are the feet of the swallow ...'

14 January   Wild buffeting gale for the last 24 hours and tonight it is still more violent. Warmth has come with it and in the first gray light this morning a pipistrelle bat flew out from under the eaves near the back door, fluttered around a little and returned to its refuge. Together tonight Mother and I watched the moon racing through the clouds and shining full on us once or twice after a day of no sky. It is the difficulty of living on so many levels at once I think that makes me sometimes seem cross, talk and behave as if I were cross, make someone suffer. Grace is in reality simplicity of spirit but I am so passion-tossed I am for the most part in too desperate a turmoil to know this. I must go with all the gales to boundless horizons, crash as waves on desolate sea-coasts.

15 January Full moon, Monday, 10.30 p.m. No, I will say that goodnight to Mother and have my bath before I take farewell of this journal in the little room of winter happiness – Now, the lights have gone out up and down the street of the village, sky and moon are covered by an equal opacity of cloud that hoards all the radiance of the midnight shining. Valentine came this morning and drove Mother and me to Sturminster. I ran from shop to shop, stood watching them where they stood at a booth in the market, a fruit stall where Valentine bought red-stained peaches. The old houses looked singularly wise. After tea I made and baked bread. A robin sang in the ash tree, Mother and I listened and as we stood by the north winter-jasmine wall there were snowdrops at my feet, not yet open but some with heads hung as well as those that stood upright showing white. How can I make a farewell of all I love here: all is in my heart.

27 June, The Beale Gum tree electrically lit from below by a sun-storm, the great bunches of foliage pendant, the clusters of grape-like fruit lift and sway with majestic motion in the wind from the west, while Zeus of the dark cloud lords it over the mountain. Gerard is sadly low, feeling all the time weak and tired; he says this is how Eisenhower felt when he was president – he is reading a Life of him. 'It is only through the deepest passivity that man can reach his highest activity.'

30 June When I had made the butter and came upstairs 'to spread the bed', this verb is used both by Homer and the Africans, I scribbled down in pencil between the sheets and blankets an 'autobiography', brief and boastful, at least as regards the conclusion, which amused me as I remembered lost Marys, saw them from without and from afar as if I were someone quite other.

4 July Katey* ran to meet us and kissed us both. And we had a little time on the grass with Martin seesawing. She is not coming to stay with us till next week. Peter* sent me sea-urchins and rocks in a tiny box, and Gerard a copy of the *Iliad* in one small volume that belonged to J.C.P. at Sherborne, Montacute and Patchin Place – 'As the race of leaves so the race of men is', Gerard read from the flyleaf; and Rose said slowly, 'leaves fall off', and added quickly and happily, 'and then grow again'.

5 July A quiet day for me of reading and writing, after an hour of cooking. Gerard was paying the men all the morning at Ndere. I think he *is* beginning to feel more up to things. With my coffee cup in my hand I took out a poetry book from the shelf and found myself in the right mood for these *Greek Lyrics*. I copied out one by Simonides in a letter.

16 July Haunted air last evening, all the evenings of this home in the forest glade gathered into one stilly nightfall. While the sun lasted we paced the forest paths, black olives gilded the loud stream. As we came up to the house the gum trees were dark as night itself, wood smoke slept in the air, the flock of ewes unshorn carried their golden fleeces across our path.

8 August On seeing Alyse again – opening the journal to write after several days, my eye fell first on her photograph and my heart gave an unexplicable bound and a fulgurant light shot into many unlit corners; not that the light showed anything, it was simply that it flashed where no other could.

13 August My quiet morning with my writing in the Fig Tree ended yesterday at noon when Gerard returned from Nanyuki prostrate again, drew the curtains and went to bed till this morning. I think it is physio-psychological, but it does always throw me into almost equal despondency and hopelessness. When I went in timidly with a cup of tea he could scarcely drink he said he'd left the satchel, he hoped at Timau, with both our air tickets and my passport in it. I went up to telephone by the Grove of the Tortoise, picking up porcupine quills as I went, of which many lay in the way, to take to Valentine. Where the footpath crossed the car track, coiled on the sallow grass, which was flattened by wheel weight, enjoying the late afternoon warmth, broad head and friendly eyes supported on the coils, a large grayling-gray snake.

16 August Paint what strikes you – and he used the word *frapper* – so in the crabbed narrowing of emotions, the serrated edge of departure, the great leaning tree smote me: the cloud-bearer cradle of stars, born and lifted into splendour, in the transcendent spaces between the black clusters – heavy hanging as ripe grape bunches. I saluted the tree that night and day has earthed my griefs – for earth transforms corruption – has exalted my sorrows, laded them on the clouds passing, oned my joys with those solitary stars – shining in caverns of light.

28 August, Mappowder Sunless and the first rain of this visit while we were walking round the wood called Crooked Oak, but the wind is still east. The twilight garden drips, the flowers of hollyhocks are papery, apples pull down their pliant boughs into wreaths and arches. Nuts are ripe but not yet slip shell. Early this morning I saw a stoat by the hedgerow and not one of the many rabbits. I have given myself a splendid present which came today, the three Loeb Classics volumes of Plotinus' *Enneads*, longing to have him in his own Greek. I read Armstrong's introduction in the church in the afternoon.

29 August Energy into words – why for me must this be – why is it, as Alyse said, my salvation?

30 August This sunless day, though there was one gleam ... the new watch I bought for myself last Saturday doesn't go. I went to Sturminster this morning. Bridge and river and a long low black boat, like a narrow barge perhaps, was moored under the willows where I once watched a tree-creeper. What does not a boat silently say. A pair of gray wagtails flew across the mill tail where men and boys were fishing. Happy with my new Plotinus in the church, his Greek is rough and powerful, carries me as poetry even through my labour of trying to translate it into sense. A long essay in the *TLS* on the Letters of Wilfred Owen headed 'No Consolation'.

31 August At last a clear sky, stars and a half moon. The rooks were still cawing drowsily in the treetops of Short Wood as we came home from our long evening walk over the fields to the church of St. Thomas à Becket at Pulham. A long walk indeed for Mother. I was so heavy-hearted when we started for one reason and another, and just *mood*, I never mended till I found a huge old horseshoe in some ploughland, hind hoof and the remains of seven nails in their square holes. I'd been reading just before we started on this walk (which must have been six miles altogether) *The Measure of My Days* by Alyse's friend Florida,* Alyse had read it in MS and O it made me miss her; the book is wise but sorrow-laden and dark with foreboding in its gallantry.

1 September A number of birthdays belong to this tempestuous day when wind, rain and rays of sun are almost equally fierce, though perhaps the gales are wildest. When I went into the church early this morning I saw a map on the ancient altar stone, with five crosses carved in its old gray face, that is beside the crusader. For clear views and clean fine-spun air this was my best walk. Two days ago, that is on Friday, Gerard went to see Mrs. Allen and he said he will buy her house, which adjoins this one of Mother's, for £4,250.

2 September Moon rising through leaves visited by passing clouds, owls hooting not near, pause at a long day's end, returned me to the loneliness of youth. All evening we walked over green meads towards Bulbarrow with its slopes distinct and cumulus clouds built above. First a rainbow came and went: and I saw a broken one as I returned from my early walk. Reading a little in the morning Florida's book and by the church wall, Plotinus. In his Greek, and with the help of Armstrong, I find thoughts, approaches, openings I was not aware of before. My mind, wakened to an infinity unattainable but true, does not easily return. 'I lose myself' – but not, I think, 'in myself, which is to lose all' – as Alyse said.

3 September Summer warmth after a fierce thunderstorm in the night. I had a letter from Gertrude this afternoon and forewent the walk to answer it, needing to be alone after not being all day ... or reading except Florida's book: 'I ask of all those who like me seem to do nothing: "Does the passion in our hearts somehow serve?"' Watching the moon through a thick ash tree in the dark garden last evening I heard owls hooting. 'Consciousness seems to be both what life tries to evolve and its greatest danger.'

16 September More rain, north wind, and news of floods: still for all we had tea outside the back door and walked in the fields and picked blackberries, coming home in mist and rain, to sit on the floor in our winter fashion. The 'sliding time' as I have come to regard it, is strong on me tonight, an experience perhaps to do with all time being equidistant from eternity, no 'point' nearer or further and each point having reality in its separate and distinct relation to eternity. Time slides easily 'backwards' and 'forwards' and now is because all that 'has been' and 'will be' is, not only in my conscious life although the awareness in this is certainly stronger. Because of this the past lives, the future comes to birth. This of course is writ by Plotinus and I will copy it here, but it is also *lived* by me now. 'One must take it all as a whole ... and apprehend, not the dividedness of time but the life of eternity, which is not made up of many times but is all together from the whole of time.' Is it perhaps intellect being active without perception that causes one's physical awareness to be (as it were) astray in 'sliding time'?

17 September   Valentine has telephoned, late in the afternoon of this glooming twilight day, to say her visit to the surgeon, postponed to 29 October because of the floods, must be fulfilled before she goes away for her holiday on 20 September. She is going on Friday by train all the way and returning, if she may, the same day. The October appointment was made through the hospital and when the surgeon heard of it he would not agree to the delay before seeing her again; and by this our anxiety is increased. Prayer is the utmost intensity of experience and this through life and by means of suffering, either joy or pain, goes straight to the source of being. To reach this inward intensity each creature is strained and straitened to the limit. In the end, it seems to me, we choose nothing, all is given or withheld, as we can endure it, to increase this intensity which is the $ἀρετή$* of soul.

19 September   A swollen inflamed ankle has bothered me today. I have had it off and on for some months – at intervals – but it has always subsided quite soon, this time it is more painful and enlarged. Aggravated it may be by a dog bite just above my boot two days ago which hurt though did not quite break the skin. Rain set in at 4 p.m. and has continued steadily for over four hours, there may be danger of more flooding if it goes on all through the night. The wind is rising. I went downstairs in the early hours of this morning and the sky was clear, all the stars shining, but not brightly.

20 September   Sylvia telephoned this evening saying they were safe home from London and Valentine's surgeon was pleased with her. So Mother and I are thankful for this, and for our happy day together. Dr. Will came to see Gerard so I showed him my ankle and he says it is a strained tendon. Still a high wind blows.

1 October   Apple-picking this gray afternoon, I climbed to the top of both the bramley trees but most of the good and rosy apples on the outer branches I was unable to pick without a long ladder. Later in the evening when the clouds were stormily torn to give gold in the west in dome and ellipse over High Stoy, we walked in the fields, all three of us, and Mother said she enjoyed every minute of it. A card came from Valentine from the place with the longest name in Wales.

2 October   In Dorchester today Gerard and I visited the lawyer Mr. Coggins in a Georgian house at the top of the town. I liked this left-handed* man who was at Jesus College. He is to prepare the contract for our purchase of the house next door. Then we went to the bank manager (who remarked he thought Gerard very young to have lived so many years in Kenya – and this cheered me up) to ask him to sell enough securities to pay for it. I bought a new skirt, which kept me from the river, but I did just walk by the clear-flowing stream and saw a gray wagtail and a fish leap. We borrowed a long ladder from Mr. Kelly, painted bright red it looked attractive leaning on the leaves, and the apples smiled above it, many still out of reach, though I climbed to the top rung.

5 October   Why is it that I seem to have to live in the most profound and sorrowful deeps my nature can explore in order to know hope. The airless air is soft as down tonight, with haze and incense smoke of burning leaves. One cottage light gives me a shadow, pins out twigs and branches; another is a chink in the murk – a curtain not quite meeting, another unseen sheds diagonal beams; a child's voice, a door slams.

1 November   All autumn grace, rare morning stars and Jupiter and Mars close, clouds coming in crowds, dividing and piled in precipices with chasms of dim blue, Bulbarrow clear as a revelation, an interval of placid tender sunshine, soft all but inaudible showers, sunset of solemn red and far-off gold. I stood by the elm tree at the edge of the valley while the colours faded and heard the rain below, waited praying until it reached me. I typed out Gerard's latest version of *South Wales Echo*; and he has been reading it aloud to Mother below me. We heard at 8 this morning President Johnson's voice and the news that the bombing of Vietnam was to stop completely at 2 p.m.

All Souls' Day   Twenty-third anniversary of my wedding day. The rain of the night made the garden a flood, but a wind from the north arose and all day blew more fiercely so that by evening there was a dryness of roads and pools and muddy places gone. Gerard and I had two good walks together, but because of the wetness, always on the roads. At dusk we stood under the steepest green flank of Ball Hill while the gale made a mighty roar as of sea or force in the hanging wood. My daily descriptions of country are (I think) first pleasure in simple observation, second in part symbolic, third exultation and liberation in the experiencing of the power of nature.

6 November   Far from the all-beholding sun. I have read in the last three-quarters of an hour *Four Quartets** and shall read it again, and hope I may return again. For he is the modern low-voiced singer of my master. Gerard and I went to Dorchester and paid for our cottage. Gerard saw the neurologist who said a return of more marked symptoms of encephalitis was not uncommon after an interval of ten or twelve years, which is what this is for Gerard. Also that what he complains of could be caused by contagious abortion, whose other names I forget. He wants to arrange for Gerard to go to the hospital in Southampton later for a thorough examination, and other tests.

8 November London Bridge has broken down. End of November afternoon, Gerard and I went into our all but empty cottage, half the staircase was pulled out to let furniture down, and all the ghosts of living dead new-born assailed my spirit, in these interludes they have their way, a little while. I was cheered by Mother coming, then her two visitors came in too. At night I read a tale of Lucy Lightfoot and her knight.

11 November Valentine drove Mother to Wells today, meanwhile the builder came here bringing furniture and paintings from Katie's house; and good Kathleen, who has stored them all these years, brought more, and took away the corrugated iron barricade at the back while the men rebuilt the stairs, which took all the afternoon. The electrician was unhelpful so we do not know *when* things will be in order – points and wiring – for us to live there. Gertrude's* three oil paintings look glorious hanging above the disordered stuff below. I went with Valentine to the bridge and as she drove off I found my hand on the head of a gentle lion-coloured dog, I was absent in mind, had seen nothing and could not think what I was feeling. He looked lovingly at me, longing to be my companion on the walk, which was a beautiful one in tender sunlight; the village a little veiled by smoke and more revealed as many leaves have fallen. I had a fine letter from Peter to read while I made bread, alone in the house.

12 November Love a wave bearing the soul beyond all reason and understanding, all known boundaries and supports of convention, a sense of being 'beyond intellect' which yet is folly to say; an awakening to liberty of spirit that would be too fearful without the companion in love, and which yet of necessity is the loss of that companion. *No real loss* – for the companion in love is an illusion, a 'lure for feeling' as Whitehead has it, while the love is truth. Gerard went away this morning, to South Wales, and to Woodbrooke.* I read *Four Quartets* aloud to Mother when we came in after our walk in the east wind, she listened with attention and was specially stirred by the part of death in the poem, and I think consoled by the quality and 'infinite' texture of the poem so far faring from village names and lanes.

14 November   'The only wisdom we can hope to acquire/Is the wisdom of humility: humility is endless.' Gales from the east drive through all shelters into each chink and crevice, coldly clean the stale stench out of the cottage. I washed some of the curtains and hung them in the blast.

21 November   It has taken me till the last few years, I fancy, to realise that life being lived by me now is all life, is of value because of that. I used to take my own 'being alive' wholly for granted, regard it often as a nuisance, to be brushed aside in the doing of duty, or rebelliously endured in pain and sickness, so I could live in what seemed to me then reality – imagination, romance, poetry, story-telling – I suppose what Auden called the 'secondary world'. I cycled to Sturminster – early – and after an hour of crimson, kingfisher sunrise that fulfilled itself in a day of tenderest hues and sunshine. I heard four separate song-thrush's notes as I went and walked by the beautiful river. Eve of Mother's birthday, warm and starry.

22 November   Unwonted warmth. A happy day, Mother's pleasure in her things; Francis calling in the morning; Valentine with us in the afternoon, going over my cottage which gave me a whole complicated crowd of emotions. This may be, I suppose, the last night for me in Mother's spare room where I have been happy in the fullness of solitude, with books and pen, for some part of all my visits to England in the last twenty years.

1969

22 January, The Beale   Once more the travelling is over and Gerard and I are at home, the land green and sunny, the country in its best mood, and the house beautifully cleaned and prepared for my coming by Mugambi. Gerard is thankful and begins I think to feel tranquillity in his troubled mind. We saw Theresa yesterday and this morning, she is coming here to stay soon. Uncle Willy looks well but his feet and fingers bloodless; he still has considerable pain in the foot of the broken limb and it is swollen also. I felt as if he was very trapped under the galvanised iron frame with a great weight hanging from his foot, and scarcely able to raise himself by holding with his hands to the iron bars above. He says he is much weaker than when he was first taken into the hospital. I wrote as best I could to tell Mother how he is. The doves coo above my head, and all is as if I'd not been away.

26 January   I see from my window mystic mingling of mist and smoke, which has given its character to the last year or so when rainy weather has ruled. Long and dove quiet the afternoon with books and thoughts led on through the spiritual thinking of men. Gerard, mercifully, seems better, less tense and distressed, his mind more alive. Theresa came to Nanyuki yesterday and we met her and brought her here for the weekend, she also is steadier, but insatiable of sleep.

28 January   House of the Winds again after the morning's dreamy stillness of greensward and touches of scarlet in the trees that wear that badge now, not as of old against the sky, but against the sky-hiding plantation of cedar and cypress. This afternoon's reading of the Farewell Discourses and the Passion Narrative* left me on the anonymous plane of spirit when Gerard returned with the letters. These indeed, from Mother, Valentine, Margaret, are the full resumption of my life in Africa. With them was one from the Commission of Lands to say a man is coming to value the Beale on 7 February. Valentine's first typed one since the middle of last month shows a return also to her old temper so that I believe in every way she is stronger.

3 February   Shootash nightjar heard this evening. I am going through my poems writ since July 1966 and typing out those I consider best, though only for myself. I find some support in this, they repay me out of the strength I put into them, the spiritual energy. All are without punctuation, disfiguring and needless in short poems where the sense, adjectives, rhythm move backwards and forwards. Line rhyme and metre are enough.

6 February   I love being in a lighted room at night with the voice of the wind beyond the porous walls, both because the place might be anywhere, city or desert or by the sea, and because especially in this attic in the gable, which is the bows of the ship, I have the sense of eternal voyaging through trackless space on a vessel that leaves no wake. And this voyaging belongs not alone to my living experience but it will continue for the grains and dust and powdery bones. Venus shines into the other unlit attic, casting distinct light and shadow on the wall.

9 March   Sitting on Windy Hill in the dusk Gerard said: 'I am going to start reading "Nature Contemplation and the One", it'll take me a long time. What I like about Plotinus is his animism, as we call it today.' My heart is full of thankfulness Gerard is reading my philosopher to whose influence I attribute his mind being in (as I think) a happier mode. Considering afterwards those three words of the title of that *Ennead* I concluded they were what meant most to me in my living, together with intellectual beauty; and poetry, on which Plotinus does not directly write. It is his intellect allowing him to interpret and express so perfectly his intuition that makes him so exciting, and his metaphysics.

28 March   Undarkened sun. I decided this afternoon the title for my metaphysical story of which one chapter and the conclusion of a chapter wait to be written, to give to it what completeness I am able. It is now much in my mind whether I shall be able to write the final chapter and type it out in time to take it with me. For in England I could not do this; and here with all my leisure I can write only in the right intensity of mood. 'Whatever the freed soul attains to *here*, that it is *there*.' Only in contact with the freed soul can I write of Plotinus.

1 April   Something to do perhaps with the mere act of taking this book, opening it, seeing the long page ruled feint, as they used to say, gives a lift or change to a mood grown dull from waiting; and from reading about Yeats who for some reason or other is not a true poet for me. I liked his father's words to him though: 'but best of all I like the music when the bird of poesy sings to itself in the heart of the wood, addressing its own soul, and thinking nothing of others ...' (*The New Poetic*)

9 April   I have just finished *The Kingfisher's Wing** – the final chapter 'Alone' and half the one before it, 'Porphyry', still to be typed out. I wonder now what I shall do without it for my writing is my living; it could be worked on a great deal I am sure, but I can no more go over what I've writ than could Plotinus. An Easter card came for me from Valentine of a car and a pair of horses on a black Attic vase, galloping off the curve of the world. These on a cup of water I gave to Plotinus. I took from the shelf *Selected Poems* of Rilke this morning. I'd forgotten who gave the book and so it was a signal to see her writing and her name – Alyse – September 1946.

10 April   I always wake, if momentarily, when the waning moon shines into the attic towards morning, the light on my window-ledge treasures, on my books – and think of Plotinus. I feel both loss and fullness over the story finished; the MS in its blue and white striped cloth I *miss* sadly; and I have come to the cottage without my Greek Testament and the Hebrew Bible. We met Konge in the gloaming, his baby boy has been sent to Nyeri hospital and he's lost six sheep.

11 April   Gay voices this morning at the cottage and there was Rose, Francis and Martin; Francis all set on staying the week-end with us. We were coming to Sirakoi to spend our first night near El Khalil so he came with us – and I write now by candlelight, light of one candle in a bottle under the new thatched roof, feeling strange and unreal, happy to know the little boy is near in his sleeping bag: stars, stars, stars …

12 April   A night of bulls roaring, dogs barking, a lion grunting, even once men shouting, so that Gerard went out to see the watchman and the ponies. To meet the sunrise we walked to the top of El Khalil. After eating mangoes and bread and butter in the sun with Francis, Gerard and I rode to Lol Mutoni, a thing he has long wanted to do, the way we went, a distance of about 7 miles to the top, grass green and good. We saw some game and a flock of something like 30 to 40 Crowned Cranes. We rode to them to see them all fly and hear the clangour. Then we went down to the river with the huge herd of cows and calves so that the mares could drink with them of the muddy swift-flowing water.

13 April   Best moment of Francis was when I came back to the cottage at sunrise and saw him drinking his tea sitting near the window with the tray before him. I watched unobserved for about two minutes the absorbed figure and profile like a miniature old man. There was rain in the afternoon, but Rose came with Martin at tea-time to take Francis home and there were some tussles between them.

19 April   The undefined intent in this score of years of descriptions of 'natural beauty', chance-sent scenes, unexpected enhancing reciprocities may be, it suddenly came to me this afternoon when I was (after Pallas Athene) thinking of other things, an attempt to bring together intellectual and natural contemplation: to see them not as separate experiences, landscape as a substitute or background for intellection, a refreshment or respite from the ardours of concentration, but rather living in mind as mind lives in itself. One light, not radiance of heaven radiance of earth clashing. This attempt is perhaps a kind of transference of aesthetics from art to nature, unsuccessful but for me inevitable.

20 April   That memoried historic room at Kisima, with roof of grass and walls of mud and the three low windows opening on green grass and limitless distance, where his three children were born, where for months I ill* lived, is now where Will is. Rose, in sailcloth blue blouse and mini-skirt, long legs and feet bare, was giving him tea when we arrived yesterday evening. Francis and Martin climbed in and out of the mid-window. Charles,* three-months old, was laid on the bed, where he rested under his grandfather's hand, and they smiled on one another. This fourth boy is a large happy one with great brown eyes. It was pretty to see Francis playing with his youngest brother while Will sang an old lullaby he heard in childhood from a blacksmith who repeated it whenever he had to ply his bellows. I must ask him to say it again (if he will), and copy down the words. The foot hurts and hurts, and to be so weak distresses him, but he looks healthy and enjoys the society of visitors. New Moon.

21 April When I walked out at dawn, as far as the red gate and turned to the east Venus was shining most exactly centred between the two heads of the cranes as they stood on the topmost perches of the dead cedar. About birds and star in the luminous green-white sky the clouds rested in long bars of crimson, horizontal serenity. Last night Gerard and I saw Mercury in a window surrounded by an angry torn cloud. There was today a large meeting at Timau addressed by the P.C.* The second time he returned from this Gerard brought me a letter from Mother. I polished all the silver this morning, and the rain that wanted to come took leave again and there is soft sunshine. Only the shingles between me and the feet of cooing pigeons and twittering swallows.

22 April Mother's wedding day: and I write now the last word here before I pack my book away, say farewell to the pictures. We go this evening to see Will in hospital, and set off tomorrow morning and if all is well fly at the end of tomorrow, 11.45 p.m. I am thankful for Gerard being better this time here. He has written some good strong letters this morning to George, Gilfrid and Christopher supporting the P.C.'s suggestion the Timau farmers contribute to a school to be founded at Kirua (Meru) and become members of the committee for organising this. I visited the cranes again at dawn, hearing them call; dancing is in their toes, as writing is in my fingers. Sleepy as they still were one could not help beginning, and the long-dead tree quaked. Then I read Deuteronomy, chapters 10–11. For all its dryness and repetition this Book has its rivers of waters also: 'a land of hills and valleys ... the eyes of the Lord thy God always upon it.'

24 April, Mappowder A happy home-coming and in mid-afternoon in sunshine as bright as the daffodils I looked at all the way home from the window of the railway carriage. The flight was good, for me anyhow, the great aircraft more than half empty so I could lie on three seats. I saw the sun rise blood-red, and looked down on Etna. At breakfast we were flying high above the Alps at 600 miles an hour, and we arrived at Gatwick punctually at 7.30. a.m. Mother was in her room talking to Austin* when I came in through the back door: her face aglow, her garden shining with flowers.

8 May   Dry: a keyed-down day and chill, but the better for bird song. I baked bread. Valentine and Sylvia came to see Mother for a little while in the afternoon: they are sad and anxious, in fact *tamed* by all their intense being and suffering; by Valentine's illness and constant pain. Both Mother and I felt sad after they'd left. A small brother and sister knocked on the door: they had bunches of flowers in a basket, 3d. a bunch. I gave them sixpence and took one, the stalks tied with red worsted. 'You *could* have had two', the boy said.

25 May   Wet Whit Sunday; through autumn-rain beat window-pane I see the lilacs rocking, a late thrush still sings in the gale and blackbirds whistle. So is my soul tossed with complexity of emotions, with love and thankfulness and a bitter cry. Valentine came to see Mother this afternoon and I did not see her. Of all the philosophers after Plotinus in *The Cambridge History of Later Greek and Early Medieval Philosophy* I can make nothing – I skip, and shall be glad when I come to the end.

26 May   After writing *that* I did meet Boethius who, as always, interested me; but there is none other. I have just heard of the safe descent of the three men from their orbit around the moon into the Pacific Ocean, and only three miles from the ship waiting to recover them. It is strange how naturally I seem able to accept this Homeric feat. More fearsome is the thought of the 'seeds of life' which can now be released from this planet and will continue on their invisible way until they come to another where growth is possible. And the idea that life on this earth must in the beginning have reached here from another world.

28 June   The ultimate gold of day, a kindly kingly gold day I have dashed by my vile moods – yet I am loved. Cuckoo, a few at 2 p.m.; at 3 a.m. I went into the quiet softly white-lit garden, as in a dream. Walking past the graveyard early in dense mist I saw a figure standing half lost among the tall flowery misty grave-fed grasses, scythe on shoulder, sickle in hand. 'I don't hardly know where to start, if t'were a path somewhere t'would help', said Jackie, looking like a Wordsworthian character. 'It be so wet-like too.' 'And if you waited a little …' 'Then be so hot.' 'There aren't many who know how to use tools like those today, they all want machines', I said, wanting to praise him. He considered this and at length offered: 'and they don't know how to use *they.'** I went to a fête at Hazelbury rectory in the afternoon. When I returned Valentine was here, with Mother. Now the swifts scream shrill and near, my small Homer lies on the window-sill unread. J. C. Powys, Sherborne, Dorset, 15 November 1890. Heavily scored under in ink the only line I've ever succeeded in learning by heart and scanning: βῆ δ' ἀκέων παρὰ θῖνα πολυφλοίσβοιο θαλάσσης.*

10 July   Dated exactly three years since I first knew her, I had a card from Valentine this morning, shaky and small writ, but clear: July 8. Briefly to say I saw the Yeovil man who wants me to see Sir Hedley as soon as may be. I'd anticipated this and already asked for an appt. Pray for me as you can. And consider Luke VIII (I think), 'Be not afraid, only believe.'

12 July   Warmer. This afternoon Nellie arrived with her children Lucy and Michael. She put up a blue tent under the apple tree for them all to sleep in, and is so happy to be here she has doubled her stay from two to four nights. She looks attractive in a cool frock of W.E.P.'s Elizabeth. I am reading *Theaetetus** slowly as well as Whitehead, so I can compare two minds seeking to define, *to know*, knowledge: 'Kant's act of experience is essentially knowledge', says Whitehead.

19 July   I have begun to read, on my bedroom window-sill this gray cool eve, *History of Western Philosophy*.* The wind has at last left the north-west and blows west south-west filling heaven with rainless rain-like clouds. And the men near the moon ... this strange Homeric feat of our times. Will exploring space, of which this is the beginning, have any bearing on Bertrand's 'individual facing terror of cosmic loneliness'? Mother and I came, after the river and fields of barley, to a ruined ample farmhouse; moving, haunted by its former living busy preoccupied dwellers, fit for a Hardy tale, prophetic (it may be) of the Beale. We ate our cheese and rolls near and stared on waving ivy, fallen roof between chimneys still stoutly aloft, black glassless windows. A strong wattle and daub wall guarded a rampant wilderness once a great garden.

21 July   'Perfect landing', writ large in Mother's hand on the back of her writing pad and propped on her Montacute tray spread with a clean white cloth with an appliqué blue flower, met my eye when I opened her kitchen door this morning. Soon Armstrong and his companion will be leaving the surface of the moon. In all I read I notice especially how scrupulous they are to have regular and long periods of sleep. *One* single gleam of sun in a day of cloud.

15 September The really exciting part of a person's character is that marginal region between what the individual is and what he could become if he allowed to become open, ever so little, to the avenues into other dimensions, or into the unconscious. One way of doing this is to trust to the guardian spirit; but the danger is great for anyone who departs from the paths of order and ceremony, society and convention, that the approaches of liberty may end him in chaos. Another way is by encounters with other minds which are kindred in their structure so that there is spontaneous communication at a certain level, and always a possibility of unspoken exploration in different directions, where one has pushed further than the other, knows other perils. The spirit enlarges itself and does not forget this new adventuring ... a breath of 'the creative advance'.

19 September The most beautiful September evening with amber sunlight and a bloom on the hills. The six cows in the field stand at peace, the apples glow. I made my first jam in the cottage, 7 lb. of plum. Whatever I do now I am haunted by a sense of the non-separateness of time, of the 'time' when the same things are done; this is not I think an awareness of tradition, rather all the time the particular thing has been done become one.

20 September A rare day of clearness and before sunrise I saw Venus. The rays of sun penetrating the garden trees glanced across the dewy air in soft diagonals. I have begun to pick the apples which have so pleased my eyes for three months, and I sorrow at the trees half despoiled. Valentine wrote Mother saying she is not going back to Guy's but will have what attention is needed in Moffat House: this is the nursing home in Weymouth where Gertrude died.

27 September Shadows on the mown grass as clearly delineated as they are in March, but not the fine patterning of twigs. I began to pick the bramleys on my tree; Mother's pair is laden so this will go on long, and the ladder is not enough. The moon here rises each eve at the same time, certainly for the last four, but it has moved from south-east to north-east almost to north. A small empty rowboat tossed among waves, planks loosening, ready to break apart, to be no more boat.

30 September Fields white with a sharp frost early. All day the sun shone and I went to the river. For a long time I was by the slow-flowing river breathing the deep smell of it, watching the surface, the trees, the withering sedges. Tiny fish rose up to take food and were hid again in the dark water. I saw marsh tits which always please me. On the far side of the willow eyot I heard a shrill scirree. The kingfisher passed, flying down stream near the farther bank so I did not see the perfect blue; but my eye followed the swift flight almost to the mill.

8 October A happy birthday. From the first when I saw the twins Castor and Pollux and remembered Pindar's singing of them, and their fair exchange, until this hour when I write after reading aloud to myself his 'Ode to the Graces'. A warm day with afternoon sunshine so Mother and I could have tea in the garden, on my grass today, and walk afterwards serenely in the meadows. I visited the church sweet with chrysanthemums at sunset; and the knight, and in Dorchester I went to St. Peter's after our time with Valentine.

16 October, The Beale In my attic, all as though I had not been away save for the sand-coloured grass. My train journey alone to London was beautiful with sunshine all the way: over the green fields and rivers, and gold-splashed trees. And after a few mistakes (from timidity) I arrived at Gatwick. The aircraft was so empty and I was the first to check in, so I could choose my seat. And I saw the glory of this night sky-faring, dawn and sunrise over the perfect curve of the desert, Southern Sudan. Often now I am called by things invisible. I woke to the instant of Venus rising over the dark rim of the world, Mercury followed, the ramparts began to flame. From some trick of altitude (5–6 miles up) or of desert the sun always first appears as if it were some distance 'in' from the horizon, a dark and smoky globe. Suddenly then it leaps back into the sky and is full golden dazzle from which I must quickly avert my eyes.

18 October Quietly in my heart, in the heart of sorrow, I make reaffirmation of poetry, though I may not speak or answer there is this grace given presence. All today is gray under gray sky, the thunder lion roars in the eastern sky, hills hang unhinged between earth and heaven ... Last evening I found Will before a wide canvas with his brushes.

21 October My search for a theme for poetry and meditation settled its lost rays on Orpheus, partly from a haunting recollection of the peerless lyric 'Orpheus with his Lute made Trees', partly from my reading of him in *The Presocratic Philosophers*;* and do I recollect some golden outline of him with lute and animals embossed on the cover of the Blue Poetry Book? He is, I believe, one whose name invoked, whose touch on the strings, is infallible for any poem. I read of pictures of him in the catacombs; and today, that the early Christians connected him with the Prince of Peace in Isaiah; that the best of his teaching concerning the soul was only understood and valued by Pindar and Plato. Close to Orpheus, Castor and Polydeuces.

24 October Great glory of sunrise over the land golden as the topaz of Ethiopia. I have come from reading two chapters of the book of Job and see the unicorns and the peacocks, and the thousands upon thousands of angels of Hebrews. When we saw Will last night he was strong and in the riches of his picture, a vast canvas propped up before him on the bed on which he'd been working most of the day. Rose, singularly lovely and ox-eyed, was cleaning his palette. Today they go to Nairobi for X-rays and an examination by the surgeon. Cooing doves cover the roof.

31 October Banging rain on the roof but Gerard and I came home (the house still ours) over dry roads. We visited Will in the hospital in Nairobi, yesterday and this morning. He did not want us to be there long, but he looks well. There was a loud knock on our room door at 5.30 this morn. I went down the long corridor seeing no one, then a small voice spoke from the bathroom 'Mary'. It was Sally who'd come up from Mombasa on the night coach and asked for our room from the watchman at the hotel. It was he who'd knocked on the door. Sally sat on a chair near the window in our room talking freely in her soft voice while the dawn light began tenderly to show us her fair head, the straight hair parted in the midst, tucked behind a seashell ear. Hair and youthful skin began faintly to shine. Day began. At noon we said farewell – forever?

3 November It comes over me at this moment I cannot bear, simply cannot bear anyone else I love to die. A simple thing, no philosophy, no poetry, no contemplation of nature, can avail me, only to know, as I do know, this wordless deep pain is the same all who love have in the ages of man. Mlefu, came to call on us this morning, he walked up through the forest with a present of a tin of honey for me, holding in the other hand a long staff. He looked in better health, I thought, and was friendly and at ease.

4 November The man came to value the stock and 'movables' or machinery, this afternoon so we may soon begin sorting and packing our possessions in the house. Another day of sunblaze and of considerable not-feeling-well on my part. Venus and Mercury were so close this morning a third planet could scarcely have slipped between them.

5 November Dark but still rainless; the valuer announced according to a note from Christopher this morning, that the farm would be taken over in about three weeks, and that we should be given two days notice beforehand. So the packing and sorting must begin, and Gerard and I made a start on some of the books after luncheon. I am supported by a letter from Mother we found at Timau.

8 November Walking back along the long polished passage from the dark attic where I pray to this lit one, from one extreme end of the roof to the other, my eye fell on the handrail we'd had the Indian fit and following its narrow gleam with my eye between shadowy joists and rafters, I acknowledged the full sweep of the pull and affection and intimacy there has been between the house and my soul which has known here its ecstasies, fears, deepest troubles and passion of love. So firm a stone house, so long lived in, is always there whether oneself is or no. I have not yet realised it will soon be no more.

9 November Yes, the house – of wood and stone, *large*, not new – it has taken all this to as it were *absorb* my passions, rages, hatreds, loves, above all ailments and despairs; to 'take' them and to restore them with the touch of reality cerebral experiences lack. At the same time the whole thing becomes symbolic; the exterior of sunny stability yet a trifle in- or with-drawn; the inside with many doors, angles, shadowy perspectives, reflective floors, windows of varying sizes and levels, facing all quarters; loose tapping panes of glass, cracks, broken floors, rain flooding in, endless ripple music of the furrow at night; 'the atmosphere of study and thought'.

12 November A day of all weathers, dazzling morning when I sat for the last time on the table in the big room eating my breakfast, watching the spray of drops from scarlet flowers as sunbirds flitted ... to Zeus the cloud-gatherer upon the mountain top, downpour, sun, thunder and lightning. Swaran Singh arrived at 8 a.m. and hammered and sawed and bored until 7 p.m., packing the few things we are sending to England. Michael in bringing him brought me also a letter from Mother to sustain me through the day; downstairs now the rooms are bare. She enclosed a card that had come to her, dictated by Valentine, writ by Sylvia. 'I cannot write. I love to have your letters but do not feel you must write. Explain to Mary the absence of letters. All my love.'

19 November Ten days since Valentine died, this I knew only now, on our return from Nairobi. There was a letter from Mother to tell me. She died in the morning, one of storm and lightning flashes, Sylvia said; and I remember Valentine was always fearful of thunderstorms, and if they came at night would put on her light and read or write. Gerard and I came home thankful to the empty Beale, to the quiet after the city. Soon it began to rain.

20 November   Much rain, cloud, fog, mist-dripping trees: the vaporous shrouds in keeping with my mood. I wrote and typed letters, unable to read. Both Michael and Christopher were here, and some of yesterday's perplexities, that preoccupied Gerard in our evening walk and kept him wakeful at night, are cleared away.

21 November   Fearsome rain in the late half of the night, torrents; creaks so that I feared the slanting gum tree was preparing to fall: this led to nightmare, a frightening presence in the empty room, and through the window of it the ground strewn thick with red grains that had fallen as rain. Rain and processions of mist all day; brief spells of earth smoking in sunshine. I have felt unwell. One word of intellect, clear intuitive thought, is worth volumes of psychology, symbols, sentiment. Moon and Saturn together. Eve of Mother's birthday. The last flock of sheep grazing in the gloaming beyond the low rails I watched long.

22 November   Mother's birthday brought sunshine, and for me three letters, one from her, the others from Peter and Nellie. Now I have been standing long at the attic window looking down on Bonnie and Jenny and her foal, and the flock of ewes beyond in the clear moonlight. Yet my heart is full of the deepest longing.

25 November   With the heaviest heart that I have ever yet begun a journal, as I feel it to be now. Not numb, but a rending and braising of nerves and fibres: an agony that must presently pass. Surely silent and still one is more wrought-stricken through thought than in any Dionysian orgy? Tony Dyer came to tea, talked for a brief time on the veranda. He told me something of the private-airline plane, which we'd heard yesterday had crashed and killed six people. The pilot was thrown clear of the wreckage and found, still living, by a pair of Africans: he asked for water, and then said '*Ndege mbaya*', 'the bird was bad'. By the time they returned with help he was dead; 'He was a fine-looking young man,' Tony said, and looked down, and was silent.

26 November   I come from praying and looking upon the Lyre, or rather, the bright star Vega. Reading Robert Graves's *Greek Myths* gives me high entertainment, both tales and manner of telling. The ego is a protection, a kind of impenetrable surrounding envelope of oneself. The least rent, attempt to tear aside, to lose this aspect of soul, and one is vulnerable; those one meets are transparent, luminous, seen as life in death, life more vivid, the 'trace' of death never absent. Every event instantaneous, unrepeatable, 'eternal'.

28 November Fine all day so we could go to Nanyuki for our business with Spiers.* The evening singularly beautiful and gold, the foal happy to be dry, to lie flat flung on sweet green grass. Mother's letter told me of her going to Chaldon for the memorial service for Valentine, the interment of her ashes near Katie's grave. Some freesias came to Mother for her birthday with a card in her own writing. A few of these flowers Mother took to offer on the graves.

2 December Return from Nairobi to silent empty green farm. Sheep gone and most of the cattle; a windless calm gray nightfall. More tests and X-rays for me in Nairobi, but I had a letter from Mother in Timau, and a brief one from Peter who is now thinking of entering a theological seminary. He is, I suppose, about forty-seven. I felt too tired to walk this evening.

4 December Sally's last night in Kenya, and I think of the child: Will also spoke of her, with concern for her now delicate appearance, when we visited him. The tractor came up through the forest this morning and the men brought news of a little girl lost from one of the many families of Kikuyu living now along the lower edge. She was last seen yesterday morning walking up the track towards the forest by a forest guard who asked her where she was going: 'to find my mother'. He supposed the woman to be cutting firewood and went on his way. The mother did not miss her little three-year-old till nearly nightfall, when some search was made. Her footprints were seen as far as the bridge across the furrow, after that no traces at all.

5 December To deal with a certain kind of seeping melancholy which runs through or 'infects' all when intellect is inactive – and without intellect energising there would be no world – is how I interpret a passage in my devotedly studied *Commentary** discovered (unmarked before) this afternoon: 'If all the "energy" in the universe were converted into actual kinetic energy ... "history" would have come to an end, and there would no longer be a "world" at all' (391). I opened *The Simple Vision** at J.C.P.'s introduction and after some of his fun with Eliot, read at the end of it: *Riveder le Stelle*, and was restored, as always I am when I see them again: when they shine for me in Plotinus. 'Leibnitz said that in every created thing there is an element of "metaphysical" evil': true melancholy partakes of the nature of this evil. We gather the opinion among the men is that the child was either sold or stolen. Gerard suspected something of this kind from her father's talk.

10 December A letter from Dr. McCaldin labelled *urgent* at Timau today more or less said there is nothing the matter with me, apart from the anaemia for which he does not suggest a cause. Many large bills but better than having ills as well. I am thankful. Gerard has decided the commotion in my breast caused by heart palpitations originated in my emotion over the disease and death of Valentine. So it may be. Fine and sunny and Christmas cards coming which for some reason I am enjoying more than I ordinarily do this year. The seven open-billed storks flew hesitantly across our forest glade this morning. I read a satisfying essay by Bertrand on Scientific Method in Philosophy.

12 December An eagle wildly screaming in the forest. After I wrote last evening I walked alone with overhead the white storks, first one, two or three, then the full company, a trail with singing wings from end to end of heaven: all in a long glide, with few shiftings of pinions, they sailed down from the mountain pastures to the dead safety of old appointed trees.

16 December Kisiom returned soon after we did from what was to have been leave. He set off through the forest on Saturday afternoon but when he was passing through the area built over by the Kikuyu a woman ran out and accused him of stealing the child. A great clamour arose and he was borne off to the headman's hut. Although the child's parents did not join in the accusation, the uproar continued and the headman to appease the crowd and to get our luckless cook out of their hands sent him on the bus to the police at Timau with the bereaved parents and the accusing woman. He was let out for the sum of 3,000/- and has to appear on Monday.

18 December, Spring Cottage New thatch, white walls, porches over the doors; sunshine and all the voices of birds. In my fig-tree niche I felt Valentine must still be *here*; and I thought much of Plotinus because I wrote many pages there; and this morning read the whole of Περὶ εὐδαιμονίας* in MacKenna's version. Most still now, with moonlight poured silverly down over all the earth, and a cicada lullaby. News came at tea-time the body of the little girl had been found near a game path through the bushes, and at no great distance from the bridge where was seen her last footprint.

19 December 'Eaten by beasts' was the verdict, and no one until yesterday, when the police came and organised a search, had really tried to find the child. The sun seems to burn up heaven which becomes as a white furnace and the grass is dizzy with the little saw-wings, as many of them as of leaves of grass.

21 December Sudden decision yesterday, we would return no more to sleep at the Beale. We went up in the morning through the forest to collect more *things*, and the cottage grows more and more full. In the evening we had a happy hour with Will. And Gilfrid flew in for five minutes. I hung up the mistletoe. Last night I dreamed of a great bull, black and formidable (after all the reading of *The Greek Myths*?), but after the way of the unicorn of legend he came and lay near me, his head on my knees and I saw then he was blinded of one eye; and by the massive hairy brow and blinking lid I understood his pain. My heart melted with pity, and all day I have recollected.

24 December For all there is no one now to send poems to I live only in poetry. All is instantaneously irrevocably reflecting eternity, *is*, just because it is, timeless. We went to see Will this morning passing on the way the children going to him. On the air-strip this one old ancient man with all Africa round him was entertained by a score of skinny brats, smelly and unabashed. They sang best their own chants with an appealing vehemence keeping time, with a still dance, bending their knees in a fast rhythm, tossing up and forward their arms. One or two clapped; the part song of the choir ran to and fro; paused in midstroke to be re-started by a half line by the leader. Each singer received a double handful of sweets from Gerard and six bananas. The play over, Gerard pushed Will back to the veranda.

26 December Boxing Day outing to Sirakoi with Will on the eve of his fall last year. A good day and we all enjoyed it, dust and all. Our furthest point, near Michael's Mount, was marked by a vast assembly of white storks and a few marabou. While he made a painting of the wild fells where they tumble onto the plains I watched the birds rise and whirl, silver as silent seagulls, black as crows. Their measured interlaced spiral, on blue, on dazzling billowing cloud, on distant desert, revolved from the green ground to heights invisible. The grass all round was dizzy with uneaten music-makers. Will sat in the car painting, and I kept looking up at his absorbed profile. It was fun to see him in our cottage, he wheeled himself about, and noticed in a shelf, with some entertainment, a book by Louis, *The Lion took Fright.** So for today ends my faithful *Powys Chronicle*.

28 December Owl in the shadowy path in the spring grove at dusk caused the red Saladin to shy. Stones in the water rattled under the ponies' hoofs. The afterglow light above the hills and Mercury shining. The Twins rising now: when I saw them this morning I thought anew how they resemble in distance apart and angle to the horizon Alpha and Beta Centauri. I grow now more admiring of the Dioscuri after feeling of old a certain coolness towards them ... We rode to see the site of Christopher's proposed dam. Storks were perching on the tops of the thorn trees there, which must all be cut down, whichever way I looked there was bird carved on the sky looking down his long bill from aloft. A flight of six duck rose from the furrow.

30 December Some quality of the piercing brilliance of the stars as they appear here enters direct the brain, explores the soul, is the utmost that can be experienced, at a physical level of 'the intellect that is without extension'. Returning from Sirakoi I saw a cheetah in outline on the gold of sunset, the spots as it bounded, one cub.

1970

2 January Quite a long Derry Day: a pair of thick-knees on the way to Sirakoi, eight kongoni, eland, distant giraffe; Mulberry picking in the shade of leaves and black and red fruit in the heat of the day: the garden with gate bowered with passion fruit, at that hour deserted by the tall old man, and sweet with freshly cut lucerne, Virgilian. Round Eland Hill for an evening ride, when I saw and heard that solitary and swift musical water lover, the green sandpiper, from Siberia. *Last* in the dusk five waterbuck, the black duck, flying, quacking, floating, landing with a magic slither along the surface of the darkly gleaming river. Stars. Journal.

3 January I walked down from the main road to the empty Beale house this morning and thought of G.M.P.* I made butter in the pantry, Gerard went to Kisima and brought Francis,* who is staying with us. The small dark-eyed boy with soft curls on his forehead came in to greet us, lighting the bare place with its ghosts and memories. Christopher's ewes and lambs on Windy Hill. No mail at Timau from over the sea or through the sky.

8 January Flocks of storks on the lower slopes of Lion Hill in three bomas, hundreds in each, close-packed, all standing with their backs to the sun sinking towards the hills. Our ride ended with Will; he was irascible for one reason and another, but pleased with his painting, oil on water-colour on wood, begun the day he spent with us. Forty sheep killed on Kisima by lion, and six lion shot the next day by Tony. He, W.E.P., gave me two letters from Mother to read. Spring Dionysus called *Anthus*. Mind cells rich with poetry as the 'crannied work of bees'. How bewildering are these inward changes, total abandon to desolation, to song, to silence, and this silence is thought, Intellect: most perfectly known unconsciously; *when* this may not be, *then* to approach by the highest thought.

15 January One of the best mornings, walking and riding. Afternoon sinking of my wildly undulant states. Suddenly after tea we had to return to the 'king-pin'. Michael had brought mail so we were lucky. We sped back here and went out with Moss and Bess and a swift shower breaking along the side of El Khalil soaked us. We shall learn the moods of this place. I have so good and precious a letter from Mother, also one from Peggy Newman;* Gerard one from Peter. Hot baths, a little supper, the letters read in bed. Zebra were coming slowly down from their night grazing on this magnetic hill as we began to go up, we saw them one after one silhouetted on the gold sky between dawn and sunrise. Mother quoted from a letter from Sylvia, beautiful with yearning for Valentine.

24 January A *TLS* of considerable interest, with reviews of more praise than usual: Wellington, Churchill, Plotinian perspectives in Augustine. Rain again, but fine for our evening walk up the turgid river. One of the things about writing a journal is the discovery of oneself in the mere choice of what to write each day. Mind skims through the hours without, the timeless moods passions wonders within, as with a magic wand ... which touches now the minute of watching in the muddy track an emerald dove, walking and pecking unalarmed – the greenness flashing.

27 January In the arms of my fig tree this afternoon I copied out the Tree Alphabet and the seasonal vowels. In our evening ride between white clouds and black, with a dim rainbow in the east and thunderclaps in the west, we came on a vulture unable to fly, thrusting forward its neck in the fashion of a tortoise. Knowing itself powerless the big bird yet made one effort, running along and spreading broad wings uninjured yet on which it could not rise. When I looked back it was shuffling into the coverage of a thorny bush. May it die undiscovered in this shelter ... Sometimes I think moods of hopeless melancholy are caused at the level of awareness by *unconscious knowledge*, within one's being, of the unfathomable mystery of suffering, an utter weariness (maybe) of process, things for ever turning into each other.

2 February   'Full fathom five thy father lies ...' Gerard drove Will out a little way this evening and he was content sitting in the car watching the cows grazing and the Angora billies. He made a sketch of the cowherd's back; domed hat with a black ostrich plume on one side, a quiver of skin on his shoulder, bow and smooth stick with hunting-crop handle in one hand, barbed arrow in the other. Pain of soul was as a flower to me this afternoon, opening imperceptibly petal by petal of some dark wan purplish hue, until the profound centre, a narrow throat with no end ... a sword shall pierce through. Not 'not by bread alone' I have to remind myself: 'not by thought alone'.

12 February   A considerable amount of remarkable reading in *The Golden Bough*.* A day of high heat. The field (2 to 3 acres) in which this cottage stands was besieged by a pair of lion for two hours last night. The two ponies ran wildly, snorting and blowing, Gerard and the night watchman went about with torches. At last, after calling out more men the ponies were caught and fastened with rawhide ropes, Bonnie to the cedar post of the porch, Slabs to a near-by tree. We left two lighted lanterns close-by and the watchman was on the other side. At about 1 a.m. we heard the lion grunting as though calling each other. Silence followed, Bonnie stopped running round her post, almost shaking the house in her terror. The old man assured us the 'home' of the lion was not far off and that they would come back. Their tracks were plain in the dust for us to read in morning light.

21 February   Full moon rosily round in a murky blue-gray sky over Muriel's Beacon Hill, where so little a while before we had walked among rocks and sparse pale-gold grasses stroked by the wind. Ruiru was talking of old tribal customs, and he said how the children used to make bird lime from the milky juice of the wild fig tree to take pigeons. But the emerald spotted wood dove must not be eaten, and if caught let go free, for this bird prays for rain. Do those single falling notes suggest the first full drops falling on leaves?

22 February   'Only believe ...' Ruiru telling so sadly those old beliefs, and others of sacrificing for rain-making, in which now no one believes, made me think how essential belief is for man: it is in a sense easy *to believe*, the difficulty is *in what*. *Not* the reasoning of theologians; gnosis? He was, however, happy today for his little wife, unlooked for, arrived, with their one remaining child, Maria.

23 February   A letter addressed to him by John* in his strongest hand lay on Will's desk this evening, on the board that pulls out and has POWYS inlaid in some light wood in it. Gerard and I were riding and did not stay long. The heat continues, often the sunny sky has a kind of underdark. I saw lightning at moonrise.

4 March   For his birthday we spent last evening with Will who was happy but sleepy so I longed to go sooner. I'd seen his car lights going up over Rock Rabbit Run at 6.15 a.m., taking as he'd planned some of the 32 bells he'd shown us to his goats. He spoke with delight of the little white kids gathering all round him. I gave him a copy of my poem 'Sirakoi'.* He read this aloud, sitting before a log fire, and to my surprise gave it praise. He kissed both my hands when we said goodnight.

7 March   The wind surging with wave music, bringing the smell of rain on dust and dry grass; for I write before dark, after putting Francis and Martin to bed. We went to pick mulberries, which stewed while they bathed. Then many were eaten in the yellow bowls, the little boys in pyjamas sitting opposite each other on stools. All afternoon we were in the spring grove. Will brought his grandsons here in the morning in his Land Rover. Martin is sturdy with broad shoulders, and often a look of Gilfrid. Slate followed my traces when I went for my early walk, I suddenly saw him running spryly along, tail up, but he could only just get home again.

11 March   I thought this morning the rejection of Christianity common today is largely an attempt not to live in the dimension of suffering: not to take it with full consciousness as the condition of living. Not to recognise, accept and endure spiritual suffering leads to an impoverishment of being. Prayer springs from a spirit broken in order to be the more resilient. Reading the Orphic and other definitions of ψυχή* and considering my own I decided in my dawn walk, with the splendours of a sanguine water-green sunrise, I would say ψυχή is the living (and to the body life-giving) relation of the individual human being and the universal; that meeting-point in intellect which is both 'we' and knowledge. Kitto in *The Greeks* speaks of 'the Ionian philosophers finding new and exciting paths of thought by their own individual command of reason': this 'command of reason' may be said to be the soul in its awareness of the energy of intellect. Remarking on the contemporary speeches in the chapter 'The Greeks at War', K. says: 'this speech is like Greek poetry and Greek art: the intellectual control of feeling increases the total effect'. And from Pericles (according to Thucydides): 'It is the unexpected that most breaks a man's spirit.'

18 March   A long afternoon in the Fig Tree with three good and stimulating (for a change) *TLS*'s. Gerard slept on his bed where he passes so much of his life. I had letters from Peter and Katey. Peter has had to forgo his wish to enter a seminary: he could not afford it. This is a brave letter written in a good spirit, and honest. He says Marian's* memory is still more gone: so grievous for him when he goes to her at the end of his day in New York – and her old Dutch wood house, falling into decay, that she so loved, her home for so long.

19 March   The day began with a comet, which Gerard discovered when he went out at 5.30, low in the east, small but bright, both head and curving tail; and ended with a burning high-hued rainbow before the sun went behind the hills silvery. We sat under a bush against a warm rock while the shower slanted down and earth and grass and leaves smelt sweet.

4 April   Ancient moon (new in two days) and the comet clear and shining this morning. Tonight clouds and much lightning, and a certain glance of my mind towards this hour next week when I shall be thinking of it being the last night in the cottage. Gerard and I went for a small ride this evening, he mounted on Jill for the first time – the first ride since his fall. I found Brownie slow and heavy and wondered if somehow she'd got in foal. I re-found yesterday and began to read, and finished today in the fig tree *La Métaphysique Orientale*, Guénon's lecture to the Sorbonne, and one of his best things, I think. I took some notes from it: 'primordial man', 'return to the source', 'living in eternity'. But do human beings generally *want* to transcend their humanity?

10 April   Fine so I could be in the Fig Tree after a morning of cooking, marmalade and cake. In the evening we went to Sirakoi and went for a farewell walk with Moss and Bess, both fat and sleek, shining black and white. How all these events strike the heart to the quick: parting and death, suffering and kindness, the patient earth bearing the multitudinous life. Mortals moving over it, responsible and rebellious: can it be the increase merely in numbers of human beings can lead to a weakening of Spirit in some sense? Not in the sense of pure contemplation, but in intensity of earthly being …? My poet Pindar is free of the self-pity expressed by some of the characters of the great tragedians, poet not playwright.

11 April   Gray with moist English air: I open my journal to look once at my pictures before I put it in the bottom of my case, to notice the patterns my feathers make, in that loose-end mood before a journey, bed strewn with things to pack and wear: yet we have few and simple ones, how can they look so many? My walk before sunrise was a satisfying one, the sky full of wild clouds and colours, the mountain massive with a crimson stain between the peaks as I have so often seen it from the Beale. Mlefu appeared to wish us a good voyage and send greetings to Mother.

15 April, Mappowder   Only one word of quiet – for I feel strange and far from myself, and from all others, and wonder at the singing of the birds: and I have nothing to say, now I have my book again in my hands, of the adventures of the way, and of land and sea and sky. Only that we flew over Crete, ridged and (as it appeared from miles above) desolate and uninhabited, empty beaches and the sea with no boats in the curving bays. And we landed at the airport of Athens between translucent waters, blue-green-glaucous, and under the steep white-speckled limestone hills, so steep they must needs be bare of buildings. And in London we went to look at the marbles of the Pantheon. Now I have been sitting on the floor listening to Mother, who is reading letters of long ago, writ by her mother in youth. For me here is a keepsake from Valentine, a small Egyptian head.

16 April   Thankfulness for Mother fills me with joy, but the day brings its customary anxieties and disappointments: the old furniture Gerard is beginning to unpack is badly broken, rats have been in the crates chewing up cushions and other things to make nests.

18 April   A coincidence? The first sunny morning here and I heard the cuckoo calling, and a curlew, as I looked over the white gate towards Short Wood: only to my grief I saw the beautiful Willow Tree had been felled. Then this evening after an April shower we unpacked the Cuckoo Clock. The big hand was snapped off and the hanger for the pendulum had disappeared inside. However, after some time we fixed it up enough to try it on the wall and it has been going for nearly an hour though I have not yet started the strike, this is for 11.30, and I doubt if I'll wake in the night. Sunshine now. Tick-tock.

21 April   Blackbird song in my head, but the oak chest is broken in several parts, a ruin of antique beauty: gray raininess all day. Gerard has given me the *Bacchae** with an introduction by E. R. Dodds which I am going to read with as much attention as I can. I must write more of thoughts and less of things if I am to continue this, for in glancing back through my old journal I quickly see the thinking still lives, the descriptions are flat, the cares and confessions meaningless, of the *ego*; though to set them out at the time may have been salvation.

22 April   One week gone: dark all day with high wind. Anniversary – 59th – of Mother's wedding day. Went to Dorchester. All Saints' church was moving into the dimension of spirit with the arcades of pale stone all but dissolving into the sombre light: the altarpiece a focus of mildly suffused radiance. Dr. Jackson's massive thesis 'Towards a Theory of Values' makes fine reading and he says some remarkable things, bold and sensitive and full of energy: 'every experience is an act'. Now and then I find it diffuse, even incoherent occasionally: but the essay I'm now reading is excellent – on aesthetics; and his phrase 'the higher immediacy' is perfect for spiritual awareness; maybe from another philosopher?

30 April   Because of the cold it may be the English April days have not gone too swiftly. At this late hour the sun shines, with no warmth but more than it has all day. When I returned from my walk with Mother Gerard was in a happy mood, laughing over *The Frogs*, which he finds the best of Aristophanes' plays. My mind this evening is absent, bent on silent prayer.

13 May   A good day for cuckoo calling; softly enfolded early and late with fog, sunshine in between. Weary, I slept all night long, waking only once to hear the light straight-falling summer rain on the lilacs that I love; dreaming through the dawn chorus. I read Llewelyn's 'May' while I drank coffee; so often at the Beale I've read these essays* desiring the English months.

5 June   The dryness is growing grievous to birds, all day the garden has been noisy with young squawkers demanding food from weary parents. Song has almost and, quite suddenly, ceased. Dodds, whom I'm reading now, is the most entertaining and light-hearted of my three authors. I should suppose by his notes as thorough a scholar as the other two, but so gay. I laughed aloud several times this afternoon in my hour of reading by Robert's tomb.* And Alyse's picture, in this journal, has a whimsical wilful look as I glance at it, as it is my habit to do, and Homer and Plotinus, before I begin to write.

8 June   I walked again in the long grass in the morning mist, the soothing dew; lay on bare earth to see the flowering heads in the sky. The day is one of heat and syringa and honeysuckle savours, only small waftures of air. Constant cuckoo calling; a wren. Sudden sharp spray of sparkling drops on the hot garden of languid leaves; I chopped off many heart-shaped lilac ones with all the while a most intimate sense of companionship. Finished 'The Greeks and the Irrational', last appendix, in the graveyard. I think the *horse*, if it were as he describes in his metaphor, saved humanity. Certainly science does nothing to counter the 'irrational' elements in mankind.

15 June Two little poems in the graveyard, to recover my customary level of sorrow and thankfulness. Ten Loeb volumes of Valentine's came to us yesterday evening, collected by Mother and Phyllis from Sylvia, nine green history ones, one red, this much-handled, read and marked I now hold and copy this word of philosophy, dotted by Valentine in her solitary studies: 'I will also fasten wings upon thy mind, with which she may rouse herself, that all perturbation being driven away, thou mayest return safely into thy country by my direction, by my path, and with my wings.'

21 June Early service. There is something to me about Mother's profile, as we walk so slow through green meads, moving in its dogged determination to contiue living and walking over the face of the earth, when both knees so ache, when the weakness of age compasses her: a testing to the limit of J.C.P.'s 'endure and enjoy': as if also all the resolution and life-force of ancestors and brothers and sisters, gone, gone, gone, were in countless intangible ways coming to succour her, this youngest one bone of their bone. Her full face on the other hand, while also showing this her endurance, expresses sometimes moods of annoyance, dislike, and other of those less attractive emotions which run their course through wretched mortals; but most often it is alight with innocent happiness, the cheeks glowing, unfailing response and joy, spontaneous as a child's: a rare combining of delicate sensibilities and obstinate will. Rosemary came this afternoon with Giles* from Sherborne for a brief visit: he will be taking his 'O' level exams for the next ten days, and intends to have only one more term at Sherborne. At seventeen Giles is friendly, good-looking, thoughtful, altogether pleasant. He wanted to know if I'd heard the cuckoo today, not wanting the silence of those naughty notes. I had – in church.

29 June 'The clotey Stour' has now borders of yellow waterlilies, their awkward stalks thrust up aslant, their leaves asleep on the surface save when breeze lifts one to flap back like an anxious ear. The white are rare and rest perfect on the breast of the river rocking faintly when the mirror is wind-rippled, holding gold distilled sun in pointed hearts of snow ... It is a thing when an old man, near his eighty-fifth year, becomes genial, mirthful, basking in his own Socratic crabbedness. A white statuette of the Old One with hand plucking his robe, Valentine's, that she gave him, and his dearest possesssion, stands on the mantelshelf above the soot-filled grate in Dr. Smith's* gamboge-painted room. 'All my books can go as long as I can keep that,' he said. Well she knew on whom to bestow her Socrates.

1 July Seagulls returning to the ploughlands, plover flying with the wind in flocks, finches much in evidence; and this wind from the north-west so keen one is glad to leave it: so begins the month of my departure. *The Pleasures of Literature*, is the work, apart from the living lectures none can hear now, which best shows forth his (J.C.P.'s) self-styled art of dithyrambic analysis, and his entering into the genius of literature at the levels most germane to my mood and present responses. No novel can I read now, of his or any man's, but the *The Pleasures of Literature* still takes my mind's hand and leads me away from the sorrow of Mary. Tiny green apples and rose petals shower down, and green leaves and leafy twigs torn off. I go over two chapters a day of *The Kingfisher's Wing* to correct slips in the typescript, but I feel far from the one who wrote it.

14 July, Spring Cottage Peter's birthday. Best not to turn back over page, or shoulder, but face again Africa. The day of the twelfth was all sun till, as we embarked on the VC 10 a dark of haze stole all the rays. And in this hazy dusk the aircraft crossed the English coast above Dover with the shores of France visible at the same time. Next morning Nairobi was cloud-swathed, the temperature 50 °F: the winter of the equator. We reached the cottage at 1 p.m. today; saw Will in the evening. He was standing in his office when I went in with his limb fixed and looking to my joy well and hale. His man was out for the day; Gerard built a fire on the hearth, coaxing the flame with his breath. Will toasted particles of crumbly bread on the end of a fork four or five feet long and spread them with butter and the strawberry jam I'd brought him from Mother. So great a struggle and woe within I try not to heed ...

18 July Lion roared in the hills at 1 a.m., waking to a level of hearing all but in the realm of slumber, I said: 'Now I have heard this voice (as rocks and rough granite groaning), I may write a poem.' At dawn and again before sunrise, but less mighty in light, the sound of the voice of lion.

25 July This evening we had tea with Will and after went with him in his Land Rover down the road to the Durdle Door he has had made, up and down what seem the sheer sides of gullies, with now and then a sharp drop to the river on one side. I'd only once before been near this fearsome granite archway in the bowels of the Ngare Ndare gorge, then riding a mule. Water from the hills in the rare rains has carved a perfectly smooth and rounded way in the rock after which it leaps to a pool, bordered by a sandy beach, in front of the rugged gate of living rock that, if it had a port-cullis, might well bear the legend of Dante. Rock doves cooed there, a robin chat sang the sun down. Will remained above with Joey.* From the veranda I saw Mercury.

26 July The quiet Sunday brought for a few minutes in the afternoon Tony, Rose and their three elder sons. Running into the spring grove, Francis cried his name, and his brothers', and sprang upon me as a small wiry wood demon. Martin followed in silence, and climbed up to the mirror of the spring basin. Next it was pomegranates, and they soon came running with two apiece of the flaming fruit in their hands.

7 August Gerard and I went riding in the morning among the herd of over 600 cows and calves onto Lion Hill: to speak to men pulling out fence wire. Then we came merrily home in sun and dust. Less than two hours later a man came in to say a lion had killed a yearling while we were out there.

9 August Gerard came in at 8 p.m. after hunting the lion, and seeing it twice but without time for a shot, in the dense thorn bush above the Mbate Drift. He and Michael passed unaware the actual bush in which the lion had hidden his prey after carrying it more than a mile from where he'd killed it. The Africans following heard him growling and called them back. This evening we saw tracks of two lion going almost up to the gate of our Sirakoi cottage, one of them exceptionally large, great pug marks of a heavy animal deep in the dust. All over the farm the wide sweeping pale-gold plains are menaced by ambushes of thorn bushes. In every least hollow, depression or dell round the base of all the hills the bush, the scrubby trees, are thick. They have covered hundreds of acres already that were clear when we came here and checked the grass fires.

12 August Mbui Mlefu, the long one, thin as a rake, came stalking in big boots up to the cottage this morning. We shook hands and exchanged all the inquiries. He handed me a present of eggs, five from his ancient mother, four from himself. While he talked to Gerard I made a sponge cake with three of them and took him a slice still warm. He was telling of the grievous poverty among the Kikuyu on Swan's farm. One woman with five children, deserted by her husband, came starving to her foodless mother. The older woman rebuked her, two of the children died. Then this woman worked a few hours digging for another: with the few cents she earned she bought a tin of insect powder, ate this, and so left her troubles.

14 August   Gunshots at dawn ushered in the day. Gerard showed me the slough of a great snake in the grass, seven or eight feet long; the wraith of a snake, every transparent scale complete, the mouth, the rings round and discs over the eyes. In the evening at Sirakoi we walked up to Muriel's hilltop Beacon. Gerard saw three elephant heading away from us up another rock-strewn steep opposite, about half a mile off. In size like the three bears; the biggest ahead, great ears spread, and all in haste. The sweeping east wind was set straight from us to them. They went faster, sending dust at the last when they were on, going over, the ridge. 'The shining figure of Orpheus' especially with me today.

16 August   In the small garden enclosure with the full moon and flowers I remember how Li Po danced with his companion shadow, and his winecup – 'the moon alas, is no drinker'. And clouds left him shadowless. Beyond this serenity, through the open entrance, over the rails, beloved by woodpeckers, scimitar bills, and wood hoopoes, all Africa. For a few moments in the afternoon a shower visited the garden cooling the faces of the flowers.

3 September   The first two evenings of this month grass and bush burning round El Khalil. Moving about on the summit of the Hill of the Friend I watched smoke drifting like mist among the green bushes, hanging blue as spirit above the dancing lines of flames and the charred land behind them. Trees and stones cracked like gunshots. In the steady gale from the east a blazing spearhead of fire roared round the south corner of the hill. Close above me a black eagle balanced on the wind with the slightest turn of tail or dip of long-pointed wing. With a small rustle a duiker appeared from a low creeper thicket, came towards me, stood so I saw clearly tiny ridged horns, turned and retreated. The first evening in the gloaming I walked alone to the river crossing.

7 October   This long day has been a harmonious one. I think Gertrude is feeling at ease. Dorothy* came before noon, looking pleasant and dignified, and talked slowly but often well and amusingly, with touches of dry humour and tartness. She seemed to enjoy the cottage. Christopher, also in a good mood, appeared at the end of tea to tell us his adventures with the Africans and Land Agent who came to value the Beale. The nights are thrillingly alive to me, with a poetry not to be written, with thin gusts of desolate far-faring desert wind.

8 October This day of my fifty-fifth birthday the diary opens at the page where Homer has had his dwelling since I began the journal in November, and this pleases me and is taken as a signal from the giver whom I saw with my mortal eyes for the last time this day last year. From the sculptured male head I turn to the white face of 'Portrait of a Child'* and marvel again at the human face divine. Will sent for this day a letter of greeting and his picture painted long ago of Vera's cottage with the great elm winter bare, and yellow of daffodils by the western wall.

4 November The whole affair of the Government take-over of the Beale, which was to have been settled today, has again been postponed. Gerard saw Christopher this morning and said he looked strained, disappointed. All the work of the next harvest falls on him; and how many more times will this happen, or may they not finally withdraw from the whole thing? I feel sad sometimes thinking of the house, my home for so many years, empty and cold. We spent a brief time with Will this evening, he was again tired, but told beguilingly of his visit to the school, the little girls sewing under a tree, and his threading a needle – to their delight.

7 December For Will and for me a kind of ghost journey up to Kisima, so imbued all is there for us with our past lives – the most important part of his – and with the ones we have loved there who seem near as the living: layer upon layer, strands intertwine. That farm is green, the thin mountain air clearing the spirit of fear. We stopped to watch many things: lucerne being cut filling the air with fresh sappy scent and a multitude of English swallows whirling over it while a buzzard glided in circles above. Rose looked delicate and lovely, it was good to see her with the four boys together. Will talked to me of his early meetings with Elizabeth, and likened her to a lioness. I must try to have a Breughel-eye for what I shrink from.

15 December Mid-month, thunder and lightning: green and gold evening sky. The Beale is, it appears, finally taken over today. Christopher sent down a note asking for a letter on farm paper asking that the money be paid direct to our lawyer – *when* this will be is not known.

Gerard and I tonight are at Sirakoi where we sleep in the bed of wood we had made for us by Harnam Singh when we first began to live in the Beale house.

18 December For our evening ride we went north and west along the track. I kept watching the dust for traces. I said: 'Now it's so dry the elephant may be as likely to be here as in their usual months.' 'There is one, and a calf with it,' he answered. Of course I had not seen them though I was looking at the gray mass of thorn bush that matched so exactly. Gerard said a white tusk caught his eye first. We halted and stayed watching a few minutes. Two more appeared nearer us but moving away.

21 December Tree hyraxes are sounding, shrieking and creaking, in the trees of my spring grove tonight; and I think I am at the Beale, looking out from veranda or attic window over the dark forest. All day I have been Beale-haunted, in the way I am haunted when some one dies by their presence, essence, emanation entelechy, *doppel-gänger* or whatever it may be, for an undefined interval, after which this particular closeness wanes and they are not 'known' just in this way again. The farm of innumerable walks, the house that has absorbed all my poetic passions, terrors, anxieties, despairs ... everything of my life there as though it were another intimately known life, so fittingly the day ends with this constant night-noise of the forest.

1971

6 January Epiphany. 'To be a light to lighten the Gentiles and to be the glory of thy people Israel.' The star guided the wise men to Christ's cradle: 'a light sees a light'. This parched land crying to the brazen heaven has not even the shadow of darkness, no cloud for sun or silver flood of moonshine. We called to see Will in the honey-gold evening when the hills were purple-smoked and the Etruscan-red thorns blazed in blue sky. He asked me to find 'a little book of old Blake's* at Sherborne' as he wanted the last wind poem – 'North Easter' – of Charles Kingsley. I met him happily with it in my hand, and he was so pleased he picked up a woolly white sheepskin cap that happened to be near where he stood, with crutch and stick, on the veranda. 'I'll give you this cap.' 'To keep my ears warm in England!' I put it on and rode home in my Phrygian cap.

23 January Trees and grass grow daily more skeletal and since this word is derived from the Greek verb 'to parch' it is correct in every way. In the evening we walked to the river to listen to the musical flow of sleek black water. The pair of black duck swam upstream, only to be detected by their silent motion against the current from water or lava rock. A common sandpiper was on the dusty brink, or wading in a bay of shallow water.

17 February The drought much on our minds: we met a lugubrious man at Will's this evening who'd been spending a fortnight in the Northern Frontier; he told of the starving cattle and children he'd seen, and of a skirmish between Turkana and Samburu in which several were killed. 'We're all wasting away,' he groaned, himself being hollow, bowed and gray of face. Gerard and I walked down to the mill – as of old – and along the furrow, then returned for me to say goodbye to Will when he was alone again. He told us Michael and Francis and another pair of age-fellows had run away from Pembroke. Rose had word, and she and Tony set off to hunt for them in their airplane. One of the other boys returned on his own while Rose was at the school, and told which way they'd gone: so they were soon found. Will's hair is straight, but he looks splendid. On his veranda I could look from him to the mountain in the clear evening sky. I think now, on the last night but one in the cottage, I will take leave also of my journal in Africa, with a merry chirruping of cicadas, in my ears: perhaps this 'happy little tettix' is the best of all creatures in the drought. I saw the kingfisher who's given me feathers.

20 February, Mappowder Snowdrops by my bedside. I had forgotten just how good they smell. All well befell with my flight, no delay, sleep, the polestar on my right hand. A mild day, and I was with Mother by noon, she coming out to welcome me in the new woolly, white and blue and mauve, I sent her for Christmas. We walked to the gate in the evening, and all was clear and gold and fair with rooks and fields of green. My cuckoo clock is going. There were poems to read of Valentine's.

21 February Clarity; moon between Venus and Jupiter, an upright crescent, golden irradiance with sunrise in Mappowder church, and a chaffinch singing through the early service of thanksgiving for Mother and Mary. White chaste light of the month of expiation. I was reading the thin paper book of poems by Valentine Ackland, called indeed *Later Poems*, although several are of long ago and some I had read before elsewhere, when I came on one of mine among this gathering chosen (I imagine) by Sylvia. How the picture of a sheep boma came here I cannot tell, nor can I ask Sylvia until there is postal communication again – if I dare to then. Still, for the first time I've seen a poem of mine in print, and in good company.

23 February White, white frost all day, sun: a goldcrest singing quick over and over over my head in the ash tree while I picked up sticks below. Mother and I walked down to the little stream, across the field to the white-railed footpath bridge and saw a pair of long-tailed tits in the sallows. When we came in I telephoned Sylvia to tell her of the poem: she said she made the selection herself, and did not seem to mind mine, 'Where the hills …'* being among the true poems of Valentine.

28 February I am sure no one ever carried their eighty years more lightly than Mother does, each thing she loves she greets with delicate responsive child-like grace: her face glows with happiness, her eyes shine. She sympathises with everyone, entering with imaginative insight into the lives of any whom she knows, who are neighbours or whose life touches hers. I was astonished at Eliot saying he had no idea what Shelley meant by the lines beginning 'keen as are the arrows' and the five following in the Skylark poem. Was he jesting? I admired greatly the last essay in the book – on Irving Babbitt, hard-hitting, trenchant, going to the root of the weakness of the humanistic attitude. It is masterly. I read it last night, and again aloud to Mother this morning.

7 March Sun all day, ten hours without a cloud, hard ice, north wind. Early church with Mother, then to Buckland to meet Francis, in Katie's cabin I suddenly found my topaz from Alyse was gone. I cannot find it anywhere. Six hour walk with Francis on the hills. Gerard telephoned from Timau in the evening with Will sitting near him. P. O. Strike over.

8 March Grass white with snow in the morning twilight, whiteness soon gone, and the day as gray as yesterday, was gay. My heart craves Alyse's keepsake, I imagine it will come to me again, as constantly the world becomes more inscrutable and more diaphanous to me. I wrote to Gerard and Will last night, to Margaret today, I read Landsberg on Death. Warmer this evening. Alyse, Alyse, Alyse.

12 March Best singing of birds: robin, blackbird, thrush under the Bear and Arcturus, while Jupiter shone and Mars faint and low – before 7 a.m. I was up early to start my grapefruit marmalade and walked the garden path. I've had a good reading now in bed, and I read to Mother that desperate chapter of *Wuthering Heights* where

Catherine pulls the feathers out of her pillow. Always to feel *guilty*, whatever I'm at, is, I think, one of my most besetting difficulties, making me restless, unsure, impatient: I'm always being driven on to the next thing with some hope that in that thought or activity, I may be absolved from my guilt. Of course I am not. Only sometimes it seems the sense is appeased for a little while.

18 March   With night the gales are laid to rest. A noble letter came to me today, six pages of foolscap writ neat and small both sides, from Gerard, a triumph of a letter full of thought, philosophy, adventure, of birds and landscape and W.E.P. and affection for me. I was proud to give it to Mother to read as we sat by the fire on the hearthrug and footstool after a teaparty. My sciatica and pins and needles continue, and arthritis is painful in the swollen knee of that leg.

3 April   Slicing cold north wind all day, all day small birds with ruffled head-feathers ply at my window. All afternoon a sick jackdaw hunched on the grass, with puffed form, dejected, only able to fly a few yards: at once my heart pitying this plunderer of songbirds' eggs. Keeping a journal is one way of finding how imaginative fears are: besetting, dominating hours of the day, that they will not be written proves them unreal.

30 April   East wind, dry as ever. I went alone in the afternoon to Sturminster. Blackbirds exchanging phrases above my head nearly all the way. I walked by the river for half an hour and saw one gray wagtail, one swallow, one moorhen, one sandpiper. The mill is deserted save by a few of the homing pigeons that still haunt their foodless home and empty cote. One sat sorrowful in a window where the glass had been smashed. I touched the cool leaves and stalks of a marsh marigold plant. My heart, even so, is stony and heavy. I liked Findlay's saying: 'Most Japanese tea-houses have a symbol for the ultimate Nothingness which blessedly underlies tea-drinking, like all finite objects.'

27 May   Sun at noon after the rainy morn, and the evening unending and golden, when we went into Somerset, all lanes and fields green and buttercup bright: best Reggie's blue eyes shining as Gerard talked to him; Mother and Gerard on Batemore looking down at Montacute from a steep grassy field with heifers and rams grazing – looking at church tower, Abbey Farm, dovecote, Montacute House. Sheep white on the slope strung as a garland between Montacute Hill and Hedgecock. A very revenant Mother must have felt herself to be as she satisfied her soul with gazing, and peopled all that landscape with her sisters and brothers in their youth and flowering. With Gerard she went to the edge of the sheer steep they dashed down on toboggans.

28 May Mabel's* birthday. A long and solitary afternoon, not unhappy, in my garden. Mother has now come home with honeysuckle, and Banksia roses, these tiny yellow ones she has been talking of, and seeking for, since her youth, and began to believe they grew no more on earth. She went to see Oliver Holt, a one-time pupil of L.C.P.* to whom she could speak of Mabel. He praised her hair until, as Mother described it, I see it again, warmly.

2 June In the nature of a pilgrimage to Shootash where we walked to the lake between flowering rhododendrons, wind flaws and ripples on the surface, mallard swimming, a moorhen clearing reedy throat: to Horsebridge where after crossing the ten bridges to Houghton we, Mother, Gerard and I, returned to the first and walked round the mill and up the flowering bank. A swan with curved wings as a great peony flower sped towards us down the shining stream, did not the Greeks call the swan scarlet? Never, I believe, in my first 22 years of life at the Mill, did I see a swan on the reach of the river. At the bend notes unheard this year till then: nightingale singing.

9 June As I woke before 5 I made my tea and went for a walk. A pair of deer were grazing in the hidden field on the dewy grass and on the flower-heads, I watched them unobserved for ten minutes, rather more than 50 yards away. I went to Dorchester alone with thoughts of V. and K.P. and G.M.P. and Alyse: and the church of All Saints behind which in the long-disused graveyard Alyse would eat her little meal, is up for sale. What will become of this edifice with its spire 'pointing to God' as Michael said? A thunder shower in the morning.

11 June Barnaby Bright is all twilight. Song-thrush clear spirit singer in this dim gloaming. 'Continuity and contentment, the unspectacular unprogressive qualities of country-folk that sustain the heretic ones, the pleasure-chasers ...' I marvel anew at the psychology the sure and poetic intuitions of Uncle Jack, as I re-read *The Meaning of Culture*: yet in the world today *even more than when he wrote*, his a voice of one crying in the wilderness, unheard, unheeded. (Why do present-day writers, by the way, eschew colon and semi-colon, those essential modulators of balanced harmonious prose?) All afternoon and evening I expected Gerard; not till nearly 7 he telephoned to tell me he was not coming, had in fact not set out. He said he had felt unwell – at which

I cannot wonder after three weeks of assiduous attention to his parents – and that there were floods.

15 June   A wren with uptilt tail and wisp of cobweb in her bill perched in a mesh of the wire guard of the church porch this early morning. She flew up to her nest, letting the gossamer fall, and out again through the lattice to the golden day. I read at the lectern in the great Bible that most poetic lesson of Jonathan and the rod dipped in honeydew: I knew then why I had come to the church and conceived a poem of the wren. Fine all day: the sun descended in an aqueous blaze of gold.

16 June   Gerard and I went to Dorchester and I kept thinking 'in ten days from today he is returning to Africa alone'. We had more than half an hour in St. Peter's. I shuddered at the two huge placards on the other main church 'ALL SAINTS FOR DISPOSAL'. I chose a new and smaller-than-this-journal at Smith's instead of Longman's where I purchased the one before this when Valentine was in Dorchester. After tea we walked in the fields, a strong west wind, cool and clearing away the haze. Phyllis arrived while we were out to stay a few days with Mother. Most often my heart and soul seems almost equally drawn between thankfulness and annihilation.

18 June   Set wet; indeed a whole solid wet day, from the south. Phyllis spent part of the afternoon with Gerard and me, in conversation – for she is full of the wish to speak, and is undismayed by any subject, person, or way of life and thought. I like watching her rarified mongolian countenance with its network of spider-fine lines, and listening also, in some degree; in saying something to make her laugh. I moaned so deeply last night, with a nightmare, I woke not only Gerard, who took so long to rouse me, but also Mother in her house. I dreamed a heavier and heavier load was being spread over my whole body: as in the experience of being buried alive?

19 June   Softly meditatively this rainless day the clouds spread. Farewell to Phyllis of the ancientest heavy-lidded eyes I have ever looked into: isolated and integrated. A poor day for me for thought and reading, I entertained myself with an account of the melancholy temperament by a Norwegian, which was salutary (maybe) as it suggested too well-known frailties and foibles; doubtful 'strengths': best summed up by 'the melancholic is the *suffering* temperament'. He is 'sensitive ... uncompromising ... hard to get on with ... pessimistic ... proud ... he has a passive nature.'

25 June   Eve of departure, stormy, wild south wind from the sea, clouds in haste allow no sunbeams to dart or steal between them. Gerard and I walked his favourite daily walk across the fields and by sweet-smelling hedges with the cuckoo calling as if it were May, clear and strong on the wind.

26 June Farewell, farewell, farewell ... but no cuckoo called this evening: when Gerard left at 1 p.m. and I'd cleared up I felt more desolation than I could have believed possible, torn but not stunned by suffering. I could only wait blindly till there was a slight lift. A tempestuous day of dark clouds and flashes of sun. Mother and I went for a walk after tea in the field of gold and purple and crimson.

9 July My eye caught on the last day of this book by the opening words, I felt a surge of impatience at myself for beginning so; moods, the hue of the soul swiftly change, a diary should be more like a sundial, though a sundial for such a one as I have proved myself to be, on a stormy day. A *chiaroscuro*, a confession, above all a transmutation by poetic thought of grief into some kind of tragic drama; of joy in the elements into song: not a trace of passing despair, of horror; rather what Socrates calls the ἔρως δεινός* of life, discovering a new manner of manifestation. A gentle large-dropped rain began as Mother and I sat in the shelter of the syringa and she read aloud to me Elizabeth Anne's* adventures, and later out of the hot sky, came thunder and last of all, lightning.

11 July, Long breathless cloudless day of heat: my best hours in the shade of the ash tree. The silence, these last few days, of the songbirds makes me feel uncompanioned. Now the sun a red globe rides down the cypress tree, meets the orchard trees and spreads among their leaves as a blood stain. I collect my many trophies and give them place in this new writing-book, as afar a thrush dares a few brave notes.

12 July Curlew woke me calling just over the roof, so I went for a walk before breakfast. Mercifully cooler with the ash leaves in tumult, the sky clouded. A letter from Gerard with a fearsome lion story which I copied out for Reggie.* Good reading in the afternoon and evening, in between my grass cutting. Mother picked fruit in her cage and prepared blackcurrants for jam. The setting sun is encrimsoned tonight with plumes and wraiths of cloudgold above. This paper is perfect to write on. I saw my tame thrush with moss in her beak.

13 July No sunless moment, yet the north wind refreshed us; no overpowering heat. Katie in her diaries, faithfully describing wind and weather, gives to each day a personality, so that it is a comrade with her in her seriously and often painfully observed routine, ritual rather, of waking, working, resting, reading. Mother reads aloud to me one month (June 1958 tonight) each evening after supper. We saw a spotted flycatcher in the churchyard, our first of this season, the bird took its stand now on one tombstone, now on another. My garden is pleasing to my eyes.

18 July Early church: arcadian and solitary morning walk round Crooked Oak; by way of the wild and flowery field where deer make paths through the grasses and couches under the bushes in secret recesses. Silver-washed fritillaries, graceful as their name, marbled whites, a comma; a buzzard was wheeling and mewing over Melcombe Park Wood; and a young one flew up close to me from the side of Crooked Oak, where it had been resting and preening, feathers and flattened grass said, with a certain clumsiness of flight and owlish softness of plumage. I clearly saw the crooked beak. Round and round they sailed and wailed together. Consider how the psalmists and prophets, in especial Isaiah, sing of newness; of the new song of the heart's desire; of a new heaven and a new earth; consider the rigidity of the Law with which the Jews forbid any newness, any hitherto untried approach to the life of the Spirit, however they treasured the songs. Then Christ.

22 July 'As it was in the beginning, is now and ever shall be' – where then, how then, the new? The creative advance into novelty, the new heart, the being renewed in the spirit of the mind, the new song? The 'is now' is the pin all hangs on, is the new, the renewal. Pretence at rain failing, wild sky tonight with drifting clouds.

23 July A lad tapped at Mother's door this evening of grace and spirit; it pleased me so well to see them looking on each other with eyes shining with affection and understanding. Simon had appeared once before at Mother's cottage with Barbara Kerr.* This time he was on a brief spur-of-the-moment walking and hitching tour. He carried a pack of about 20 lb. and was going to find somewhere to sleep in the fields.

24 July Rain in the night for Simon, soft straight rainfall; cool day with south-west gusty wind from the sea. I heard the willow-wren that has been for some days in my garden singing. Mother and I walked to our field. In the evening her diary and Katie's for March 1959 told of Mother going to Kenya to help Gerard and me at the time of his illness. All dry again now.

2 August Two letters from Gerard this morning, happy in Africa but missing me. How can I tell him I never want to go there again?

Dorothy (Isobel's grandchild) has been playing in the garden today, she returns to London tomorrow. I loved seeing the starry-eyed little girl suddenly at my side as I wrote, running over the grass, climbing the apple tree.

4 August   Plato's catharsis – 'the practice of mental withdrawal and concentration'. This no doubt is essential if one is to live at all when one has the 'way' of seeing each thing as a $\vartheta\varepsilon\acute{\omega}\rho\eta\mu\alpha$,* and for the first and last time. Mary Barham Johnson* left early this morning. The day was stormy not to say tempestuous, with all manner of clouds in endless procession before the soft south wind. At our 7 a.m. breakfast in the garden a veil as of muslin crystallised over the blue heaven; at other times amorphous gray and cumulus clouds majestic with snowy domes. With this month the wood pigeons have fallen silent: a silence as of fasting and abstinence morning and evening. Only at intervals in daytime wren and goldfinch sing gaily.

7 August   The soul becomes most serenely contemplative, knows that she is herself contemplation, by the river. All the qualities of moving water, all the adornments of weeds and willows, and flowers; the behaviour of birds in the reeds, in the air as with many twitterings they dart and prick with beak points the light-imaging surface of darkness; upon the current itself as their chill feet ferry them across the eddying river, all these are a preparation for the distance, the ultimate luminous reach, the bend to nothingness ...

25 August   For me the white mists spread low over level fields with cattle grazing so stilly, as we went by, in or on or under them, and the view of the Abbey from the hill above, and the tower, as we stood by the yellow-lit walls, cutting out heaven of Madonna blue; and my companions – were the most signal events in the *Son et Lumière* last night. To this I at once recollect I must add the singing and playing of Sir Thomas Wyat's farewell to his lute. Peg* went away this morning to Sylvia, her two-day visit in every way is an unequalled adornment to Mother and me. I write this in a smoky eve with peach-bloom west, my mind half turned to the Japanese after reading of their art.

27 August   I watched a heron marching along the river bank at Sturminster, gray and goose-stepping as a German; I don't think I've seen one walking in this way before. I bought a pretty lamp for my evening reading and it won't light at all. When I came home two book parcels had arrived: Yeats's *Complete Poems* for Gerard. Cornford's *From Religion to Philosophy* for me (first published in 1912). I have for long wanted to read him after notes and references to him in Inge's *Plotinus*, and elsewhere. The power, quality, human emotion, need, idea – how define the particular ingathering and exalted approach to the glory of the deity – *worship*; I find myself often considering this state, which pure may be one of the simplest and most complete. As I read the first chapter of Cornford I wondered whether it might be, not denied its access, but transmuted into thought.

29 August Clouds and grayness of momently changing depths and obscurity. Only enough rain towards nightfall to cause leaves to glisten in the electric light – what 'he' calls a westerly air stream. Gertrude is here for two nights; she has brought her fire picture. We walked to Melcombe Park, that haunted tract of primaeval woodland, the blighted late summer foliage black as midnight, frequented by a multitude of ring doves, cooing upon cooing. I saw a deer where the stream runs under the gate, and a hare; heard the scream of a buzzard and picked up two barred feathers of these wild ones.

7 September This flight of the Alone to the Alone is an exhilarating thing, almost a physical sensation in the depths of being; one that makes me feel as if my eyes flashed like Athene's. Though I am not really alone (I know) any more than any other wretched mortal, while I eat bread on the earth. May it be rather a flight of thoughts *through* the vivid seen to the unseen, a constant awareness of 'the trace of the One'? I simply and stoutly deny that 'in this ecstasy thought denies itself', as Cornford declares in his last paragraph of *From Religion to Philosophy*. It returns from this ecstasy with youth renewed as the eagle's.

18 September Twelve hours of sunshine; I read the introduction to the 1955 edition of *Visions and Revisions* while I drank tea under the ash, and took note J.C.P. pronounced *Lycidas* to be the – for him – finest poem in the English language. In the evening Mother and I went blackberrying, warm and peaceful by the south-facing hedge. I continue to meditate on the nature of the soul, of man, of the all: the 'I am' of each one, that (as one grows old) becomes continually less sure of its separateness.

19 September Fourth cloudless day. I read the *TLS* under the Warrior* in windless heat, with a background of chattering of starlings. An interesting number – Graham Greene, Wittgenstein, Barth, and others. I have wrapped it up to go air mail to Gerard, 16p postage. Mother has begun reading *Quentin Durward* aloud in the evenings, keen as when she read it the first time to me in childhood, her voice just the same. She has made jelly today, blackberry and apple, rich and dark and sweet, the very taste of autumn.

25 September I read, after all the essays, the conclusion of *Visions and Revisions* today, it was a re-entering into youth for me as some of what I felt at nineteen or twenty stirred in my brain corners; and for John, who must have been about forty-five when he unleashed the passionate intensity these authors and poets roused in him. Yes, as far as I can tell I plunged head first into Uncle Jack's books in my late teens, and I suppose he has been a more potent influence in my life than any of the ones he writes of so ebulliently and discerningly. Though most of them too have had their homage or their way with me.

27 September Harvest Festival last night: the latest sunlight touched, fingered a moment, a small area of one pillar as I went into the church. Afterwards I watched the singular luminous Italian-painting-sky through the east window above the burnished brass, the white and pale lemon flowers, of the altar. Phyllis has arrived this evening, the taxi we went to meet her in was late, so had a fine chase to Sherborne, then the long crossing was closed for the train, and as that pulled out, for another. At last we saw her black figure and small sallow (if not witch-like) countenance as she stood just outside the station. Still no letter from Gerard: but I had a friendly one from Sylvia Warner, a most rare event.

28 September Letter from Gerard today; and my date for flying, All Hallows' E'en. Sun all day after the morning mist intangibly born, *after* I had seen Orion and Sirius from the garden. *The Complex Vision* has defeated me, it is dead, inchoate; although it may have helped J.C.P. to clarify his own thought and attain his masterly if prolix style.

29 September The gray day, the south-west wind, sorrow-laden. Phyllis in Mother's little twilight room bowed over the electric heater, a tragic black figure, I found on my return from Dorchester. She talks so gently, gracefully, amusingly, a pleasure to hear and observe, yet all inclines to the negative, to the shadows, the realm of regret that so it is – that our human predicament is as it is.

30 September A day of being moved to the very deeps of my being; and because of this spiritual disturbance I have received the riches of the serenity of this blue-skied autumn day also in the depths, until I am (if that were possible) satiated. Mother and I went to Sherborne to say farewell to Phyllis, going first of all to the Abbey, as Mother had planned it, so I could see again Wyat's stone and the Saxon bones, as well as Phyllis and Mother side by side in the green-gold luminosity of the building. Phyllis said her days here were as if she were in Paradise.

1 October Sun, blue sky with apples in it. I had not long been up the ladder when the telephone rang; I hastened, then had to wait nearly 15 minutes, knowing the call was from Kenya, before Gerard spoke to me. I could barely hear, it was as though he spoke from another world but I did have his message; and he said, 'Will's all right.' Mother's bramleys are enormous this year, glowing red, without cracks.

2 October The parterre in the spell of moonlight later last evening. An owl hooted between moon and church tower; and I heard it again in the misty dawn. The fog vanished before noon, then all was sun-warmed till now, 6.30. More apple picking but the most fiery still burn, out of my reach, the reddest of all at the topmost twig, as Sappho's girl unwed destined to be plucked by the storm winds. Three tea-chests full in Mother's larder, and herself there in the coolness reading the poem 'Apple Picking'.*

13 October The first rain, the first wet day of the month: night with a rising wind and rush of rain, black darkness. It is in his briefest thoughts, side and sly thrusts, Pascal tends to be most original; so it may be best he never made a whole reasoned-out connected work; some of the long paragraphs of conventional defence of the Christian religion fall flat, though they are part – to himself – of his 'cosmic wrestling'. Of the soul, inherited, in love, in intelligence – as the intellect of the body. For all they say, Plato and Plotinus and the rest, this is the mystery of mysteries.

14 October Sun's swift return, with beautiful clarity of Vale and Hill. In my scarlet jacket I raked together on Mother's lawn the leaves that lay shed there, a blazing weightless cargo for the wheelbarrow; gathering them up with my hands – bright also with new blood sprung from scratches of rose thorns. On the wall here where I write a noiseless dance of leaves, shades on yellow of the ash nymph's fingers.

15 October From the manner of his writing of prophecy it seems to me Pascal believes in linear time, as if he were unaware that all is one in eternity; and one pole of our mind is outside (or independent of) time. In their prophecies the seers of the Old Testament were influenced by what is – or 'before Abraham was I am'. Yet although time, in the aspect of eternity, is one so that all can in a sense be foreseen because it already is (although indeed from the apparent point of the present there are usually flaws or obscurities in *all* prognostications), I am not a determinist. There is freedom: the wind bloweth where it listeth. This is a difficulty. Pascal says well: 'to prophesy is to speak of God from an inward and immediate feeling.' A feeling is universal, perhaps. It is not thought, and he says elsewhere, 'Man without thought is inconceivable.'

30 October   A sunny ceremony to conclude and close my journal, after this eight months in England. Light flickers over the page, the garden beyond the window I have newly cleaned, flickers, shimmers with silver on green leaves and grass, keen as metal: other leaves, unborn when I came, are worn thin, translucent, hang as paper lanterns of jade and amber, form motionless designs in bronze and brown (and wait life-giving wind) on the dew and rime of the lawn. I end with this tone of Keltic green, of autumnal thankfulness, with the eyes on me of the small nut-eating birds, the very same hue and with blue for happiness: with mind coloured by this from Mother's companionship. 'Peace ... a quality of mind steady in its reliance that fine action is treasured in the nature of things.'

5 November, Spring Cottage   The desert wind arose last night and blew for some hours with soothing rhythmic violence: I saw it as waves of the waterless regions it swept across, waves that broke in the trees near the cottage. This evening I heard a single whip-poor-will of the rainbird, and saw a flash of sheet lightning in the dip in the hills by Rock Rabbit Run. Mercury has joined Venus and Jupiter; red Mars at the zenith broods over the stricken earth.

8 November   The first letter from Mother with the Star Chart for November. There was a fierce thunderstorm here in the afternoon, the more tremendous for being dry at its height. Some rain fell later. Walking round the spring of the great fig tree just before sunrise I saw a bird on a yellow bough ruffling its brown feathers and emanating satisfaction, back towards me. But full soon it perceived it was being looked at, turned on me the penetrating gaze of an owl without fear, then glided away among the shadows of the grove.

11 November   Gerard has arranged to sell nearly all our drought-stricken cattle, 1,015 are going off tomorrow morning. He is thankful to have a buyer prepared to take them in their present poor condition. It does seem a sad end to our farming in Africa. But it is better than watching the animals die of starvation. Gerard is counting them now.

16 November   The terrible beauty of the dawn sky born of the rainless rainy season. Gerard paid the men who are going off after the sale of the cattle; he said they were all pleasant-tempered and made no complaints over losing their employment. In the evening we went to Sirakoi, there is a film of green there and on the instant, with this one small shower, certain flowers with pure white bells, scentless, appear singly in the grass.

1972

11 January Lightning and the rainbird calling: it is two hours since nightfall. Cathy* and I had a particularly satisfying walk this evening, talking fast and happily, we put up a green sandpiper, always something of a fairy messenger for me with its tender thin fluting call. We picked bitter oranges together and Cathy carried them back to the cottage in the nosebag. I think now of the mercies of sleep.

20 January Gerard, Cathy and I rode to the Derobo Beacon this morning, and beyond to a promontory facing west below Kuku Hill. Bonnie put her foot in a hole when we were cantering home and fell down and I fell over her head. Only when I reached home I realised my knife, worn smooth by nearly 20 years in my pocket, had slipped out and was lost for ever in the grass.

27 January A good day with much laughter, ending with a song in the moonlight by Cathy. Gerard and I walked down the river to see Will; we were with him ten minutes and in that time he told us a fine row of stories of animals and Americans.

1 February February Filldyke, for there was heavy rain this afternoon and evening, and the rainbird, when it was over, calling to its heart's content. Yesterday I was in the grove when the tempest set in motion the great fig tree, and beside me the green water-snake watched, and darted infinitesimal double tongue when I leaned near to look at the round black eye in the flat head. A heavy cloud sky tonight with the red eye of a shepherd's fire on the hills, and a hyena.

2 February R.G.H.P. 1945. 'Give them candlelight, they don't need food ...' I slept well and felt serene and happy all day long, in the garden, in the spring grove, walking with Margaret* ... now, with Cathy in her red shawl sitting on my bed. The tree hyraxes are calling tonight in the tortoise grove. Last night the cranes called.

3 February Gerard, Cathy and I rode up through the forest this morning when the glades were still silvery with dew. We saluted the house from afar, as the gate in the vermin-proof fence was chained and padlocked, and then rode along the top edge of the forest to Ngusiru, and past the Buffalo Dam where one big solitary one had left his tracks, there was a yellow wagtail and drifts of butterflies along the muddy margin – and up to the Samangua Ridge where suddenly all the landscape was blue and boundless below us. Slate came gaily all the way, I never ceased wondering at his ancient energy, gaunt and grizzled as he is. How blue the sky is, clear the mountain air above the forest, the peaks blazing with snows. Mary the revenant.

22 February A sad evening of muffled airs with faint gold wash on sky and water. On the far side of the dam as we moved towards it alongside a wall of reeds were eland and zebra. Small meres divided by green walls are all there is in the bottom below the great earth wall: swallows, English and rufous, sipped and dipped; a crane called hollowly in it, climbed to the top, duck were here, a hammerhead, sandpipers, a greenshank, and at the last as we walked in the meagre brave crop of wheat, colour of clover honey, and after the sun had gone behind the hills, a pair of spur-winged geese flew round and round at no great height over the grain, a silent salutation to the day's end.

23 February Thunder but no rain, the clouds stayed all evening, although at the last hour the mountain showed. Cathy called me to see a glow-worm in the grass not far from the cottage, an intense green globe below Venus ... 'the planet and the glow-worm', the earth-born, a luminous star.

24 February A long morning ride up the Hyena Valley and then on the ridge of our rampart hills. Winds blowing from the north and east raced up the steep, fanned out like palm branches, swept over the saddles in the fells and away. The sweet skimpy grass of the yellow, gold, red, crystalline granite was airily flowering, feathery, like seeds on curled hairs as the English quaking grass. Multitudes of small deep gamboge Compositae ... Rose called with Mrs. Mackintosh, who is returning to East Chaldon on Sunday, and we heard of the Irish bomb-throwing at Aldershot, at the very paratroopers who were in Nanyuki last week; no names given yet. Goethe, in his talks with Eckermann, has referred more than once to the Irish independence and said there would be no solution to this problem for England. He often proves a true prophet.

2 March Rose came to me in the spring grove this afternoon with a telegram from Peter. Marian is dead. Gerard and I went to see Will this evening to give him our good wishes for his birthday. He had Gerard open a bottle of red wine and himself proposed the toast 'to Marian, to help her on her way to heaven.'

3 March   Will spoke last night of the god I sent him from England, which is the Head of Homer from the Louvre, saying he had not copied it yet. Gerard brought me a telegram from Peter today, also sent to Timau. The leopard called again last night but not so close.

10 March   Gerard and Cathy and I went to Sirakoi at dawn this morning, they walked to the top of the hill and saw the sun rise. Then Gerard and Ian Craig* counted the cattle, the last of our cattle, which David has bought, and Ian took them over. He has a giraffe about a week old which was caught in the wire, we went to see this later, a most beautiful creature, perfectly gentle now, ready to caress and be caressed. Full dark plum-like eyes and erect chestnut mane and the geometrical designs in white on the bright coat, sheer wonder at its being made us look long at it. Gerard and I went to see Will at the day's end. This was a happiness.

19 March   A clear dawn this morning so we saw the mountain Kilimanjaro from the balcony at Limuru before the sun rose and drew up mists from the plain. All the way home, Mount Kenya was clear before us. We visited Will in the evening. Lines from 'Dejection' I read in the Spring Grove this afternoon and applied to myself.

> But to be still and patient, all I can;
> And haply by abstruse research to steal
> From my own nature all the natural man –
> This was my sole resource, my only plan:
> Till that which suits a part infects the whole,
> And now is almost grown the habit of my soul.

20 March   A letter from Peter today at Timau with his account of his mother's wake and funeral. She died on 1 March. He sent also a sheet of printed press-clippings about her death from New York papers. Lightning at dawn in an anvil cloud in the east, and towards sundown stormy radiance reflected from a blue-black rainbow-spanned cloud electrified the fever trees, the rustling green maize – a most intense and brilliant bow. Still with Coleridge.

21 March   I came in from the spring grove this sunny sultry afternoon to the refreshment of a letter from Mother with so many good things in it, true, simple and loving. I think she is a peerless letter writer, touching lightly on the essential. I gave up Wordsworth and Coleridge under the palm tree and looked at the glassy glancing water; can one be said to see translucency? Yet what without this roots and enfolding moss, yellow and umber leaves gleaming under? These broad leaves as they float, sink, drift and lodge influence the face of the water's flow, change the spray and tiny fountains, the whole dance of it. The rock I call the head of Orpheus is one day dry, another dark with water dammed by leaves bright as sovereigns.

23 March What distinguishes Whitehead for me when he writes of religion, as compared with other philosophers who touch on this subject and who are not avowed Christians and writers of apologetics, is his freedom from malice and that superior tone of the twentieth-century man freed from ancient beliefs and doctrines. On Sunday Nellie arrives in Nairobi at 11 a.m., now we learn that the Queen is due there at noon that day.

24 March Africa seemed to say to me in the night, I will not let you go until you bless me. This blessing, I was given to understand, was to be in the form of a choral, elegiac pastoral composition; that I should leave an accent or trace of (it may be) something Virgilian on this intellectual wilderness where, stranger and pilgrim as I am, I have sojourned so long. I can only write personal poems.

28 March All has gone passing well. Eleanor arrived on Sunday half an hour before the Queen and benefited by the proud high-floating flags. Gerard and I both had happy times with Cathy, and with each other, at Limuru. This evening we went to see Will with Nellie; he gave her a brave welcome and fed her on butter and clear honey fresh from his bee boxes, and told stories to delight her (or, he may have hoped, dismay her) of cattle thieves and their deeds, and how he admired them. It was good and strong, and she came away satisfied ... with having been with her father's brother.

1 April The birds as always call me to talk of them at the end of a day of blue blaze and bleak white light. How now the wind sings, moans, sea-surges through the trees, the jacarandas grown so tall above the cottage. From somewhere high in them a sunbird's nest was blown down today, the cobweb cables this down-lined hammock swung on could not take the weight of the young klaas' cuckoo. He was nearly fledged, most gay to see with tiny bands of emerald and buff on head and back, and survived the fall, but it seemed beyond us to keep his rosy gape filled. At Ruka's Drift at the Beale we watched over the sparkling water a pair of thick-billed seed-eaters enraptured over their nest of green lichen. With wings aquiver they admired their skill with the strands of glaucous lichen. One would settle in the cup with faint sqeaking, the other fly off and return. A party of red-billed wood hoopoes came near with outcry and ran up the trunks and branches. And at the end of All Fool's Day I sat in the red dust by the Impala Drift and for half an hour watched a pair of black duck at their silent sequent water sport.

2 April   Nellie took an Easter egg Michael had given her to Will, and he broke it and ate, and later when Gerard and Nell came in from the dark and the stars after following the leopard that grunted so close, we also took fragments and ate of the chocolate shell. I wrote a dithyramb in the spring grove.

14 April   Cathy's long-awaited flute, posted in England in November, is with her again, her last night here for this present, and she has been playing to us, sitting outside the door so the sweet notes entered the lamplit room from the black night. Gerard and I went to see Will for a moment tonight and were happy to find him restored again after a night of sound sleep. The sharp spasms of pain in his leg had faded away. He was in high spirits because the price of wool is rising after two or three years. It had seemed as though there would never be a future for natural wool; now the market has improved surprisingly.

26 April   I was woken last night, rather as was Odysseus sleeping at the river-mouth, by a high-pitched outcry, troubled inarticulate calls, and clamour of children's voices through the ambrosial night. I imagined some dance or rain-making ritual of the starvelings on the cooperative, a bewailing and invoking of Ngai, long-drawn-out. Mugambi told me in the morning this was a response to a moon-light raid of the Derobo on the lean and poverty-stricken cattle of the peasants, which they keep in bomas close in between their dwellings of mud. The true rain-making ceremony, he told me, in Homeric language, is the slaughtering of a sheep or goat in the mountains and the offering of its fat on the shores of a dry tarn. 'We know,' Mugambi added, 'God likes fat.'

28 April   Chapter VII of my mystical Orpheus romance I decided, as I read it over by the clear water moving between roots and leaves, is long enough. The title I have found for it is from *From Religion to Philosophy* – 'both alive and divine' (page 138). Is it of necessity, that is to 'make' me write, that I can no longer read?

2 May   9.15 a.m. Packing, so I write now in soft morning air my word of farewell, while the flute notes of last night, the thunderclaps and dazzle of lightning are still active about my head; and with thankfulness for rain which almost unperceived followed the storm to the amount of half an inch. So I write with more than I would have expected. The first token was a toad on the door-sill two or three nights before. Then the rainbird began; now the dolorous black cuckoo. The gray one I have not seen, maybe with the rain he has gone on his way after living near the cottage for 18 days. A breath of woodruff comes to me from the journal, I shall not be too late to find this in flower on one of the hillsides, unless there is yet another change. 'God in the world is the perpetual vision of the road which leads to the deeper realities.'

2 June, Mappowder   Sunshine: two cuckoo talking, echo to echo, early. With evening the west wind rose shepherding back the companies of cloud, the long-drawn twilight is autumnal with promise of rain. Sweet bird voices, there is a revival of spring as they, the winged ones, mate again and prepare for new nesting. I cut grass round crimson peonies, pressing my face now and then into theirs as I did 50 years ago. I like the coarse oriental things with their clumsy attitudes and leaves better now than I did then. They have a strong emanation.

5 June   Dry all day long; cumulus clouds, vast white, asail in cerulean sea; violent sun falling between, driving their shadows racing up slopes of moving grass; flickering, glittering on leaves, leaves on walls. Mother walked slowly, not easily, all round the field where Pat Kelly kept her sow long ago. Blackbird and thrush unwearied sing ... 'the immensely subtle combination of things, which always and everywhere include an actual infinity.' I also read today of the 'minute perceptions' – which are the signs and constituents of personal identity. (Everyman: *Philosophical Writings of Leibniz*, p. 150)

7 June   Aunt Dora* said to Llewelyn in 1920 'it seems extraordinary how you all go on writing and never get anything taken, it seems INCONSISTENT.' It surely does, certainly for me who never have and never will. Yet our way of life is our life, and mine is this 'inconsistent' writing. I am entertained, as usual when I re-read the letters, by the way Lulu's reactions to Africa run parallel to my own in so many ways. A copper sun in a copper sea has sunk from view.

14 June   First day of summer, north-east wind blowing strongly, sunshine all day. Gerard and I went to Weymouth, pleasant at this season with only scattered groups on the shingle, small children here and there in shallow pools, running along the wet sand. We walked past 3 Greenhill Terrace* on the wall between Lodmoor and the blue-green waves, looking over them to White Nore. Then I called at the Hydro for my appointment with Clarkson, the osteopath; he said my sciatic pains are caused by arthritis in the base of the spine, and gave me a mighty pummelling.

16 June Tomorrow Gerard sets off for Woodbrooke, a journey for his own interest, if not pleasure. Yet my heart is heavy; for all my cardpictures, communion with the past, claustral garden, chanting of birds beloved, I feel I could cry for a chiliad, a chill lament which would never find fulfilment. It is, maybe, in part to do with *fin de famille*, the only child of an eleventh child, myself childless, all but the last two gone, dead and gone, of the proud eleven; all of them so strong and real and life-absorbed, before (as it seems to this late-born one) the age of shades set in.

17 June Bonfire night, both because I have been burning grass on a mountain of rubbish, gray smoke swirling round my gray pate; and because sad sky and soughing wind are more autumn than mid-summer – more autumn than words can show, unless in the way of a poem.

18 June At the very end of a day of dim cloud and thin drifting rain sun floods the west with watery silver, a single thrush sings. The rain has quenched my Beltane fire. Rosemary brought Reggie and Edith to see us which was a true happiness, a brightness before the lost sun found the land. Another was looking up into my ash tree seeking a tiny singer and finding the rose glow of a bullfinch's breast; the minute agile songster, swifter than a phylloskopus warbler, was a goldcrest. Letters stronger, tenderer, more magnanimous in the last years of Ll.P.

19 June Most full of light of the days of this mid-summer month with a high 'white' north-west wind; sheets of burning white flung from heaven, consumed by storm-clouds, tempest whirled. I watched the guinea-gold sun meet the horizon to the north of *Silver Hill*, this will be its furthest mark. The curlew has loved this day, and my eremite life has been undisturbed. Llewelyn's voice is in my head, the last brave letter lately read. I suppose where Theodore triumphs as a writer is in not preaching; he tells, after his quirkish simple fashion, tales and fables. J.C.P. and Llewelyn never forget their message or 'moral' – and those words are far too weak and mincing for their shining iterated philosophy. There are some masterly sentences in old Leibniz. I keep opening his Writings and re-reading marked passages. I saw Jupiter last night and the Scorpion – Africa.

24 June Cool winds, clouds, reluctant roses. A reading tonight of *Late*

Greek Philosophy.* Origen: the right to think and reason from a Christian standpoint. Plotinus: thinking it through in the light of his own experiences. Rest in sleep brings the undifferentiated activity of consciousness, the vigil of the 'Orphic' soul. Each morning's waking now is painful in the sense of causing a return to directed energy.

10 July In looking back it seems to me a mysterious thing that I could have filled so many journals with silent words. I do not remember the year I began ... This is the birthday of Charles whom I saw first at two years old and last at twenty-eight before his life ended. The sun shines on me, in a brief time it will begin to be eclipsed by the new moon, but set before it is half hidden.

11 July Orange-brown sun among clouds, but we did see a corner of shadow in the dull yet angry crack between a barrier of cloud and the horizon, Mother and I looking in turn through smoked glass in her spare room. Tonight heaven is eau de Nil shot through with white radiance. I have worked quite hard today and yesterday cutting grass in the ditch and along the road verge, thick unsavoury stuff.

16 July North-east wind, dry; white light, so the mown grass appears spread with hoar-frost. We all went to visit Dr. Smith at Heathcote this evening: he looked fine and more than ever like one of Rembrandt's old men; his features all over are startlingly mobile, lines and wrinkles sown with life, only the inward expression of his eyes seems not to change with their complicated surroundings. When his mirth is at its height the eyes are swallowed up in quivering flesh. Mother enjoyed the visit and was happy because he accepted the tiny round basket of strawberries, topped with a leaf, she brought him. Ceaselessly the wind sang in the pines. A queen wasp entered and hummed round the room, so bare but for books. Dr. Smith gave me back *Process and Reality*,* I was disappointed as I don't think he could read it. Another sunset of copper and reflective glitter.

20 July In the last of the twilight I met my hedgehog last night, he came snuffling softly over the grass under the Warrior tree, visited the birdbath, hustled slowly to the area where I throw scraps for the birds, came close to me. I stroked his spines and this so bemused him he neither stirred again – as long as I watched – nor turned into a ball. From a little distance a black cat observed.

5 August Eve of the Transfiguration: transmutation of ever-living fire, quivering blazing tongued and formless, fearsomely ascending into pure shining, limpid serene, the substance of flesh into substance of being.

Sunset last night reflecting in tossed thin clouds the fires of Sinai. The agitations of molecules, as passing into vibrations of light – quanta of energy.

21 August   Full summer sunflow all day, with a delicate twittering chorus of martins darting this way that way in the dim dense blue sky. Isobel telephoned Peter this morning. He is coming here from London via Stonehenge and Salisbury. A greater spotted woodpecker came to one of the bramleys at tea-time when we were sitting under the acacia and tapped loud and strong. An almost unrelievedly grim programme we listened to in the darkness last night of William Cowper, called 'The Castaway'. There was no word of his hares, his dog, the consolation of country life as in many of the poems it is quietly revealed.

> The poplars are felled, farewell to the shade
> And the whispering sound of the cool colonnade

Cowper is so much a man of his age, enclosed by the attitudes, education, way of life of his class, in the eighteenth century. I miss the awareness of apocalypse, the prophetic eye of the poet who alights in one age or another, knowing in his soul the manners of them all.

31 August   Now he has gone away from Mappowder, I ask myself why, when I am with Peter, I am at peace, fulfilled, satisfied, although he is one of the most nervy, unresting, not to say demon-driven of men, as I am well aware. It must be that my demon, or daimon, is not 'cast out' but transmuted. The two visions of Peter that return most often, and involuntarily, are both with his face, his figure as it were triangularly and dynamically opposed, unseen: when he stood utterly still looking upon Wyat's simple stone, when he sat again in an attitude of life-giving motionlessness on our grandparents' grave in Montacute. Was it realisation of my unique being not in time?

1973

24 January, Spring Cottage   Certain events cut through all crusts, protections, defences – and the most human and potent of these can be words – direct to the seat of suffering: that sword that pierces the soul, of Jeremiah. For me this evening it was the sudden bleat, a most penetrating appeal, of a small fawn lying perfectly folded together as they do. With head raised, ears alert, the little creature from the weeds of a shallow drain watched us as we paused at this unwonted cry, watched us pass by. I think of Andrew Marvell's poem, the maiden lamenting the death of her fawn, and the drawing of her darling in the Blue Poetry Book.

25 January In this 'tour' as the English Civil Servants used to call their stay in a colony, the food for my mind has mainly been provided by the two deans,* of St. Paul's and St. Patrick's; with some reading from both almost every day; high-wrought spirits both men have, both are too expert in describing, or 'ironising', horrors, disquiets and revulsions. Yet, how well they write, how they entertain. If literature is abolished, done to death, in the universities maybe the love of it for pleasure, for understanding the art of life, and life itself, will grow ever stronger outside their walls.

1 February Walking down to the river to see Will, we found him in the office writing up his diary for the day in the presence of his glorious canvas of Lolokwi,* while outside the men were being paid. Will was exhilarated by a long day out in the Meru country, he went early to Kisima, then on to Meru with a goat to give an old cook of Elizabeth's. It was after 6 p.m. when we arrived, and he said he'd only just had his lunch. We had a good walk home toward the amethystine mountain.

2 February Candlemas. R.G.H.P. 1945. 'Life is a continuall burden, but we must not groane.' I have a considerable admiration for Donne's spelling which appears to be spontaneous, and according to context. The words have an individual air, as human beings. When is life, one's own, not a burden, or one is not so aware of the burdensomeness: I think when for a moment there is a sharing of some other being's light-hearted activity of living, of, there, a breath-taking fleeting fairness.

9 February The grass before dawn smelt sweet with approaching rain: in the evening the mist of it drew over and veiled the hills a moment, again earth and dry vegetation breathed for the fragrance. Jomo Kenyatta passed through the farms above today, pausing briefly to address the throng and promised the land would be distributed among the Meru tribesmen who have none. But Mugambi, when he returned, said this was all false and nothing of the kind would happen.

13 February Nothing is more profitless, a more useless squandering of life and energy, than thinking, talking, preaching of sin: this is where I part company with Donne. It is enough for any religion to say with Kierkegaard – as before God we are always in the wrong. Or better perhaps: in whose sight shall no man living be justified. Keep silence and then turn to the positive. The preaching of sin in a church where people are gathered to worship a Redeemer who has taken upon him the sins of the whole world is in itself a travesty. This theme is one to turn from Christianity those who are most willing to recognise the need to pray and worship.

14 February   When I stayed as a small child at Bridge* (a great house now demolished) with Monica, her father, an old retired London lawyer who shuffled about in carpet slippers, with small pointed beard and occasionally emerged from a darkened, and for me forbidden, library, once said he thought a bird might build a nest in my curly hair. Well may it have done so, judging by my lifelong joy in these winged loves.

16 February   My father's birthday: after sunset seven wild geese, spur-winged geese, flew over our heads as we walked, and at that moment above, they spoke. We watched them as long as we could see, Gerard was amazed at their speed. For the last two nights with this huge moon we have heard lions; to one sequence of grunts the toad near the cottage promptly replied. The landscape near and far has been brushed with a giant powderpuff, you might say, so thick is the air: the mountains lost, hills blurred, grass robbed of colour, bleached, starched, isabelline. The thorn trees either entirely arid silver spines or clouded with hoary flower bales. Moonflower fragrance hangs on the hot air.

17 February   The stifling heat ended this afternoon with a whirlwind when the air was full of flying dry particles and I felt myself to be in a bastion under fire as hard cases of the jacaranda seeds, double like castanets, kept smiting the tin roof. After a welcomed shower of rain there was prolonged thunder rolling continuously overhead. This morn the lion gave a growly roar just as I put my teatray by the bed, a *purr*, Gerard said ... I had a blissful night's sleep and woke cured of my cold; but I'd had a host of dreams; and one inter-slumber visionary understanding of why there must be the resurrection of the body ... to preserve the individuality we recognise here, because 'soul was never in time'.

20 February   Gerard was talking to a charcoal-burner in our evening walk, asking how he built his pyre, where the ventilations were, and how he kindled the fire, how long it would burn. This ancient craft is always of interest to us. The smell of the acrid far-drifting smoke disturbs immemorial responses, thoughts are lost in pure experience of sensation. As we parted from the man, black of himself, not smirched by his toil as those who worked in the forests of Europe, he said his final word, and repeated it: 'If a man does not use his blood he finds nothing.'

22 February   In the evening we went to the Barana Lake, and there was a surprise for me there. As we walked along the western shore a Land Rover sped along the wall of the dam, and soon there was Gilfrid standing with his blue eyes and glittering hair in the wind that blew so cool over the water. He thought the birds on the eastern side were spoonbills, after he had gone they flew up, the four white birds, and so they were; unknown to me before.

25 February   The difference – and difficulty – of external living and living within: the interior reality, self without act, distraction, suffering even; knowing with no effort how all will fall out, for time is not a sequence. The outward conditioned from the beginning by so many controls, and unavoidably of a different figure and nature to every other person encountered: no marvel, we wretched mortals take refuge in distempers of mind and body in an attempt to dodge all this tricky composite involves. Today we went down to the Uaso Nyiro and saw a good number of elephant close to the great turgid river. To Will this evening; he was in his office with easel and palette, talking to an African called Menene who was nursery- and houseboy at Kisima when I first went there in 1946, and used to bring our early morning tea. Will said 'I've had a perfect day.'

6 March   With Tao te Ching, with John Donne, with Pindar I prepare my farewell, for this morn came the news of the flying-time being advanced from late evening on Thursday to the morning. Here is great heat and strong sun, all afternoon a rocking of laughing doves … Stragglers of the sunflower forest still encircle the fairy-tale cottage, and spread ragged rays inviting bees. And I feel now a strange standstill of each instant, sound and fiery vision in the pervasive furnace air … fare well.

9 March, Mappowder   Thrushes singing, the flight over and forgotten. I came by coach to Sherborne after a night at the Victoria air terminal because of a rail strike. The drive gave me much pleasure all the way, bare fields and trees, elms in especial. I had nearly an hour in Salisbury, time to walk down the shining chalk-clear Avon to the church of St. Thomas à Becket and the Cathedral. The sun shone all day, all the way. Stockbridge street appeared unchanged from when I walked up it from the station half a century ago 'to do lessons'. I liked seeing Wilton again after years; and the queenly red-brick house of Milford Post. I was at Mother's door before 3 p.m. She had a fire in the hearth and was expecting guests – Thankfulness.

10 March Thinking is not taking up certain attitudes to what has happened, may happen, would happen in certain relations of other things, it is the individual creative in the object-subject fusion which is, in each instant, his life. This is also relation, the most direct that can be between human consciousness and the life-principle. Experience, response, rest, energy diffused and re-engendered in work, in aesthetics, in being identified with the whole gamut of emotions, in the concentration of silent prayer, all are for the deepening and heightening of consciousness, or better perhaps for the intensification of it as focus, burning-glass or universal centre. All outward gestures are symbolic and directed to this, whether they are quasi-mechanical or not without mental awareness, watchfulness; although the monitor itself must be implicated. For the poetic temperament the hardest things to suffer are its own unavoidable spells of 'whoreson lethargy'; and things that have to be done in the 'cause' of social duties, as pleasures, entertainments, and so on that are abhorrent and seem to go completely against the grain; and yet *are* others' ideas of satisfaction and what is desirable ... All kinds of adventures today for Mother and me together, moving to be driven over much of Valentine's country, though we scarcely spoke of this. Francis and Sally* called in the evening, and when they were here news came over the telephone of the death of Mrs. Cobb in West Chaldon.

15 March Ides of March. Gerard's birthday, fifty-fifth. A good day, long letters came from him to me. Just before I woke about 5 a.m. I dreamed I had a letter from Alyse, clear as my heart could desire was her handwriting on the blue paper. I could read though the words are forgotten: only on the right side of the page a large piece was torn away, the shape of what was gone and the indentations resembled the Horn of Africa. When the postman arrived he brought a parcel for Mother which I opened for her, and drew out the book. This was *The Cry of a Gull*, a collection of writings from Alyse's journals made and published by a man called Kim Taylor. The book is well-produced with sky or sea-blue binding, and linocuts of Chydyok and the downs. On the end papers a few lines in Alyse's own calligraphy appear, drawn at the beginning from an entry in the journals, at the end from a paper written on the night of her death. So I consider and interpret the dream sent me by my spiritual, or maybe she would prefer literary, godmother, to whom always I feel to be so closely akin.

16 March The answer is, I think now, to 'no one understands, no one *ever* understands' that this precise impossibility of any human understanding the soul of another in all its complexity is of the mystery of being. So indeed, in this essential integrity, never to be fully comprehended, each one should rejoice, exult even. Not fellowship, goodwill, intimate companionship and sharing of all things, not the communion of saints, can annul or exceed the alone, the solitary in the core of being. Mother read aloud for an hour from *The Cry of a Gull*, bowed over the book, intent on each word, listening as it seemed to me for the lost intonations of a loved voice. 'And what heart knows another? Ah, who knows his own?'

17 March No return to what today might be termed 'the simple conviction of St. Patrick'. Although it is by the company, for all that, of the single-hearted that I am best fulfilled. The company of those early Christians who were willing to identify Christ with Orpheus, who painted their beardless saviour under a tree softened with foliage, with doves on a bough above and mild creatures of the wood at his knee.

4 May Nellie sent me, which arrived this morning and I read today, *Letter to a Priest* by Simone Weil – the reasons why she did not become a member of the Catholic Church. Is there a hint of intellectual arrogance here, all she says would be familiar to a Catholic theologian. If she desires as she claims to in the book, categorical answers, I think she should ask 'categorical' questions and keep to the central and essential dogmas of the religion. Reading Goethe last night: '"Nothing", as he says, "could rob him of his love for the Holy Scriptures and for the founder of Christianity." He therefore wrought out for his own private use a Christianity of his own; and as everything which took possession of his soul always assumed a poetic form …'

5 May Also: 'Let mental culture go on advancing, let science go on gaining in depth and breadth, and the human intellect expand as it may, it will never go beyond the elevation and moral culture of Christianity as it shines forth in the Gospels.' The young girls of sixteen with whom Goethe habitually fell in love were for him, I have a notion, like the spring into which Hera dipped herself in order to renew her virginity. Sea gales from the south-west with rain blow hot and cold. Mother and I went to Sturminster for shopping this morning. I visited the graveyard of St. Mary's church above the river, which somehow oppressed me with damp and gloom and funereal odours. On top of Bulbarrow where Peggy* took us for bluebells I heard a lark sing, my first lark.

6 May 'And the worst is, that all the thinking in the world does not bring us to thought.' The tempests, cloud storms, hailstones, sun lightnings of the day, outflanking gales and stinging rain squalls, fallen into limpidity at the shrine of the crescent moon. The wildness thrills the curlew; rooks make clamour in the longed-for darkness.

7 May Green Pater-Leonardo light at dawn, 4.30, when the singing of birds began: an hour's rain followed, gentle, undisturbing, as I drank my tea. Later the day was a turmoil of howling winds and now as the sky to the north-west assumes again the green tint with indigo clouds the cottage becomes a ship battered by storm-winds. An air letter writ in red, as Gerard always does them now, came by the second post to tell me he has put off flying from 11 May to 1 June, when he hopes to be able to travel with Spiers. He was in Nanyuki when he wrote and found himself weak and shaky, unfit for travelling. O I hope he will be careful in these three weeks. André Gide, in his journal, admires Goethe.

12 May Between 6 and 7: garden warbler singing by the way into the secret field, singing with that abandon, fervour and exultancy that belongs to arrival, the unmistakeable note of having attained after long flight over land and sea the heart's desire, so sang the sylvan bird this frosty morning when every pointed leaf of grass was tipped with a crystal globe, a world, a drop of dew. On the way home, a spotted flycatcher as if a trifle strange and muzzy-headed to be here again was on an elm twig by the graveyard. When I was almost at the white gate into my garden a pair of swifts flew over my head: I have heard them screaming now and again in the day, and seen them again, a single pair. The exciting, tremendous, agitating thing in *Faust* ('that mad thing', as Goethe called his masterpiece to Eckermann) is the relationship, the interplay, the lively deadly discourses between Faust and Mephistopheles: the scenes when they are entirely absent, or one is there without the other, are on a different not to say inferior level. When they speak to each other all is inevitable, certain, present. Lewes both adulates and sternly criticises Goethe who is not a born playwright but a supernatural dramatist. How much in *Porius* John* is indebted to certain scenes and adventurings in *Faust* – as with Merlin's 'creatures' for example.

14 May Unequalled spring day, soft drizzling, mizzling rain from sunrise to noon, then sun sending off every cloud till, after his setting, vermilion-cheeked as a Homeric ship, the sky became a sublime blue-green translucency with soft crimson bands at the horizontal meeting of earth and heaven. Some good reading of Goethe, and grass-cutting, slaying with no pleasure tall hollow-stalked hedge parsley. Africa a strength behind me as the Wilderness of the Israelites and the Fast, just *because*: 'from the ends of the earth I have cried unto thee from the depths of my heart.'

1 June   Sun king all day: a whole day of light with a cool west wind. In my first walk I saw a fox walking about a close-cut paddock looking for things to eat left by the mower. I could watch him close and near before he was aware of me. I had a second walk in the evening. The daylight is unending, the sky never dark at night. Mother is reading aloud Valentine's poems from *The Nature of the Moment*, we are saddened by this, many of these poems are not of value, weak, unsustained, without melody; not worthy of her, or giving us the feeling of her. Gerard flies through this swift night.

2 June   Wild winds as of autumn with a scud of rain now and again, a flood of sunlight at the day's end filling the cottage with brilliance as though all the lamps were put on suddenly. Gerard arrived by the bus at 3.10, thin and appearing now ill, now well and aglow; he is certainly as well as I could have expected: and he spent some time with Mother giving her all the news of Will. Trailer loads of silage rattle up the street all day long, bright green and tender grass, still there are some fields left 'up for hay'.

23 June   Cloudless, the sun liquid copper, molten as lava with black leaves afloat in it, now rayless and evaporating in haze. The culmination of the year with treasures of earth given forth in fragrance of hay and roses. I am reading my old friend *Philoctetes*,* which is the easiest to read 'as a play', rather than Greek Tragedy. Today I am happily haunted by the shining river. Thrushes still sing shrill and Jenny wren and hedge-sparrows.

25 June   I have the sensation now so often of being beside life rather than part of the mystery of being in the company of the quick that it can be singularly satisfying when a moment of reality is fulfilled: as today in the Norman church of St. Nicholas at Studland. I have long felt a need to be there, after what I have read, and also seeing the sister building of the same period at Worth Matravers. That desire to be in the house of the Lord I saw there, painted high up in Gothic lettering.

At a moment of being of this kind it almost seems there is a true fusion – not one left indeterminate – of Whitehead's 'two distinct modes of direct perception'.

26 June No two village churches could be more of a contrast than Studland and Norton below Ham Hill, to which we went when all umbrageous Somerset was veiled in steady mist-haunted rain. This was after we had seen Reggie and Edith and were searching for somewhere to eat our midday meal. For this unexpected visit we received a rare and unforgettable welcome. Reggie, looking especially handsome and eighteenth-century, was seated at a round table peeling onions and scraping new potatoes. Gerard has gone to Dorchester to meet Isobel this evening. I read some poems by Valentine.

28 June Now in the heart of the rose of summer: sky nude of all but screaming swifts in the luminous approach to the nightfall that lifts into dawn before there is any dark. 'All comfort in life', says Goethe, 'is based upon a regular recurrence of external phenomena.' And explains this as: 'the change of day and night, of the seasons, of flowers and fruit ... these are the main springs of our earthly life. The more we are open to these enjoyments the happier we are.' Mother picked 4 lb. of gooseberries this evening and nipped them for jam-making.

30 June Of the total eclipse of the sun witnessed by many from the Northern Province of Kenya ... of the cuckoo heard by me calling this morning as I walked in Lark Rise ... of the last day of the Queen Month of the year ... of the writer of the Night Sky in the *Telegraph* who calls the bright star Vega in the Lyre of Orpheus *the Falling Vulture* ... of our plan of going to Romsey this evening to hear a performance in the Abbey of *The Messiah* ... of these *and others* taking thought I make my farewell to June with the prayer of quiet.

1 July 'One feeling which was very strong in me, and one for which I could never find adequate expression, was a sense of the past and the present as being one: a conception which infused a spectral element in the present.' Part III, Book XIV, *Poetry and Truth.** We drove home under a skyful of stars with Jupiter rising at the last ... so long since I have beheld the stars. The performance in the Abbey was powerful and satisfying: 'How beautiful upon the mountains are the feet', music and words, pleased me most. The whole programme lasted two and a half hours.

8 August A mottled gray sky this afternoon, severe rainless gray with a mode of imparting undercurrents of strong light ... the time comes to take a silent farewell of my Goethean summer, the stone-walled cottage and garden. I have finished the first volume (Everyman) of *Wilhelm Meister*, stifled by the final 'Confession of a Fair Saint' ... I thought to leave the second here for my return but I think now to take it for company on my journey. *Faust* is the most agnostic poem in the whole world and yet it is the most religious ... it de-dogmatises Christianity, turning its nobler elements into the beautiful mythology they are; not treating them for that reason as untrue, but as humanity's culminating symbol in a world where *everything* is a symbol ... The essence of religion – that is to say the feeling of wonder and awe in the presence of life and of the unknown powers behind life – 'is the supreme and highest virtue of man'.

20 August, Spring Cottage   St. Bernard of Clairvaux. Joy maybe – with due honour to 'the pious apathy' of the saint – is the best word for what I felt with little Francis. Neither love nor hate, rather the quality of a living poem: the boy in his red jersey; often, with dark head bent, with the very air and attitude of the elder Charles; ceaselessly busied: I see him sitting against the stem of a yellow fever tree; curled up in bed, his lean back bare drawing by lantern light. With unabashed confidence we shared our mischief and mocking, our not infrequent spontaneous references to the dead that in our hearts and being live for ever more. Only with so swift dry abstemious a child is my own old austerity at ease, my criticism, and involuntary captiousness at others' attitudes, lost.

27 August   Eve of Goethe's birth, for me one of meditation and recollection, alone in the cottage, a discovering of hand-holds in dry silence. In the morning I sat long on my root-seat. The robin came near; fed, pruned a wing. What does it feel with those two so distinct white crescents above its dark eyes set in dark feathers? As I moved homewards a bush-buck stood before me, raised horned head, nostrils glistening with moisture twitching. I thought of Odysseus and Orpheus before the creature sprang away, with a soft bark.

22 September   Mlefu appeared when my hands were covered with meal from making biscuits, gray at the temples now and shrunken he retains his old air and charm of manner with fewer words. He brought us a present of five eggs his ancient Mother in Meru asked him to provide to help Gerard recover: she is so old and frail now she lives only on a little honey. And five small apples, a special rarity here, from a tree he grew himself on his land above the main road. Here is a Virgilian episode come to life. A slate-gray evening with early dusk, the bushes on the hillsides put on with charcoal. Sultry and heavy-aired, though at last a languid wind gave a few flaps as the cock turned.

5 October I think more and more that the human personality is an unassailable mystery. The transference, as Jung calls it, is only brief and those who have experienced this mutual and satisfying interchange, or reciprocity of being, often quickly diverge again and become incomprehensible one to the other. Yet for most contacts and companionship are necessary, semi-mechanical though they be. This morning I made a light pencil sketch of the cottage on part of an air letter. I enjoyed doing this in the first warm sunshine before windrise.

6 October Awakened by an odd snicking sound close-by like something tackling the thatch, I presently raised my head and saw a buck just outside the window eating off sunflower, a bush-buck appearing black in the moonlight with a pair of sharp mephistophelean horns. The bee-eaters with their peerless flight and calls gave me pure joy in the evening walk. As we were on our way home in a particularly arid place among the thorns, lifting each foot with some effort out of the dust, we saw a Land Rover coming towards: Will and his driver. He told us thieves had tried to take his vehicle in the night. His wheelchair had been removed and certain jagged stones put in for ammunition. The men had evidently spent some time trying to join the wires to start the engine and failing had given up and departed. Will had been out all day and now in the dusk was looking for traces of these intruders, the way they might have approached.

9 October A crumb of pure poetry, a single line in a scarce understood tongue, can feed, content, restore the soul. My true task in Africa, not self-imposed but involuntary and, when I am in the country, inescapable is to give a soul to this wasteland, to those regions especially that are, to my mind, God-forsaken, and also those known as God's own country because man's hand and foot can indite no sign, leave no trace upon them. Gerard read aloud to me from *Hellenica* a description of the altarpiece by Polygnotus in the temple of Delphi.

16 December, Mappowder Wrestling with '*Der Schwan*'. I suspect a fine poem, but Rilke is more difficult than Goethe, whose singing voice carries me even if I can only translate one word in six. When I hear a poem read aloud, musical, powerful with rich language, I think I should seek to write more eloquently instead of in hard-grained objects that tend to be without grammar or tense, tangible as Chinese squares yet lacking their visual elegance and allusiveness. I made one today of a dream that would return as vision, to exorcise it. One interpretation that came to me was that the double creature seen from, perhaps, a crusaders' castle in Palestine, was an image of myself. There was more to the dream than the poem could take, 'there' I called Tony to explain the doublet.

17 December   When I entered the room at the point where day and night part beside the elm tree a single cloud-mass formed an exact outline of Mount Kenya as it appears from the plains. Gerard lay on the sofa invisible, his tray of tea beside him, a faint gleam from the west reflected in the china as though it were water. At my call he raised his head and together we looked at the mountain and tree, with thoughts of our parting-to-be in three days. Since then I have been reading Wang Wei's poems: as always with the T'ang writers many are on the theme of fare-well.

26 December   The fairy lights, red blue green amber, strung in an inverted V across the holly tree over the road softly illumine the mistily vague village street, even obscurely my two upstair rooms, in a manner that would please a child left to sleep under the patchwork quilt of million-stitched blue and white triangles, and not finding sleep easy. The tensions between desert and industry continue to strain, give slightly, are drawn more tightly, and I cannot avoid a profane glance at being anointed with the oil of gladness, and at the widow's cruse of oil which never came to an end. Indeed oil, as I think of Athenian olives, Old Testament and New, appears as *essential* to the life of man as bread and wine. And that word in its turn reminds me of G.M.P.* and how she explained to me the significance of essential oils. A return to the Spanish mystics I was reading once at the Beale when Gerard was away ill with Gerald Brenan's *St. John of the Cross*.

28 December   One sunbeam when I was with Mrs. Jackson,* none in my walk, when, as I walked over soggy ground by brown hedgerows and trees with black ivy leaves waving from trunk and branch, the thought visited me, the relationship between two living beings, even the most loving and closest was as unknown and indefinable as that between life and death in the soul of the living: that is 'the tragedy of love' though we feel ourselves to be as close and inseparable as life and death, and love is as strong as death ... this relationship, contact, intimacy that consists 'simply' of the reflection of one soul within another. When I was cleaning the window of my 'front room' this morning the postman came along the red tile path and I received from him a single envelope in a fashion, that reminded me of the frog and fish footmen in *Alice*. I knew the handwriting. Inside the wrapping was a card with *Happy New Year 1974* printed on the outside, and within the fold a poem called 'Winter Illness' by Valentine, a greeting from Sylvia: this lies by me now on the table.

31 December   'God is pure negation.' This plain sentence of Karl Barth I read last night in his rhetorical paradoxical *Commentary*;* in which, I sometimes have an idea, he says anything (and nothing) to startle, to jostle and finally empty the mind of delusions, 'the hard irreducible' facts we live by. On the whole I prefer the Bible, or Whitehead: 'God is the infinite ground of all mentality'. But I will give him the last word on this year's last day: 'It is as true to say that God transcends the World, as that the World transcends God.' The bright stars shone all night, the morning was lit with rime which dissolved only in the direct sunshine, freezing did not cease any more than the sun ceased to shine. After its setting we, Mother and I, watched the figure of the man opposite walk back and forth, back and forth, and growing ever darker against the western sky. He carried a prong on his shoulders hung with lifeless leaves and vegetation of the summer gone which he dropped on the smoking pyre, the hidden fire patiently at work consuming the leavings of the season of fertility. Long we looked, and I looked often on Mother's face, the dark eyes and vivid red lips.

1974

1 January   Moony night, grim gray day, neither freezing nor thawing. Ancient Charlie Smith and his daughter Rose called. I felt the old man was not as strong and up to the mark as on his last visit and his chest was troubling him more. He returned *Owen Glendower* which he found he could not read, he took Jeffares' Commentary on Yeats, which I had just finished, instead. They gave me a sprig of witch hazel, bare save for tiny yellow cells which may enlarge and open. No word from Africa for some time. No New Year poem, I will try in bed.

2 January   Deadly dark all day with a wind in which one shrinks, shrunken and weak though it be. These two, in one gloomy mass save for their points, Van Gogh trees I look upon each day when I have drunk my tea and blown out my candle. Four letters from Gerard arrived, two in the morning, two in the afternoon; this is the last day for afternoon delivery now while fuel saving is continued. Miners and train drivers have undergone no change of heart, indeed the former are likely to increase their strike, after today's talks. The whole atmosphere here is sinister with strains and tensions that befoul it.

5 January Flowering of light, sky flowing with gulls in flight, rain blown over, blue sky above, cows champing great trusses of hay, two ponies racing over green hillside, round and turning, tails and manes dark on storm cloud, friendly south gale smelling of sea. I took Mother out for a small walk to feel this new clear on her cheeks, for her to see birds and washed world, water pools in fields, rain-made shallow pale mirrors.

6 January Continuing brilliance, of stars, sun, moon, for the shining forth of God. A dancing hailstorm in sunshine turned every trunk, branch, twig to silver glisten, glass clear with a living shimmer. Hail, which I always salute as coldest of grain, is a brief-lived dancer. Warm too, wren singing, great tit see-saw; fieldfares and smart jay I saw in my watery walk. Translated *'Auf dem See'*; *See*, feminine, 'sea', *See* masculine, 'lake'. A long reading of that desperate taskmaster Karl Barth last night; I think life is more mysterious than sin and death, sir.

10 January Mother, a little old woman now when she stands with her arthritis-wrenched back and bowed and twisted legs, but fine and glowing when she is on the hearthrug with books at her side and the warmth of the electric heater at last allowed to be switched on to give her warmth, has been engaged in making marmalade most of today, as well as baking bread in the morning. Gales again with rain all day till the evening when the rain was driven away and I hurried out for half an hour in the wind strong and gusty but soft as in the far west of Ireland. Babel of rooks in Short Wood.

11 January Awe-struck, even now, by the war of the elements in the hours of darkness. Darkness at its worst not without the presence of the moon however cloud enveloped. The day following the tempest has been one of tranquillity and suffused with pale gold sunlight. I woke suddenly at midnight and lay awake with no touch of sleep for nearly an hour, rocked by the roar of many winds near and distant, turmoil, conflict, counter-blast. Then lightning began its blinding play, and thunder waged war with the wind, winning with tremendous reverberations so that the cottage, which had quaked now and again in the gales, shuddered to its foundations. Hail and rain lashed the window like a storm of pebbles from West Bay, the glass was misted over with impenetrable ghostly whiteness. The electricity was off for five hours. I kept thinking as I lay of the psalms and the terrible Jah riding the storm winds, seated upon the floods; and of Miranda in *The Tempest*, and her haunting words – 'Oh, I have suffered, with those that I saw suffer.'

12 January   Cessation of wind, a soft pattering of rain momently on the roof: the stillness in my ears is strange; Mother gave Rose and her three elder sons a lovely tea by the fire, and they had an interlude of quiet talk when the boys were out of the room. They were, when I returned from my walk, engaged in single combat on my lawn with plastic swords, and Francis sported a gilt Viking helmet. He is still not too old to suck his thumb and to clamber up me as a pretend monkey on a tree. I suppose *some* people are born to inhabit a phantom world, as I, or is it a half-conscious, half-unconscious defence, withdrawal; essential if anyone is to create their world and not quite accept the ready-made one of other human beings: an evasion, a not-growing-up, or 'a bid for freedom'.

4 March   Grass spangled with frost or 'jade dew' yesterday, today grass green, garden beds white with a shower of snow in the night. A calm gray east-wind day. A letter from Rose in the afternoon did not give a very good account of her father's foot which causes him considerable pain: she visits him often and Gerard nearly every morning. It appears now that Heath will have to resign ...

6 March   Darkening down the daylight hours after the white-frost beginning, falling finally into drizzle as the rooks fly home. The starlings are in their holes long before sun-down, shuffling and squeaking, and I am as lazy as they are: not even playing with my pen but reading on the rush mat. There is a Lenten service in the church at 7.30 tonight. Mother and I have had our minds much engaged with Will in his latest ordeal that one would take to be beyond the endurance of any other man of eighty-six. To help us Mother had a letter from his own hand this morning, writ on his birthday. O dear, this Powys blood, if but a single drop, has some substance in it of electric vibration that is alert to something in the universe that is unknown to other men; an incommunicable communion that is active in the dead as in the living ...

7 March   Fine and warm, Mother walked round Lark Rise with me, we saw one lark and heard a curlew. Three letters from Gerard arrived for me this morning, posted by Rose in Nairobi. On the back of one she had written: 'Foot better, no op. yet again'. Gerard's letters are good ones, but *not* for the country and climate. He says it is very very

very dry. And the Africans who had received plots on the Beale are cutting down and burning all the trees along the stream, the beautiful ancient trees with rugged trunks; the young cedars tender and taper as girls, which Gerard treasured and watched over as if they were his children. This destruction of trees and forest goes on all over the country now, and for the Africans there is no connection between this disafforestation and the constantly decreasing rainfall. The music for a lyric, Uguritic, or Sumerian, in cuneiform on clay tablets has been translated, or transposed, into present day musical notation: music composed they say about 3,700 years ago.

10 March Lenten weather: sunless, raw cold, wind north-east, snow powdering the ground early, soon becoming black wetness: even so the distinctive white light of March strives with a gloom of December. Bird song fails. I listen rather than read, seeking now, it may be, a refuge from words: only the lessons before breakfast, and *War and Peace* at intervals.

16 March 'breezes loud and shrill/dancing dancing daffodil' Letter from Rose, her father has had, as she put it, 'the blooming toe off': so all day long he has been in the forefront of our thoughts. I am haunted by Will as Africa, Africa as Will, rich in flocks and drawing water from the rocks. Dazzling sunshine, warm; distances, airs soft as in Ireland. High buffeting western wind now bearing small rain: all clocks advanced so 'twill be dark again when I make my tea, indeed this is the first morn I have *not* lit a candle. I live so much – for so long I have – in what Auden calls 'the secondary world' I am unfitted for any other. Much keen reading today: Plotinus, Plato, Hebrew (small but strong), Greek New Testament, German poems ('*Zauberflöte*'), and to crown all the first essay in *Obstinate Cymric*, 'Welsh Aboriginals', mostly read aloud by Mother triumphantly. But what tossed my spirits highest, *War and Peace* – Natasha at the hunt, adance, aplay, singing, sleighing.

17 March No Jovian day for the first of summer-time; still for early rising I heard in the garden the freest bird song for a few unmeasured minutes. All day dark and rainy, with no come-hither of wood and field. I spent much time on the rush mat working at the poems of Georg Trakl in the Oxford Book, which were agreeable to my Sunday-after-early-communion mood. I miss the lofty carefree flight of seagulls, which have ceased to tack across this inland skyscape. It is a problem for poets – having to let all soaring and sinking impulses of soul *go to the limit*, feet winged in air or straight in grave, in order to feel the crafty play of things that are 'symbols for words' and transfer to them a singing life: to experience also all times if not as an instant, yet closely overlapped or infolded upon themselves, not sequence, brilliance.

21 March   First day of spring, so warm calm sunny after some hours of fog. The new light pierces into every crevice of the cottage; I see objects, colours, for the first time. Out of doors haze blurs and softens giving a velvety effect. A digging fork leans agleam in the level last sun rays, aslant in the fresh turned mold. Francis's sixty-fifth birthday, he came to tea with Mother. I listened to 'Tattered Banners' which today dealt with the war with Japan and premonitions of the revolution in Russia, up to 1906. Brilliant and terrible contrasts to shake the imagination.

30 April   'No lust there's like to poetry ...' I am keeping close companionship with Herrick as I walk, work, wander in meadows, rest in bed, write my ephemeris. This is a brilliant dusty day for the last of the month. What I expect, look for, wait upon – I decided this morning – is constant highlights with no shadows to set them off; with my own cottage, country on all sides, health, music and imagination I achieve (some days) a poetic exultation to transmute everything. With much solitude I can carry over into company enough, I trust, to convey some gaiety. How distracted, preoccupied, agitated, self-absorbed mortals in general are. One has first to learn to *throw away* the soul.

2 May   5.35 p.m. A gentle rain has begun to slide down the breath of the sourish east wind. My first and only letter this week today, from Gerard; and one from W.E.P. enclosed in Mother's. I went to Dorchester and delighted in the clarity, herald of rain, the haze of many days totally done away with; pleased with a picture card of tapestry I found *à mon seul desir*. A good programme of Dvorak last evening to commemorate his death on 1 May 1904. I saw both Venus and Jupiter early this radiant morn.

3 May   Wet day, cold but beloved by the birds, the English ones, no curlew or cuckoo; goldcrest singing ceaselessly. At this late hour, 8, the clouds thin and grow threadbare showing between them the light from above; I typed out my Lent poems, from 20 March to Easter Day, 14 April, though who could read them who could say. Strong growth and thriving in the garden over the road. Mother's cold is better, but she is weary with the weakness of old age, not being able to do more, to walk, to work in the garden. A mist of distance-blinding soft rain drifts over again.

24 July News of a civilian Prime Minister for Greece and the end of the military junta. The latter part of the day shining and wind-swept by a boisterous west wind. How in some moods the world, life rather, seems totally unredeemed, so full of trouble, evil, suffering, it can never be justified, any more than man before God can be. Then in other moments of vision the flame of beauty soars to so leaping heights all that is not of the heart's desire is consumed. I had the delight today of hearing 'The Cuckoo and the Nightingale' concerto by Handel.

25 July The date we were to have returned to Kenya, a brilliant morning, blue sky, then a swift advent of round snowy clouds. Tomorrow Gerard and I are to go to Cheltenham for the two day meeting of the Powys Society, Friday to Sunday. We go by coach from Sherborne, which sounds to me romantic and eighteenth-century. The thrush woke me at 4.30 and I saw it singing on the point of the roof in a luminous sky of gold deepening to apricot. But each day the speckled one sings less now, and the constant goldcrest is mute.

29 July 'My favourites at the moment are *Richard II* and *A Midsummer Night's Dream*', said Wilson Knight,* 'but they may change after lunch.' There is no doubt that this humorous old man was the making of the Cheltenham conference.* He enjoyed each thing, quietly savouring it with closed eyes, or suddenly, after some remark in his subtle-toned voice, with his whole face puckered up in mirth. There were about 26 people, most of the time, with others straying in and out. I was happy to see Oliver Wilkinson just for the first evening. Gerard read aloud the last part of John's essay on the *Odyssey* at that time. We slept at the top of one of the white stuccoed houses. In front of the terrace there was a sweep of greensward with trees of tremendous spread and stature. The Gloucestershire cornlands, Bath Abbey and Wells Cathedral, with stormy sky-scapes were the chief accents of our homeward drive: and there was the sadness of stark January elms, and elms with every autumn tint of yellow and umber splashing their foliage as the mighty trees and their slender children prepared by the shedding of leaves for death.

31 July Flowers and leaves in my garden awhirl tonight as in a Van Gogh painting so fierce is the booming wind from the sea ... I finished just now the sympathetic study, written almost as a monologue, the artist speaking to himself. It might be called 'Two Brothers', so close and intense was the bond between Vincent and Theo. I started a bonfire in the multitudinous wind and now as smoke rain races by. How this simple undemanding life in contact with the English elements is a benefit and blessing to my half-lost soul ... now Gerard takes the heavy key with cloverleaf-pierced handle and goes bowed up the concrete path between the tangly borders to lock the door of the church. In flurry another month ends.

2 August I walked at dawn in my leaf-fringed garden, Jupiter to the south, Venus in the north-east, both shining as calm lamps in the nacre sky; masses of dew and total voicelessness of birds. I write nothing now and no wish arises to make a poem at all: although more and more I have the sense that only creative work makes life live. I must have something which my whole soul can embrace, into which it can fling itself with that motion of spontaneity that for that instant, as when the swifts scream, is the endurance and annulment of pain. To see the swift flatten wide-winged on the stone wall opposite and vanish under the eaves takes all the breath from one half of my 'double-soul' of the poet.

3 August Kathleen Ryall's birthday. Gododdod escaped from battle at Catterick in Yorkshire (as he sings) 'bleeding by grace of my blessed poetry'. By the grace of the poetry in my nature I might, I believe, say I have escaped from the most grievous, sordid and hopeless conditions of life – or as yet I have, by this inward gift of making despair a taut lute-string, although at this present I do not write, I brood themes for verse that somehow inveigle my mind through sorrow.

9 August Richard Nixon made a speech last night in which he resigned the presidency of the United States after his prolonged Watergate 'agony'. The newspapers are all criticism and appraisals of his life and work as President. Whether the prosecutor brings a case against him will be seen in time. A stormy day of hurrying cloud battalions: early I saw them traversing the moon, with evening they thicken causing swift nightfall.

10 August West and north-west wind throwing down Warriors, scuds, wild white sunlight, heart-dissolving-into-glory cloud-scapes. When I walked ahead of Gerard up the muddy lane towards Cadbury Camp a golden retriever dog joined me, a fine friendly animal, and kept with me until I was on the wall-encircled height, when Gerard caught up. The wide prospect from the impregnable Camelot this equinoctial weather was something to make one forget all the inevitable smallnesses.

11 August Haunted this Trinity IX by Somerset, deep-soiled, lugubrious with leaves, with doomed elms, with (despite the richness of orchards and cornfields) an alluvial desolateness about the moors, an unsympathetic outline of certain bare hills. Always so, whenever I revisit this region of Wessex, I am drawn to write, to deal in some way with the impact of the land that gave birth to my father, that with its layer upon layer of human history in earth labour and legend may be considered as the holy land of England. Ovid's king-bird, if I remember right, the woodpecker, was on the summit of Cadbury, doubtless ant-hunting. I disturbed it twice from the ground and afterwards heard its voice out of the towering trees.

7 September   Gales, so the grass is spread with green globes and pyramids, the solid reassuring confident shapes of apples: apples at rest as in a still-life but so newly torn off, so close to those rocked aloft as to be instinct with movement and with a tendency to be disposed in patterns to the eye that kept returning to them. Ten bound copies of Gerard's writing *South Wales Echo* arrived this morning by post, carried by Mother into the cottage. He has given one of them to her. I wrote letters and read *John Cowper Powys: Letters to Iorwerth Peate*, the frankest and most candid and close to his true nature he wrote, I would say; apart from some to his family.

8 September   'Free full and absolute pardon' for Mr. Nixon, the best part of the Watergate scandal which may now be forgotten. Sunshine and clear air for a few morning hours, but the rain clouds reassemble; gale warnings continue. A dreary evensong with the most dismal deathbed hymns not one of the few (the 'two or three gathered') could sing. I ate plums and climbed into the tree to recover.

10 September   Every morning star shone in heaven and in head this dawn, so that all day I have felt the irradiance, or felt it at scintillant intervals. Most starry also is Mother's myrtle with white many-stamened flowers and distant fugitive fragrance. Alan Clodd* sent us Kathleen Raine's latest book *On a Lonely Shore*, a sequence of poems which although I cannot read them through, I am roused by enough to fancy taking up her theme in some merrier manner: somehow in this book stars, graves and rain are exhausted, there is need for new metaphors and symbols that startle. 'An intense experience is an aesthetic fact' I know and believe, but let the communication be as the crack of a whip with a touch of the stinging tip of the cord. Feel the dark collar on the warm and delicate throat of the dog that is never off the chain.

11 October, Spring Cottage   All gray afternoon, the painted starlings run about the grass, take bents in their bills, run again, discard the gray stalk and spy with gold-rimmed eye for some other scrap, fit for a nest.

Children chant and chatter, most of their speech (as with children in England) falls into rough rhyme with short lines. Beyond the children impala grunt and bark; the bell-bird sings.

31 October   Month ends with the moon full, a night as bright as though the rugged features of Africa reflect back the shining upon them of all full moons from the beginning. I have just shaken hands, and said hail and farewell, to two friends of many years' standing, Mwerebua the gardener – the waterer of herbs – and Mugambi the house-servant and cultivator of flowers yellow red blue white, the manicurist of grassy edges who went to school for '*siku moja*' (one day) and is all the more friend for that.

9 November   The cloud curtain is lifted and lowered before the hills as in a theatre; now a scalloped vapour hangs above their heads, now conceals them to their feet. A grizzled man, spare and lean-limbed as an Indian sage is engaged in cutting down tall trees, the yellow-branched acacias, not far below the cottage. Trunk, branches, twigs are cut and arranged methodically; the first two for charcoal burning. This morning in the misty atmosphere blue smoke rose up from palm trees he had kindled living at the base to clear some ground. Here is a sorrowful sight, a trunk crowned with fanning fronds being consumed upright and quick in rich smoulder and with sudden cracks, as of a pistol shot ...

18 November   A pleasing day, beginning with mist cloud-puffs low lying, with three drops of minute drizzle bestowed upon each already shrinking curling green grass tongue. Followed by a collection of letters contenting to desire and reciprocity; by posting my Christmas mini-greetings; by shopping, not unsuccessful in the present world shortage of many foods, or at least what Gibbon names 'luxuries'; succeeded by an unsoporific reading of the part on 'Will' and the 'Will to ...' in *The Dictionary of Philosophy*. I grow ever more interested in Kant, who states in more present-day language (to my mind) much of what I have learnt, and assented to, in Plotinus.

22 November   Mother's birthday. A visit last night to El Khalil, Our Friend, the red hill by Sirakoi, dry as clinker, bare save for many green leaves of some flowerless lily corm. Looking out over the storm-lit landscape from the warm rocks on the top I moved, as usual afloat in time, to the acts of the hand-axe makers and the builders of cairns. Two or three painted-lady butterflies were our companions on those porous scoriac rocks, no bird sang or crossed the infinite sky. Only on the homeward way facing clouds stained as by the glow of a furnace we saw by Eland Hill three owls hovering diving gliding, now high now close to the gray grass of the slope.

6 December 'The spiritual discipline is one with the poetical.' A visit to Nairobi accompanied by a reading of *New Bearings in English Poetry* (1932) brings this 1973–74 Ephemeris to an end. As the purpose of this journey was, for Gerard, to bring to end his Kenya 'residency', which began in 1938, there are backward looks for both of us. Retrospect, regrets, recognition (it may be) of what oneself was, the failures in life-making; but predominantly of thankfulness for having for so long beheld the light of the sun, if for few other things of *my own*, in this double-entendre, doppel-gänger bodily existence between England and Africa. The Nairobi night began with rain and my soul in sleep was soaked, drenched with delight. And behold, the whole land was rained on to our own door-sill where we splashed in mud.

1975

14 January, Mappowder Polishing silver and brass to bring a gleam sunbeam or moonshine into my house as I set back the last piece a brass swan the yellow sun flung light the clouds were gone. And later on this first light-after-tea night when I typed Littleton Alfred's* poem to the West Wind for Nell Gerard called me out to see new crescent moon, Jupiter, Venus most low in a net of dark twigs etched on primrose. The wind is stilled, I sit with lamp at my black window.

30 January Without literature who would know how the circles of the same and the different differed from generation to generation in the minds of men? A whole day of sea-mist rain with wind rising as darkness creeps in: the second (we read) warmest January in one hundred years.

8 February Smell of spring upon the warm air this afternoon, daffodils everywhere. I have been typing some of my poems for Gerard chosen by him; stepping back into other scenes, inscape and landscape; all day I step up and down living on this level or that, realising and losing immediacy, overhearing the soul's dialectic. In bed at night I read an act of *Julius Caesar*.

12 February Ash Wednesday. *The Architecture of the Intelligible Universe in the Philosopshy of Plotinus*: I cannot say for how many years I've been trying to buy this book, now it has come to me easily from Blackwell's. I will read it the first time without making marks. Armstrong refers to Marcus Aurelius to whom I was devoted in my early twenties so I have him beside me also. Yes, I did mark *one* sentence in my new book which is: 'the boundaries shutting off the self from the universe are largely illusory, and disappear in the higher stages of perception.'

18 February   Completed my second reading of Armstrong's *Plotinus* with considerable satisfaction and assent: he is one of the few ancient philosophers whom we can still honour, though not uncritically, as a master. I remember Alyse saying when I wrote or spoke to her with enthusiasm of Plotinus – he is your master. Mother is happy to have, at last, a letter from Phyllis who says she is feeling better each day now. Something about the way Phyllis wrote of herself and her re-awakening life made Mother's chin quiver and mouth droop as she came to the end of the letter she read aloud.

27 February   Interrupted to go to the church here for an icy cold Lenten compline with a discourse on humility. I always see Theodore's long upper lip and hear his voice repeating the compline responses. 'I am enamoured of this journal' wrote Sir Walter Scott in his: Phyllis has sent Mother two small Nelson volumes of his journal, begun towards his life's end. I've only as yet read a page or two, how I delight in his language, choice and placing of words. Gerard and I heard the curlew as we walked home in the gloaming.

8 March   A letter from Gerard this morning, writ in Cardiff Museum. A quiet wet day again; only sparrows have scrums and chirrup merrily: reading *Pindar* (Bowra's) and Cornford. Mother is always cheerful when I go into her room; 'spring-cleaning' the larder today. Observing her minute care for all her 'little things' I am reminded of Whitehead's words about God's infinite concern that nothing be lost.

25 March   Digging up grass roots among my daffodils below the ash tree I pondered many things in my heart: fitfully the blackbird sang, the one that for days has practised hoarse notes with ruffled breast receiving the blast of the north wind. When I had washed my hands I entered Mother's fire-bright room, she started round on her perch by the window where she was watching for Francis and exclaimed: 'O Mary, King Feisal has been murdered ... by his nephew ... he came into the room to speak to him ...' Francis arrived, I went out and continued in prayer.

3 April I wonder at Sir Walter's energy to 'gurnalize' when he was in the midst of his debt crisis and writing – 'my own right hand shall do it' – at top speed to produce new works: last thing at night I find myself well-pleased to be in his company in this self-communion as I was in childhood to live in his romances. This is the most April day all moods, and storms, fairyland brilliance and bitter bleakness: transfigurations through earth and heaven. Eleanor spent the day with us till towards evening; we walked and talked, laughed and were serious ...

17 April Soft soft sea mist all pervasive celestial wetness. 'I know a bank ...' two or three cowslips their last and only refuge, scentless but sweet to the eye, with one lark's song and a curlew cry. Taylor's *Plato* almost finished, well enjoyed ... Consideration – in company with stars – with contemplation, entry into the mind's inmost sanctuary, or the temenos of soul as the suggested derivation hints: it seemed to me on a sudden last night I might write a Contemplation on Contemplation. The capitals of Cambodia and Vietnam have fallen to the Communists.

7 May Mother tells me they (whitethroats) are becoming scarce, these airy singers above the hedges with their wayside gaiety. I walked among bluebells and stitchwort this morning and standing by an oak tree, with hazelnut shells in the chinks and rough crevices, listened to a garden warbler. Kath has dug the heaviest part of the garden all day in a maniacal north wind. I look upon the countenance of my Louvre Homer in my journal, at the copy of the head said to be Plotinus' Phyllis sent me, for consolation, for confirmation that the eternal values will remain when, it seems, the threats against freedom of thought have never been more determined and purposeful. All minds are at risk, whether or not directly exposed to controlling 'influences' and 'philosophies'.

18 May Sunshine all Whitsunday with none of that rushing mighty wind the Pythagoreans imagined could blow the soul away. I have been re-reading my markings in Taylor's *Timaeus* Commentary, an unfailing quarry for my enquiring mind. Pink peppery lupins have come out with this new warmth in my garden. I question constantly within my soul but without response.

19 May My best joy is the voice of the turtle in the fog cloud of morning, three distinct croons reached my ears wrought in my heart, although from far, and that, I dare say, is the first and last I shall hear of the turtledove this year; the fullest serenest most fervent caress of coming summer, the grace of my river days. Beside this a book ordered from Blackwell's arrived, *Eros and Psyche* by John Rist which I began to read in the garden this day of warmth now ending, as the sun god falls in liquid fire.

22 May The May morning burning with the spirit, bright long-desired light, shout a shrill *Mailied*, fell in ashes at a word on the choral air, destruction in the dark element of fire of a sculptor. Death or sickness is apt to set my word-hoard in Greek epigrammatic attitude now: fatality decked with no future hope, no rebelliousness, a simple mockery to sharpen the mind's edge to cut clean the thread of life, a moment's pause at the gap before both ends are lost. The news reader began the daily jeremiad with a conflagration in Cornwall; the home of Barbara Hepworth burnt down, herself within. Did the fire begin with her wood carvings for kindlings, her stone ones remain for her monument in all the great cities of the world.

26 May According to Sir Walter Scott, Dr. Johnson in advising Boswell to keep a journal told him not to record the weather and similar 'trumpery' – a pet word with Scott who, as I do, partook of the nature of the weather almost equally with his own life but resolved (after reading this counsel) to omit allusions to his ill-health, discomforts of body and lack of psychical well-being. I try with him to dodge this, but it is better to write as a last resort of this than to talk of it to any companion ...

29 May 'O the twenty-ninth of May/'Tis a most glorious day' begun with cuckoo, Corpus Christi, and swifts' screams, and the Peripatetic's talk of the Platonic ideas as 'twitterings': anything to do with birds or suggestive in this way causes a glow in my heart. Mother and I went to East Chaldon this shining morn in high royalty, white and gold on either hand, all the way through: then with Rose up Chalky Nap to Chydyok and the haze-dimmed sea, the windy capes. Ghosts on all sides, over the ocean, aslant the sunbeams, riding the strong wind from the land, striding the green earth. 'What are ghosts?' Charlie inquired. 'They're what you don't see but you know they're there.'

1 June Continued cold from Greenland, sunless also. In the morning we visited St. Catherine's church in the undercliff with the grassy ledge of graveyard. Young and glossy blue-black and satiny white magpie tumbled into the rosemary bush. A regatta of small white-sailed ships, yachts rather, filled Weymouth Bay, like a flock of sheep, Gerard said. Their changing patterns and groupings indeed exactly resembled grazing new-shorn flocks. The undercliff always haunts me for the rest of the day. How often the psalmist exclaims 'Sing a new song to the Lord', and how faithful he remains to his so constant and dwelt-on themes. Can it be said whether mortals most desire the new ... the latest ... it's just out ... or dread it as something not recognised, a possible menace to order and continuity, to feeling safe. Once a new mode has been accepted by enough people it is smothered by endless discussion and examination. Yet in another sense each time psalm or poem is read or chanted it is a new song.

9 June 6.30. a.m. Parched edenic days, cuckoo and curlew since 4. I have now read to the end of Scott's journal, the conclusion and farewell to life in the Appendix, taken from Lockhart. Last evening we went to the small church of St. Mary's, at Holnest. Mother and I shut ourselves into a white-painted box pew. The sun cast a diamond upon the deep gold Ham Hill window jamb. Taffy,* who returns today to his college, gave a talk from the Jacobean pulpit. Earlier I had shown him the first pink wild rose growing by the wall. There is a large grassy area round the fourteenth-century building, freshly mown. The evening before this we were at Salisbury. The virgin spire pierced a cerulean heaven with swifts, black specks from their lofty altitude, in endless satanic dance about it: a demonic eternal whirl of the tireless ones. No scarcity of nest crevices for them with a whole, built in heavenly space, cathedral for breeding cote, a rare columbarium.

10 June Flaming: good dewy walk, a pair of deer, one barked in the recesses of the wood; I heard also, and even saw flitting from a bramble patch, a sweet singer of thrilling notes, a garden warbler. Followed the minor inevitable griefs and heartbreaks day brings: of course, I am absurd in making a full Greek tragedy in the silence of my soul over certain minor yet to me brutal calamities. Even now the swifts' screams can scarcely over-ring the hideous irregular excruciating rasp of a fire billet cutting circular saw across the way. Near the end of my early-to-bed day Rosemary telephoned to tell us her mother is to have an operation, probably next week in Yeovil hospital. 'As soon as possible' Edith begged the surgeon. She is eighty-five and has lived by pure determination, or will-power, for Reggie's sake more years than anyone knows. Rosemary's voice sounded hard and dry, her only complaint was, 'I find it difficult to concentrate'. Kathleen has been here, staunch, as much a son of consolation as St. Barnabas. For want of Sir Walter Scott's Journal I could not read at all last night, he is my first and best hero, to know all and love to live …

11 June Barnaby Bright all day and no night: indeed cuckoo calling after 10 p.m. last night when Venus was high in the white west, and before 4 this morning, with Jupiter afloat over the roseate glow in the east. 78 °F in my western room this hour, 7 p.m. A little owl looked me in the face as he sat upright on a gatepost this early day … well after sunrise though. Yellow-eyed bird of Pallas Athene … Crooked Oak is girdled by foxgloves and I saw two hares before it this morn. All plants wilt in the continual cloudless heat, the north-east wind is warm once the dew is gone. Mother moves with more difficulty and pain in her knees, but she was gladdened today by a letter from W.E.P. after he'd breakfasted with Rose and Tony at Kisima.

14 June 'There is a willow grows aslant a brook,/That shows his hoar leaves in the glassy stream' – here Mother came and sat upon a bough that lay supine in grass and buttercups; for we today made our midsummer pilgrimage to Romsey, and up the Test valley to Horsebridge: first debouching to visit Little Somborne, the antique church of flint which has been by the Queen declared redundant. So the weather; the trees that root beside the walls and stretch above weighty and perilous branches, the hole-haunting birds may have their will of this sunny tabernacle where once we saw on the dusty leaf-strewn altar a new loaf of bread and country wealth for harvest festival. And in between the swift shining pellucid streams and rivers, and this place mad main roads, iron dividing the pastoral corn-grown downs. I heard no turtledove, even along the river and now begin to think these smallest ones have been ousted by the collared doves that are ubiquitous and strong. A snipe flew over the Horsebridge meadow calling and three young peewits flew up silently. The yellow iris were in full flower along the banks, better than once royal gold on dress and banners. Beehives again in the water garden.

20 July Swifts' screams in the consecration of the Host; song-birds silent, even the last thrush that practised in the *Dämmerung* with unsure jarring preludes. Read in an essay on Freud in the *TLS* the first sentence 'since Freud's discovery of the unconscious …' which made me merry, and led me also to suspect that I am not, as I've generally supposed, without ambition. Have I an 'unconscious' ambition to offer an elegy to each day, with a glance at Donne's 'Valedictions': 'of the Booke' and 'Forbidding Mourning'; with a hint or two from 'Urn burial'? That nothing be lost, *pereunt et imputantur*,* rather; and the other inscription, the dedication on sundials: 'I record only the sunny hours'. Yet the sundial is still there when clouds darken. Gerard is away for a week at Woodbrooke.

21 July In twilight with a cloud-gathering to deepen the gloaming after a sunny day with west wind blowing. With my alone meals I read *Crime and Punishment* for Dostoevsky is always, because of J.C.P., a challenge in the rereward of my mind. But O sorely and savagely against my will. A small improvement *so far* on *The Brothers Karamazov* is the solitariness and soliloquising of the sick man: almost anything is better than the interminable tedious aimless talk of Russians one to another. Last evening Mother and I listened to a radio *King Lear*; three hours, good voices, the familiar characters alive in them.

23 July Winds and shatteringly clear sunlight. I walked early in Lark Rise. 'No one remembers the tall parlour maids in Red and White', Mother said reflectively, as she was telling of her visit to Montacute House this afternoon. She took late tea and talked of the paintings and rich treasures; sun flashed in and out of the room, clouds as canopies hung aloft.

24 July 'I was never more religious than during the composition of *The Creation*. Every day I fell on my knees and prayed for strength.' So Haydn. This evening I heard the oratorio sung in German, an experience long desired. For all the choral splendours I was most spellbound and transported by the orchestra, except, it may be, by one particular period of the soprano. Full moon last night, Mars and Jupiter towards dawn, Venus low after *The Creation*: the sun filled my room with gold during the last part. I walked to the Haw and the Watergate this morning, to see butterflies and on the thistles I did see three fritillaries as well as many meadow-browns, a few tortoiseshells and whites, a small copper, a skipper and a peacock. A biologist was speaking when I turned on my radio immediately before Haydn's *Creation*, and he said, 'There will be an atomic war and most of the human race will be wiped out', in parenthesis as regards the rest of his discourse, but in certainty.

28 July These glaring sun-sped days have some sinister effects upon us older ones as they wax and wane in unending equatorial sequence, many odd twists and shrinkings and shiverings and shrivellings dizzy or cow the mind: the elm trees in their parti-coloured dying are fired by the sun and are consumed piecemeal, a bough here another there yellowing, hotly tawny, malachite foliage gone to rust in a day and a night by mere aridity, one catches oneself believing rather than deadly disease. Charlie,* when we called yesterday, gave me a valuable present – Bréhier's *Plotinus** in seven volumes, heavily but neatly annotated by Charlie himself. The sun has fallen now into a splash-edged pool of blood and sinks from sight. Timothy Hyman* left us today to visit Wilson Knight near Exeter. My beloved ἄποδες* have descended from invisible heights and scamper and squeal round humble human roofs.

30 July An evening pilgrimage to Winterbourne Tomson, this sultry day, the magenta sun-globe low now. There on the chalk fields and gardens appeared more starved than here on the rock: cornfields on the way in their fulfilment of red and silver and tawny gold; harvesting just begun. When I said good night to Mother she said this is the date, sixty-one years ago, her own mother died, and so she was glad on this day we visited Bertie's church and burial-place.

6 August Transfiguration, a beloved and meaningful festival. Ἀλήθεια* – unforgetfulness – is different from memory, remembering, recollecting, calling to mind, it is rather constant awareness, conscious or unconscious, of the wholeness, the life of the All; it is indeed contemplation, a waiting on reality. Gerard and I went to Blandford; town crowded but we walked on the banks of the broad black Stour, looking across the water from a level field to the trees that grow to the very brink. A few yellow waterlilies still among their flat leaves and the beautiful three-petalled satiny arrowheads, white with dark eye.

13 August All ways dry; wind after days in the south-east has veered to north and is now north-east. Louise,* the sailor in Greek waters for the last two years, arrived last evening to visit us. She is a Dutch woman who grew up near Amsterdam, she cannot remember her father who was killed in the war. Her favourite author is Dostoevsky. That which plucks from me my whole soul, that to which on an involuntary impulse I fling my soul; the inward response or motion which leads to this surrender or gesture: these are closer to life, that trace of the One, than any other of my commerce with being, that I now know. Llewelyn's birthday ... the heritage in gold grain. Letters from W.E.P.

17 August Long straight rain till all is soaked, shrouded in obscurant dampness, this early coolly dove-ringed dawn. Across the road the yew tree is so veiled with mist the eye recalls hoar-frost; greatly grown, slow though yews are, this one now out-tops roof, draws sprays with languid fingers across windows. Gerard took out for the day our two guests, Louise and Taffy, to see the wonders of Dorset: Maiden Castle, Chesil

Beach, Cerne Giant. For my part I read *The Poet's Calling* which by luck came through the post, after I had disposed of the unendearing picture on the cover of Robin Skelton; the man is disarming, simple, candid, painstaking; the book a weaving of quotations from near and distant poets.

18 August   Rain at nightfall hastening the dark, hinting at an autumnal scurrying of shed leaves, the cerise fish increase, cherry leaves on the lank grass. Taffy went away today and we are sad at the empty space; large broad tall bearded he is now with dark eyes old as Africa, as the Welsh mountains; looking through one might think from the Dark Ages. This monologue is all I can now, how write poems when each thing at touch becomes poem?

20 August   Sun south of the elm celebrating the return to autumn with the most impassioned display that I must not stretch after with words. Louise left us today, and we miss her sadly. I write now where she drew and painted the Cerne Giant. She sent me by Gerard from Sherborne a true present, a compass bought from Mr. Cheeseman joined by herself with a clean-smelling leather thong to a disc of the same size of Grecian olive wood. Yesterday with Louise we visited Glastonbury Tor and Alfred's Tower again in wind and light intermittent rain. The peaty ground near Stourton was sopping; the clay in the gateways slippery at Glastonbury; Sherborne Abbey at the last, and Wyat.

21 August   North wind and all the burning clouds, pure light, transfiguration that goes with this keen white wind; renewal of life. Fields green as Paradise. Louise's tokens with her sprig of rosemary in silence on the table. Little reading, head empty of words as welkin is.

1 September   Glen Cavaliero has returned with us from Weymouth, and has been talking of modern poets and their writings, as well as listening to *South Wales Echo*, and admiring Will's paintings. He has, I am sure, much of the well-known Italian suppleness, the restorative gifts of a father confessor and his skill in deflecting the mind rather than meeting it with ram's head resistance. We all walked twice round Maiden Castle this morning, then I left the two G's at the base of the Cerne Giant's hillside, to climb to the summit, and came home. The T.F.P. Conference* was more successful than we expected, with about 40 members and varied lectures. In fact a modest unobtrusive life and work was ransacked.

2 September   Perhaps the most valuable part was the reading aloud of considerable passages from *Interpretation of Genesis* and *Soliloquies of a*

Hermit, by Harry Coombes: these still sound in my head. Last night in the darkness of the night, the interior mind dark, I knew a sensation, that was also in some way visible, unperceived hitherto and so not to be described by comparison to any other touch or utterance: only in words can I say imperfectly there was a tension, stretched, extended, not inimical, wan or black, as a chord both visible and experienced; silent but concerned with the letter C.

1 October   A day of shining: stars, planets, Crone moon; continuing with towering clouds, silvery showers, sunshine ever clearer more caressingly mellow, until by the evening twilight the sky was clear, is clear, as pre-dawn, luculent, awaiting the stars. This French impressionist atmosphere has pleased me, so has a rainbow with a few stray house martins aflutter on high. I have been recollecting the old domestic servants I knew in childhood, wondering if my own content over the small diurnal offices of the house – my own house it is true – is at all owing to their affection for their tasks and loyalty to those who employed them: some unconsciously recorded awareness of this?

19 October   After the 8 o'clock service Peter put into my hands a small ancient Common Prayer given to L. A. Powys* by his father, rector of Stalbridge, in 1858. This book was great-uncle Littleton's encheiridion throughout his army life. Although pages are missing at the beginning and the last pages of the psalms, the list of places where his regiment, the 83rd, stayed is complete at the beginning, from Chatham in 1858 to Agra in 1874 before his death in India from cholera. There are also two sentences copied in opposite his name: the first words being 'Keep innocency'. I am moved by this gift and I love the little book with clear print and red margins and headings. Dense cloud early through which presently, gradually, the sun sent wan yellow rays to finger all yellow things on the face of the earth. The afternoon was all sunshine, russet leaves and harebell blue haze; Peter and I walked fast over green fields to Ball Hill up to the top, back through a plantation of young bright tinted beech trees to the pines and yews where once stood the pilgrim's chapel.

21 October   By some witchery Alyse arranges her four feathers in a design of meaning and beauty for Peter's last night in the cottage. He is now with Mother. A day of storms and wildness, some open and some overlaid with silence and poetry, of chill easterly winds, Kath gardening, Peter charging off, after a long passionate converse with Gerard and me, into the fields on his own and up to the level land on the summit of Ball Hill. He returned two and a half hours later at the same pace, bearing down the mown grass over the leaves in his black and red squared jacket. I hear his voice now in the dark outside as he says 'Dear heart, goodnight', closes the door. He enters, mounts the stairs, closes the door of his room after him: to be alone.

22 October   Third gray east-wind day: starlings noisily at work in their two roof-holes bumping and banging as though preparing their winter quarters. Sitting again at my table where Peter wrote his journal, and copied his *I Ching* oracles, I miss his presence in the cottage with a double sense of desolation, for his departure which forebodes my own, and because he is sad: alone, as he would not be and for all his numberless friends and acquaintances. Painfully he is taking stock, revising values, preparing for another kind of life in the hut in the woods he is to rent for the winter. From the news: Arnold Toynbee has died, the Russians have landed a space-craft on Venus.

1 November   Τότε ἡμῖν τέλος καὶ ἀνάπαυλα* as I read in Charlie's *Plotinus* with his translation above. And now his Socrates leans above my right shoulder. For today our friend died, not long after noon and when Gerard had been with him for a little while. Yet again when he died neither Charlie's Rose nor Gerard was in the room. Gerard indeed had picked up a copy of Barnes's poems lying on the table and opened it at random and read the lines of Hardy's, who saw across the fields a flash of light from the coffin as it was carried out of the house, a signal from the dead poet to the living.

5 November   Charlie turned to ashes in the morning and how many stuffed Guys after dark ... Mild and rainy, but some stars appeared when Gerard and I walked to Beaulieu Road (1½ miles perhaps) to see a mighty bonfire with the luckless effigy surmounting the flames on a long stake. The crowd, 200 or so Gerard reckoned, were standing in silence with upturned flame-lit faces, there was an atmosphere of awe over all, as though we were witnessing an execution of a living man. A flame sprang from Guy's foot, soon after that he toppled, the pole went down with him into the heart of the fire. Children began to run round here and there holding hands: the rockets, star showers, silver fountains, all the pyrotechnic display began. We left on our homeward way.

11 November, Spring Cottage   'A touch of reality. Heaven help me' ... 'where the intuition of the universe is always present'; with my journal in my hand again I re-read the pieces I have copied into it, in order both to remember and to forget. The travelling is over, the cicadas resume their song; the moon is near heaven's height, the hills are quiet. Will was in the room he has turned into a studio leading off the central room of the house. Two wooden rails all round the walls carry his newest bright landscapes, a lemon sunset reflected in still water on the easel; in his hand a postcard size tablet onto which he was copying the head of Christopher* and his girl Nancy's profile from a photograph sent him by Mother. Will was fine and vigorous, he sang a verse of John Peel ...

13 November Simplicity between the poles of Lucy and Gerard my life presented itself to me last night before I slept, but this simplicity and intensity have nothing tangible about it. These visionary experiences in words have a momentary truth, that is all, vividness that can only belong to single instantaneous impressions that most often are totally lost, leave not a wrack for the light of day, nothing of themselves except, by chance, a passing sensation, a form presented itself from the void. Exceeding wetness of jade dew this breathless aesthetically colourless daybreak and sunrise.

14 November Crystal sphere day with cloud splendours, bubbling snowy curves and archangelic angles, rays ruled keen, fleeces, marabou feathers stroking all heaven. Gerard read aloud for a while, the first time for a whole series of days, from the chapter in *Pillar of State* dealing with Wellington as Chancellor of Oxford University: how I find myself envying the confidence of continuity among these learned dons and divines. Indeed the whole leisurely intelligently occupied way of life of the well-to-do in the nineteenth century.

25 November Mugambi returns from town with one letter only, from Louise in Paris, she tells us her and Joost's ship the *Justus* has sunk off Sinai, with the beloved boat her spirits have sunk into deep waters. As the *Justus* was going down, she says, an exhausted seabird alighted on it. Joost presently took the bird in his hands and tried to take care of it through the night, after the ship disappeared: but the seamew died before morning. Here is a tale simple and complete as a Greek epigram.

26 November This cranny of Africa is an aviary for Mary, or should I say rather a caged-bird walk? Do writers make themselves regional for want of originality, I wonder. What is the spell of Greek epigrams, ironic mini-tragedies rhymed without sympathy or sentiment for the victims' untoward destiny. The best of them somehow evoke a new response to inevitable end; something about the witty unsolemn resignation of the voice from the tomb, no self-pity, a hint of enjoyment in warning.

2 December   Commemoration of death of Ll.P. in Switzerland in 1939. I remember dancing under the birch trees at Shootash when I heard the news thinking I am alive. A totally gray but rainless afternoon, lit by letters, two from Mother, with hers from Katey Grey enclosed, and two or three others. So I've been writing in reply.

6 December   Return from Nairobi to a rainy afternoon and evening, soft snowy ceaseless, like a shower that is just about to end and never does; there is a silvery light through and indeed upon the rain, a sheen on rails and rocks. We heard today the Beale house is full of African school-teachers and buildings for classrooms have been put up round it.

13 December   St. Lucie's Day. To mark which I read Donne's 'Nocturnall'; ' ... and I am re-begot/Of absence, darkness, death: things which are not.' If there may not be poetry (for me) there is prayer: 'Let mee prepare towards her, and let mee call/This houre her Vigill ...' Prayer *ἀδιάλειπτως** is light upon St. Lucie's Day. 'that soule that is accustomed to direct herself to God upon every occasion ... as a flowre at Sun-rising that soule sometimes prays when it does not know that it prays.'

1976

10 February   Is it because 'In the beginning was the Word' that I have this faith in the nature of words, the very art of writing, to in some way make suffering endurable, to be received in seemly wise by the soul, that in some moods, at some signals, feels to be shredded into separate sensitive nerve-endings that have no other mission but to enhance pain. Words as living and aesthetic perception must be my 'avenue of solution'. That is for consciousness, although most is unsaid. But I must not join the Russians in their habit of self-laceration.

12 February   I have at last put together twenty lines for *butorides striatus*, putting, no doubt, myself into the green-backed heron in this piece of water music, for so I found I felt as I considered the bird. This morning Kimatai rode away through the *mlango** on the mare Jill, born here and named by me, he took her up by the old forest road to the Beale to give to Rose.

13 February A small herd of elephant moving up the ancient way from watering at the Giraffe Drift appeared as boulders among the scattered thorns in that hollow ground. We saw this, near Sirakoi, on our way to Kisima. A shower moving across the hills, burning light and dazzling storm-clouds made this drive up and down full of splendour. All the ripe cornlands, where harvesting has not begun, sprinkled smelt divine – true grain of Demeter. A little rain here too and the robin sang more richly at daybreak to Venus and Mercury, Arcturus and Spica, Alpha and Beta Centauri. A note came from Will to say his foot was bad, he was resting it in bed, and asking us to go to see him. Two letters from Mother. Something sorrowful about those slow-moving primaeval elephant on their centuries' old beat in the empty no-rain grasslands in an alien inimical age.

15 February The thorn tree before the cottage, the home of birds, is topped with scarce white stars of bloom, lit here and there on the great vault of blue. This droughty year most of the whistling thorns are black and bare with only their hollow baubles and spare shrivelling leaves, but a few have a sprinkling of may and I remember other Februarys festive, perfervid with blossoms and scent, my mind leaps then to England's white thorn and black. Stormy heats and gusts churning the dust with brief sultry lulls between and jacarandas singing clear above. One call afar at dawn from the rainbird, and in the early afternoon burnt air a few imperfect whistlings of the unseen emerald cuckoo.

16 February My father's birthday. Full moon last night; when I set off for my dawn walk, soon after I had gone through the *mlango* I began to be aware of tracks heavy and circular in the dust where I put my own feet down. I returned. Gerard and I went up together at sunrise and saw the traces of about three elephant which had skirted the cottage in the night, come out into the road through the thorn trees, and continued up to the maize field and on to the Orpheus group. Will looked more handsome than ever last evening as he sat talking to us by the fire. He has given us presents, paintings and sheepskin jerkins, to take to everyone. We set off after breakfast tomorrow.

19 February, Mappowder Strange to be under the cloud blanket after yesterday sitting all day in the sun on high on the west side of the aircraft, above the Rift Valley, the Desert, the Mediterranean, the Alps, until the cloud like a gleaming fleece thickened. With a bump one went down into it and after what seemed a long time discerned in deep obscurity and end-of-day twilight the roofs and roads, rivers and reservoirs. There was no fog. Mr. Clarke drove us home in not much more than two hours. The porch light was on and the light in Mother's sitting room, so the journey, 7,000 kilometers, 'all day long till set of sun' was safely accomplished, a happy homecoming. Hedge-sparrow, thrush, blackbird, robin song, three curlew calls in the dusk, the call from beyond the grave. A pair of duck flew over with soft quacks.

22 March To sum up at sixty the contemplation and the art that is my being-in-life: 'to dwell in the house of the Lord all the days of my life, to behold the beauty of the Lord, and to enquire in his temple'. To explore the nature of the soul where it is closest to intellect by the way of those before me, and by vision in the light and shadows and darkness where words are poetry.

23 March Hard frost 10 °F below zero – waning moon like an orange pig, scanty notes of song, daffodils fallen like dervishes after their dance. Sun in haze all day, strong rays on one cheek, ice breath of north wind on t'other. I visited trees with rooks nesting aloft to listen to their endearing confident caws as they perched above their proudly exposed well-built nurseries. First ground-ivy blue, far and far off the spring cry of plover that casts my heart in fragments to the winds and restores it whole, aglow.

27 March Griseous day with rough-maned wolf-whistling wind from east and west, and on this 'Cimmery-Land' day, Saturday, we went with Mother to Witcombe where the pastoral my life has been began. For here sixty-six years ago when she was living with Will at his dairy farm my father courted my mother; riding over to visit her on a horse called Blue Bonnet and fishing in the River Yeo. So the place is an idyll, better an *eclogue*, a scene of youth and liberty, milking and cheese making, baking and *sans-souci*, that *is*, once in every lucky life; when the work-play balance is so perfect there is no slant to before or after. Witcombe is a word of magic vibrations. The house, still with thatched roof and stone-mullioned windows, is doubled in size and no longer a farm, but still the last in the lane just before the ground finally falls away to the wide green river flats known as Witcombe Bottoms: often flooded in former times. But in this rainless era we could drive down the track to the bank of the canal-like Yeo and the high-flung foot-bridge, called by Mother The Bark. Two pairs of wild duck flew up ('Willy used to shoot them'), larks rose and soared into song, the first of this spring for me, and a redshank went away on the wind on the further side of the deep-down water with the musical call that is voice of forgotten memories.

14 April North wind, battering without bewailing within as the book of Lamentations; cold white light with fugitive wan gleams as though reflected from an unheated bronze cauldron. So for Wednesday in Holy Week, and my mind released from the tensions taught by the appointed readings makes play with the shadows called thought and poetry, looking out as the black cat on the window-sill across the road looks in with fur ashiver, waiting for day to begin for man ... 'who knows the end of life and the god-given beginning'.

18 April Easter Day. Sun with hazy distance and heat all day. A happy day with Mother and Gerard. Early Gerard lit on a Greek eighteenth-century Easter poem which he swiftly translated, wrote in red for Mother, and read aloud in church at 8 before the Communion service. In the green and mellow evening we drove to Bingham Melcombe church, finding it most beautifully decorated within. By the clear stream with green banks and tall trees birds small and large flew and sang; it was paradisiac in that hallowed dell.

3 May Moisture in the air. Goldcrest song from the too tall dark dense cypress tree by the post office where last year magpies nested, near the top. The cuckoo calls, swallows and martins twitter and flutter over the farmyard this morning. Odd how the *Laws*★ can be amusing ... I am feeling now more interest in Aristotle too, and have sent for the *Metaphysics*, shall I be able to read this 'collection' in Greek?

15 May Flurry of petals on the east wind this morn, begins the apple snowstorm, but the twigs and boughs are still thickset and encrusted with whitening bloom, and even yet coral buds. The sun goes down in a gold flood after this wild-wind day, and the Argonauts would sail and row on gold sea waters. 'And after these things I saw four angels standing on the four corners of the earth, holding the four winds of the earth, that the wind should not blow on the earth, nor on the sea, nor on any tree.' This in Revelation I have now read, after our return from an evening drive, over Batcombe Ridge with abundant bluebells, and to the church between chalk downs and limpid shallow stream, ancient to Saxon times, redundant; where four angel heads keep the tower's four corners.

4 June North wind, cuckoo in the morning. Each individual's reality depends, I think, to some degree, on what is *instinctively* taken for granted through the day, throughout life: 'it couldn't be other than this however I look (or do not look) upon it'; and what seems always wondrous, new, *made over* as it were into miracles, poetry now, immediacy. The more reality that is 'taken' the harder life is.

29 June   Continuation of heat, brazen heaven: weary tramp of cattle up and down their scorched pastures, or they gather in tail-swishing despondent knots: the driest year for 250 and there are no records any further back than this. A willow-wren singing sweetly in a field corner.

5 July   At night thunder with flickering sheet lightning. A morning mist to give brief rest from the bald heaven, to enhance the universal hoariness. In the shallow dish I keep for small birds to sip and splash in sits in the half an inch of water a gaunt gold frog faint from hunger, his long legs no longer serve him to hop: an example under my eyes of the countless creatures parched and dead of thirst day and night. I read the lessons carefully chosen for the refreshment water is and recall daily Ὕδωρ ἄριστον.* Last evening we were cool for two hours driving in the car from village to village, patterns of dwellings and tower among trees below khaki hills: church bells ringing, organ and singing. One arrives always for the first time and goes away for ever. 'Our poets must feel that their work is prayer', this prayer is to redeem ... by tension spontaneity and stability, the soul according to Heraclitus is these qualities, its relation in being.

6 August   This day of sun and on the cliffs south wind, 'the wind from the sea' although inland it continues to be north to north-westerly, Gerard and I and Louise made what has for us now the nature of a pilgrimage – our visit to St. Catherine's church on the undercliff, and walked afterwards along the path on those white sea-capes to Chydyok. Our companion was a collie dog which joined us at Holworth and kept with us all the way, drank gladly in Llewelyn's pool, his wishing gold-fish pool, and returned, ranging far over the stubble and burnt-up pastures as collies do, until we were within half a mile or so of his farmstead when he vanished and we saw our jaunty companion no more. We visited Ll.P.'s stone* and also, on our way to the cliffs, Charlie's Heathcote* which was surrounded by a herd of Guernsey milch cows in the heath.

7 August   Vision of an angel in Romsey Abbey while listening to music in the garden at the base of the cypress tree my eyes closed. The figure was statue-like but vivid, the robe long and traditional white, but adorned with red in squares or angles, robe stuff you could know how it would feel to finger. The angel held a gold sceptre of no great length and the head was bearing a tiara or crown of gold rays as those in a sun image. Nothing was said. The music cello and piano.

9 August '*Unter der Linden an der Heide*', after our walk to the Dorset Gap, mainly distinguished by (in certain parts) abundance of butterflies, and an hour by the rustling limes in Melcombe Horsey Valley, I heard Michael Mann speaking on the diaries of his father, Thomas Mann, which were not to be made public till twenty years after Thomas's death in 1955. I liked M. Mann, the arrangement of his talk, the way he presented, and quoted the sayings from, the journals, 1911–55 with a gap of twenty years or so in the midst; the subject is naturally interesting to me, this recourse and experience of keeping private notebooks, I also learnt enough to consider I did not want to read the journals, any more than the novels, from the hand of the devotee of Goethe and neo-Olympian.

10 August 'By God, Severn, a man needs some superstition to die decently by', and 'if I had a Jeremy Taylor I think I could believe'. No *Holy Living* and *Holy Dying** could be found in Rome however, and Keats's prolonged and agonising dying was without either of these consolations. I read this this evening leaning against a cherry tree, fanned and cooled by the north wind after a particularly hot day, in the letters of the Cambridge Apostles collected and linked into a fat manuscript by Mary B. J.* A laborious worth-while effort I believe, as well as a work of love on her part. Some of the letters are ablaze with intellect, and the Apostles write much more of literature and the literary figures they met, as well as of philosophy and theology and the borderland where these two overlap. The moon, full last night, has risen and an owl speaks, the small sharpish notes recalling the buzzards, four together, we heard mewing over Ball Hill this afternoon as we returned under the northern slope with fat blackberries in the satchel. Earlier we had watched one alone soaring in spirals, floating, wheeling, gliding far and wide in ample heaven with moveless wings as at the will or whim of every flaw and invisible air current.

11 August Today in Sherborne we parted with Louise after a happy week, I think for us all. She is better than last year, more reconciled, more hopeful. Tonight she will be on the sea crossing from Harwich to the Hook of Holland on her way to her native land. I am still absorbed by the 'Apostles' and by Mary's hard work. The letters teem with quotations all translated, (the Greek is copied by hand) and authors and works cited are given in notes. Occasionally she comments on the style of the letters but to me as I read or skim they all seem close in style; I could not recognise one or another of the young men by their 'speech' which is often swift, free and alive, often akin to this age. They, these fluent letters, are all writ between 1827–37, and in reading them I feel as though the whole Victorian age had simply fallen out, as though there were nothing between myself and the writers. At the same time I completely enjoy their masculine intelligence, the absence of feminine scholars which for all their accomplished work in this century is in some way a contradiction in terms. A talk last night by Geoffrey Grigson set me to reading the few poems I could come by by Fulke Greville: G.G. spoke of the dead elms in Warwickshire as symbolic. Now I have with chilled heart to say I see yellow leaves on my signal tree.

29 August Beheading of St. John Baptist, the Hebrew Orpheus. Fog early thick even to causing a thin drip from the trees: remaining all day impenetrable overhead. Holy Communion. My usual reading. Picked plums, shared a perfect pear with Gerard. Woke with the sense-words in my head: 'all is mystery, all is nothingness'. Why do I forget over and again that all is mystery? That being is inexplicable at every level and degree, can only be experienced by living. By the fatal, inevitable habit of comparison the very personal experience is taken for granted as the monotone fields, stone walls, roads, withering leaves, Socratic soul-tendence.

31 August End of summer this gray day sinking from the beginning into evening, most hushed and heavy-lidded. About midnight we woke to an owl, so close, on roof or on cypress across the road. Whit whit whit to whit to woo oo: many repetitions till my sleepy head was filled with this Pallas' bird's musical hooting. Thoughts dwell with Will.

1 September Drought with drizzle instead of sun: forecast is for the no-rain to continue through the next three months, no autumn rains, which were never more needed ... Gerard is with his mother. Each letter from Will now adds to our distress, to the sense he is moving beyond the earthly things no other had so retentive a grip on, realised more vividly.

2 September Sun again, north-west wind, cold, clear. Owl returned at nightfall and was scared away by neighbours, misliking the bodeful call of 'the staring owl'? With much pleasure I listened last night to piano music by Liszt who played (I read today) like an 'inspired poet' which did not surprise me, but that he ended his days as a Franciscan abbé did. I made plum jam after tea.

9 September Totally in the dominion of the North Wind, winged son of Dawn; cloud chase white sun race, blue cubes and ledges, sudden dimness underlit with manifest brilliance, an accumulation of suppressed unflashed lightning. An apple carpet below the Warrior as the aged rigid boughs wrestle with the gale. Apples batter the wall, one now and again strikes the door determined to enter. Cattle crawl along the field-hedges questing.

7 October Squally morning, the last of the apples are being cast down, torn off with leaves and buds. I think in retrospect there was not enough emphasis on 'joyful lips' in that conference on Poetry and Praise. There is nothing to do with merriment in most modern poems, I am tempted to say, which doubtless matches our present mood, and it is 'easier' to make wearily and drearily than gaily and with light and good hope; yet to do this, in other words, to redeem, is the poet's impossible task. Before death (it came to me last night) to experience instantly and completely the happiest moment while I breathed, and one new and hitherto unknown, to be compared with nothing before or after.

2 November All Souls Day. Wedding Anniversary: 1945-76. Tempestuous. Splendid riotous day, dazzle and dark, hail coldest of grain, heaven washed and hung out anew, new hues new rifts and pools, spirals and horizontals: a good day to clean drains, mop floors, sweep sheds, mow drowned mossy lawns ... which I did do: while snowstorms as seagulls whitened fields, floated danced intersected paperlight upon russet yellow-red woods. Read Auden between times, with love, with torn heart, brain singing, again in total non-understanding.

3 November White frost, sunshine all day. I walked down over the sodden green fields to the river in the morning. Gerard telephoned last evening to tell me his father was in hospital resting and looking more at ease. Gerard plans to return here on Sunday bringing his mother for us to look after. Yeats wrote: 'But the passions, when they cannot find fulfilment, become vision.'

6 November Happily Guy Fawkes Day was fine with sunshine, high white clouds, evening dry and warm for fires in the open, squibs and local rockets. Gerard telephoned, his father died in hospital in the night of the 4th.

17 November Warm, fine, no stir in the air. All moods from childish rebellion and fractiousness, to the heart knoweth its own bitterness, the dignity of grief, the ghost of a cackling laugh, retribution: then again total forgetfulness, no past or to come, the present blurred: so I see Margaret, never expecting to see a face more ravaged, lined, tormented, as long as I behold the light of the sun.

21 November   Perfectly calm and gray. I now have neuralgia night by night, beginning at precisely the same time. The cock bullfinch came again to the French honeysuckle berries only a few feet from my window, the berries resemble black boot-buttons or the eyes of mice. The bird's colours breathtaking; I saw him in I suppose about two minutes, take thirty-seven berries, pulling them off one after the other and then nibbling them in his beak.

26 November   My life is always a love affair with the heavens, the visible sky by night and day and the earth structures that poise or outline upon it, the phenomena and the elements: but first cosmos as sky with luminaries and vapours. Untutored by intellect it is this which I begin to record spontaneously, the appearance, the reflection in mind, my responses as lively but muted impulses. The lion's teeth and claws continue their ferocities in neck, shoulder, biceps. Two word visions came to me in one night's wrestling with this demon that touches my shoulder instead of my thigh ... regularity is cruelty; spiral is spirit – the abstract mode of the spirit manifest?

29 November   Phyllis's birthday, aged eighty-two, she wrote to Gerard. To my surprise I had this morning a cheque for £8.25 from the *Anglo Welsh Review* for the poems of mine Gerard sent them and they published. I suppose the only emotions one can neutralise by intellect are one's own? Mother had an air letter from Will, the saddest yet, he is in pain and distress with both stump and foot now and keeps falling asleep.

1 December   Black rain-lashed window tonight; last, stars and the window cast as light on the wall opposite by the moon. Strong awareness as I write that what I write is inwoven with unknown other elements, with much untouched by the senses, those John-named 'imponderables'. And how breath-swift, mind and limb wearily, this year has run down the spiral stair, half-turning now to bid farewell appears at the top. A difficult day for Gerard with his mother, who insists she is taken home ... But though distracting to our 'way of life' she has doubtless done good by over-toppling or undermining with her desperate psychosis our reason-ruled rigid regimen.

2 December   A much better day in the chess-playing ploy with dear Margaret. She has been both more herself and more docile and has agreed now to go as her offspring wish, to Theresa, near Chichester.

Gerard and I are to stay three nights near the creek at Itchenor, which may be fun.

9 December   Calm and frost glazed all day, sun not absent, sky opalescent touched with fire as day faded. I baked in the morning, returned at long last to Aristotle in the afternoon. Considered with pleasure my postcard picture of Izaak Walton, from the stained glass window in Winchester Cathedral. I have now read all the studies in Simone Weil's *Intimations of Christianity*. She has, I believe, some rare and valuable insights and the passages from the Greek writers are admirably chosen and so set out by her with comments as to make a strong impact. The title *Intimations* I take to be fair, but she often goes beyond this term to force her conclusions, to press her parallels and allegories too close or too hard ... the forerunners are 'motions and incomplete at that' as Aristotle would say. Christ is the consummation and from these later days do we not read back our Christianity into Plato, incomparable as he must always be? Head aswing now with the voice of a boy soprano played on a record Gerard bought in Winchester Cathedral.

10 December   Aunt Dora's birthday and I have by chance as it appears been reading a letter about her by J.C.P. just this moment. Half a dozen letters to *her* mother, Catherine (Bodham Donne), were sent by Mary B. J. to Mother to read because the literary agent Pollinger wants to copy them. Mother herself was much stimulated by this contact with her brother, and became wonderfully animated at twilight tea talking of him, and of other Norfolk cousins.

11 December   A slight rain last night freezing as it fell makes it impossible almost to stand, let alone walk, on the concrete. Still, the day was sunny, I walked in the fields in the afternoon. A small party of larks rose from the slope of Lark Rise; wagtails ran among the frozen clods; a wren sang once its full song. Gerard is reading aloud Izaak Walton's *Lives*, the first is John Donne's. Tillyard said (in the small book on the the Elizabethan World Picture) Donne was not *sure* in his religion as they were, there was a note of doubt. Did he desire by his fervour, this passion of the whole soul he threw into his sermons and other writings, to overpower, to be triumphant over, doubt? Intensity, concentration, the labour of intellectual being ... living to the limit in intellect, take their toll. Then there is the genius for friendship, the gift of winning hearts this Life by a contempary proves.

12 December   Fields white and crusty as if with snow, a reluctant thaw imperceptibly disposed of the rime but left most of the ice, and the 'bone in the ground' below the slippery surface; water in the gateways where yesterday I trod proudly on hard clods. Life of Donne finished, why was he, so eager for his life's end, so actively preoccupied and obsessed by death?

24 December   Eve of four days' holiday. Clear sky tonight, new moon first seen, now Cygnus sinks in the west, all stars shine. Gerard finished the Life of Herbert today and felt he couldn't read the last of Walton's *Lives*. Piety and religiosity can be a surfeit; I have always felt this with Walton. Mother had an evening call from Francis's son and daughter-in-law and her great-great-nephew William. Then Gregorian chants.

25 December   A good Christmas Day, blessed beyond all contradiction with sun from the rising till the setting thereof. Morning cooing of pigeons, afternoon peewits with seagulls in the green fields – thrush, pied wagtail, a pair of yellowhammers, from my window, bullfinch, Jenny wren. Now is to sound *The Creation*; my reading solely in the *Ecclesiastical Polity*;* this I owe to Walton.

29 December   Continuous frost, no more snow. We went to shop in Sturminster for a few minutes; the trees, all trees, in low-lying or riverine fields enchantingly frost-encrusted to the tips of the finest twigs, the Stour motionless pewter colour with ice along the banks, the six arches of the bridge black as holes into nowhere. Considering Stoicism and Christianity ... Mr. Moilliet has sent Mother the journal of her great-great-grandmother Amelia Moilliet to read: 1810–25 about. This she finds to be a patient, painstaking chronicle with all feelings, emotions, excluded except occasional expressions of anxiety for her children or for 'Mr. Moilliet' who was a Swiss banker. On the table before me lies the shagreen-covered slim Book of the Psalms she gave her daughter Amelia, exquisitely inscribed in an Italian hand 'Emily Moilliet from her Mother, Christmas Day 1821'. Doubtless generations of restraint and repressions leave their mark, in more ways than one, on those born in an age of other attitudes and societies. Now and again Amelia confesses to weariness at the huge lengthy dinner parties which must be attended when her mind is under strain, her spirit grieved. In the Goethe – *Selected Verse* – my eye was caught today by this couplet:

> Was vom Christentum gilt, gilt von den Stoikern; freiem
> Menschen geziemet es nicht, Christ oder Stoiker sein.

I wonder. Anyhow, speculation is idle by one who is, in some degree at least, an inbred Christian and Stoic. And what would Goethe himself have 'been' or 'done' without these powerful antagonists to free the world from? He is, I daresay, a 'prophet to the strong' as that character of J.C.P.'s in *Atlantis* regarded himself. Byron also. But what occurs when 'the weak' are liberated by these prophets to the strong is not always (it may be) what they would find agreeable. Gerard has begun to read aloud Lewes's *Life and Works of Goethe*.

30 December   Year's end near, a roaring and soughing wind from the south-east throws rain on the window-panes. In the night I perceived absence of creeping cold, by the end of the morning the snow had vanished, the ice followed. Valentine's cousin, Peg Manisty, called on Mother this morning, attractive, delicate-looking, vivacious. I read Amelia Moilliet in bed and this afternoon Gerard read her journal also, we all feel fond of her.

31 December   Last night there was a final flourish from the year, a fierce hailstorm pelting the black glass of my kitchen window, two blue flashes of lightning with a single roll of thunder between them; silence succeeding the second light flash. Today all dark gray, damp, trees, twigs, stones glazed as with snail slime, a very sombre nocturnal conclusion to dissolve the soul.

1977

21 January, Spring Cottage   Haunted during a somewhat wakeful night by those six hours in Addis Ababa: the appearance of the city and its mixed dusky inhabitants, many in the gayest clothes and in curious contrast to the fifty or so blank-faced identically uniformed Chinese who in speechless rows dominated the airport. This building was unready, all loose sheets of corrugated iron, crooked and scattered notices, smelling of raw cement with forbidding flights of concrete steps both at entrance and exit to the airfield. The hotel where we waited some hours was decorated with crude posters as: 'the land for the tillers', 'the people's militia', 'to defend the land', 'to liquidate reactionaries'. One of the hotel staff ran his hands over every Ethiopian who entered to feel for weapons. 'In a world where everything consists of symbols', I thought as the bus had to reverse to avoid a twisted-off light timber telephone pole with its wires sagging low across the roadway; and further on avoided a traffic control sign lying on its side among the shattered glass of its lamps. Because of street Arabs and haggard-faced starving sellers of local craft objects we looked at Addis, sparkling with recent rain among sunny mottled hills, from the wide open window of the Ethiopian hotel. We left London on Monday night and arrived in Nairobi on Wednesday afternoon, instead of the usual 8 hours non-stop flight. The trouble began at Rome. Here all is shimmering apple-greenery, dancing shadows, carefree birds. A rain-bonus has been given out of season, winged insects and other saw-edged creeping ones are plentiful, the air sings and the 24 hours fall into two neat halves of dark and bright.

22 January Literature: when it is escape, compensation, experience at a safe distance, clarification at the price of simplification, to give direction, to enhance thought, to refract the intolerable white light, to string on one's own song notes, catches, snatches of other birds' metres as sedge and reed warblers, to pass into another world in great literature and to return with a burden a life-bestowing refrain, and in humility. Pleased last evening to watch black cranes and learn their dabchick trill and croak. They are said to line their nest with green leaves.

28 January Fast, says the Lectionary, so I did at noon, Gerard away. I discovered the oriole's nest high above my window, hen sitting, much visited by the musical cock, he perches on the same twig below which, at the tip, the grass-green nest is suspended; he calls, moves along the bough to kiss or give food now and then. Made a poem for this. Signal from Will in the form of the *Nation* with the news that Ian Smith has Shut the Door on further conferences at Geneva regarding Rhodesia. Then, heralded by thunderclap and a shower, Gerard returned and brought me the first letter from Mother to gladden my spirit.

29 January As the rain ceases, 4 p.m., the oriole resumes his cool call, a quiet Saturday afternoon, the child-chorus much diminished. Will's note today asked how he should address the Bishop of Tasmania when he writes to thank him for the account he sent of the Montacute in that island.

30 January 4 p.m. Heavy rain to the west, sunshine over the land to the east, as I sit between two windows in this curious cross-light and turn my head from side to side. My minds runs back over thoughts and fears in a day to be no more. After his life's service to books Gerard confessed today he is no longer enthralled by the ones he was sure he could always return to for succour and pleasure. A pure white egret floated upwards from the waterside of the nearer dam this morn as a diaphanous spirit-bird in its feathery snowy mantle.

31 January Brilliant afternoon, first (almost) since we arrived without shower and thunderheads: so the first month of the year ends, and looking here and there into books with dates, forty or even fifty years ago, I marvel at my long stay on earth, consider age, the dead who are so strong, so incontrovertible in their time and now *pereunt et imputantur or* all or nothing.

1 February Candlemas Eve. Reddening pomegranates hang and swing like Chinese lanterns. Month begun with various non-events as: Kimatai ill with a fever, the faithful house-man; the man who was to come to empty the dip does not come; news of yet another car-theft so that we have sent the pick-up to a shed where it can be locked, which must cause a slight delay. These moonlit nights I often lift my head from the pillow to see if the vehicle is still in its place. Read with a crib Schiller's *Cranes of Ibycus*.

2 February Anniversary of my father's death: recollected with 'full fathom five', and a Marcus Aurelian meditation on the man and what I owe him, the mystery of fatherhood in the Gospels: 'He who sent me, the Father'. A certain regret, he also may have felt, that my mind was not more simply directly West Saxon instead of, even in simple-seeming responses, being aware of employing a complicated inwrought structure (convolutions, he would have said) to 'make' attention immediate and spontaneous. As I wrote 'mind' here, exactly on penning the 'nd' a black-headed flycatcher perched on the open window's notched latch, a clear gaily seen omen, head proudly crested, chestnut-red mantle, even to delicate fringed overlay of feather, sweep of long tail; beheld and flown on the instant. Behold Behold Behold – Old Testament keynote.

3 February Second letter from Mother. I read now my flycatcher is 'fearless' in attacking shrikes and larger birds of prey, so the rush that preceded the epiphany must have been an encounter above, and out of my vision, with shikra or other hawk.

3 March W.E.P. 89. Gerard spent the night under his roof and I went to see him on the veranda at breakfast. He was pale, the feverish flush gone, but without appetite, skin transparent, the skull hollows visible, so little left of him and that so eaten by suffering. Still he had himself propelled into his studio and set about finishing the latest painting of the all-dominant mountain he wishes me to take to Mother. We met

Rose on her way to spend the day with her father as we returned, in a quandary as to what to do for the best, whether a nerve-severance, another amputation, or simply to have him endure as he is. Following my re-reading of *Agamemnon* I find myself defeated by the Aeschylus *Libation-Bearers*, not only by the difficult Greek but more by the brother and sister inciting one the other to vengeance. In reading and presently in leaving, this intolerable three-thonged three-tongued whip Orestes, Chorus, Electra, it seems to me at the human level 'the vengeance is mine', and 'love your enemies' the most important Christian teaching. However little it appears to be heeded, it *must be* within our consciousness, act as we may. I take refuge in the *Fragments*, even more impossible to construe, sharp-edged, tantalising.

5 March 2 p.m. Alone in the airy grass house with leaves fanning, sunbird twitting, white flocks thickening in the blue above, shadows deepening on the bushy hills, I provide this little ceremony for myself and my journal before it goes into the bed of the case. The last bread is eaten, the guest has taken leave, the red lily has opened her first flower. I submit to a sense of suspense, near and far transpose themselves. How can it be:
   now and never
   now and ever
What power 'saves' some impressions, lets others go into the dark backward and abyss of time: it lies at the point of intersection between conscious-unconscious.

8 March, Mappowder Why so desperate a headstorm this warm serene spring evening when the day began joyously with full chorus of bird song and Mother is here and prepared all for me with daffodils in the rooms, tiny posies of primroses with a celandine in each? The acute mood will pass, until then I can only be patient and thankful, think and pray; the drive last night down from London as we left the city lights was below a clear sky with stars, planets, soon moon shining, the roads growing narrow and more deserted. This was something long awaited after a journey of 3 extra landfalls, but which commenced with a particularly clear fine view of Mount Kenya with its lesser companions and foothills. Gerard was unwell on the flight but is now restored. We've been to Sturminster and had tea with Mother in her room.

19 March Still stormy day by day, floods from heaven both as white light and water which, spread over the land in calm meres, reflects the sky as if one lived between a double mirror. As on Sunday we visited the Frome, we concluded the rainy week by visiting the Stour at Hammoon where the bridge divides a straight reach from an S bend: this also was full, turbid, noisy with much white foam churned round and drifting away from the vortex along the green banks. From time to time when a journal is under review in the *TLS* the question is mooted *why* do keep people journals; the question is left or some unsure speculative reply put in: for myself the answer is simple after almost a lifetime of indulging the habit, and remembering Alyse's words about writing: it is, humanly speaking, my salvation. In this current *TLS* is an essay, delivered originally as a lecture to the Slade, on the Sistine Chapel roof, by Edward Leach. I found it valuable, this structurist vision of theology in fresco. But it did not make me 'take to' the work of Michelangelo any more than previously. There is talk now of a possible general election next month if the Government fails to win the vote of confidence on Wednesday; New moon today and clocks advanced one hour.

24 March Day merciful and mild as Mary in mediaeval carol; so calm so tender a light, flowers are still as the stones they grow in the lee of chinks of, primroses amid crinkled moss-green leaves. What is the yardstick or touchstone upon which notions, hopes are tried by querying mind; is it the true nature, unchanging of the questioner: is this trained by experience, or what? Is it rather, for the one born under the sign Libra, an innate balance that gives judgement both for matters proposed by conscience for discrimination, as well as for those weighed unawares? Is pure thought, imponderable and not having place in space, exempt? And prayer: 'the soul's blood ... something understood.'

27 May Sun all day in azure sky, temperature 70 °F again. Air letters from W.E.P. this morning. At noon Rosemary telephoned to tell us her father had died, so there ends another epoch. He must surely have been the last country miller still 'left on life' until today. 'When the fields are white with daisies I'll be there' my father used to repeat: now, so they are. I was thinking last night of Avalon, the many associations with this apple word: with death, with the west, with King Arthur, with my own childhood. I think of Reggie fastening a gold bracelet on my wrist when I was a five-year-old bridesmaid at his marriage.

31 May Cold winds and sunshine, all Queen Anne's lace and white may blossoms as we, Gerard and I, went into Somerset for R.A.P.'s cremation. We drove round Alvington and then went into St. James' church at Preston Plucknet, so it was we followed the hearse into that place; where a notice in the car park said: WAY OUT BY CREMATORIUM. Edith, Rosemary, Bruce, Giles, perhaps half a dozen others unknown to me; somehow I had expected there would be many after Reggie's long life in Somerset. I am odd in the theatrical setting, plush and carpets, coffin on the stage. After brief readings issued into a court full of the sound of water (purification?) which I at first hearing took to be fire crackling: μέγα χαῖρε.* We went back to Sherborne, ordered a book on Birds in Greek Life and Myth. Then ate bread and cheese and onions, 'no cider for me, g'i' I bread wi' eyes in 'en, g'i' I cheese wi' no eyes in 'en, and g'i' I a drop o' good cider to meäke both eyes to spearkle.'

2 June High summer, whitethroats adance above the hedges, the eye of heaven from 5 until 9 in the evening. I read little, there is no need now. Gerard continues faithfully his discipline of walking and reading at the appointed times. *What I could* I read in my honeysuckle bower of the essay on Relativity in the Encyclopaedia; cosmology is most attractive to my mind, the door I batter upon the boundless. Better to listen watch pray. Receive a token for good.

6 June Jubilee holiday, hallooing wind, cold round rain on the pane, curious double horizon formed by a blue band in the grayness, level, parallel with the tipmost bare and leafed twigs of the elm; continuous slight shifts in light intensity; ready to be wilder, a cock seeking the station to crow. Puzzled how it is the physical and psychic emanation or 'recollection' I would have expected from Reggie after his death has, in the last day or so, vanished. I feel after this, I find my father's instead, or perhaps superimposed on that of his youngest brother standing beside whom in life he appeared so diminished. At the same time in these days my spirits have been exceeding low, downed to a new nadir, submerged, rarely rising to inhale life-giving revivifying breaths. There is a natural comparison; the two millers each with an only daughter, the mill-wheel and turbine; waterpower.

11 July Warm summer day bringing silence, almost silence from birds; wren, green and gold finches, enduring omnivorous sparrows, swifts to enchant my soul on the pure luminous brink so imperceptibly protracted into brief night. Yes, as I grow old it is ever more those visions, and sounds, that claim my whole soul, upon which I bend as it were, into which I am momentarily rapt, that become the only fulfilment, unsought though they are, that sustain me by their intensity through what befalls each hour that is undesirable, that makes weariness and anxiety rule over failing spirit, loss of ardour in response.

26 July 'When I look out of the window – or at a landscape –' insisted Delacroix, 'I see no lines.' When a poem forms I see no punctuation marks, the lines infer thoughts, some are distinct aphoristic, others overlap, make small leaps, hesitate on the edge of the unexplored, perhaps the unexplorable? Constant reading of the Bible, in particular the Old Testament, has a way, in recollection, of pulling you up with a jump when the mind is running downhill, refusing to take comfort, as on those dreary *longueurs*, evil rulers and so on, when suddenly a line that is pure poetry, a metaphor that redeems all, is all the more because of what has been passed through before this sharp light, green spray, wing touch.

2 September Unresting wind through the night with dash of rain now and again. I woke clear-headed at 4.15 and made my tea. Now more than two hours later darkness still prevails, the wet wind weeps while robin wakes and trills. A talk last night on Simone Weil, her life, learning and thought; the speaker, Louis Allen, ended by saying 'she is the Antigone of our time'. Were her studies, without the stronghold of the Church, too great a strain for her? He referred (as those who speak and write of Simone always do) to her frequent mention of the poem by George Herbert: 'Love'. 'The soul always exists to some extent in advance of the body', but only of its own body, except in the case of true prophets. The loss of awareness of this 'advance' is one of the modes of temporary despair.

3 September An excellent masterly discourse last evening on *The Myth of God Incarnate* given by a Cambridge theologian Donald Mackinnon who perfectly and politely confuted, not to say annihilated, the seven writers of the book. Gerard heard it also in Sherborne. A most beautiful late summer day with morning mist, sunshine hourly, bland and warm, and with the addition of clear distances, near hillsides, pastures outspread to bathe in the sweet light of the sun.

5 September The Sherborne Powys Society Conference is over, successfully 'they say'. For two days visitors called to see Mother; now this Monday morning Gerard has returned with Glen who is remarkably prosperous and armed with a copy of his newly published book on rural writers.* A work of literary criticism, lively and controlled, dealing with the first 40 years of this century. I like reading of old friends – Henry Williamson, A. G. Street, but a page or two of Whitehead restored my (for some reason) jaded nerves more, as of the New England Puritans 'racked with the intensity of spiritual truths intellectually imagined'?

6 September Dim until day's close when one sun gleam, a wanly lit rift in the clouds to diminish the sense of departure, conclusion, the hesperian melancholy. My crippling ankle was X-rayed in Sherborne by an Irish radiologist who was at school in Skibbereen and knew Union Hall and Castle Townsend well. I felt so delighted to recollect my spells in County Cork. As I left, this gentle therapeutic gray-haired woman added in her soft voice, 'The Irish love a fight.' She had told me before this she 'could not wait' to leave school and come to England fearing the war would be over before she could play her part. Glen has played *his* admirably with each one of us, listening and talking just as was most needed; telling his pranky tales.

26 September Fine, warm, misty sunshine, flawless autumn day with faded earth-hues, deep and royally rich flowers. Silent observations upon age in myself and Mother, heart-breaking to me in her the eternally youthful and childlike; reflections upon unattached suffering being necessary to stimulate intellectual energising. How many parallel 'lives' does a separate human creature experience, moving from plane to plane above the abyss, below the starry heaven, tugged this way and that, flinching, misinterpreting the signals from the soul that is always extended in time and space beyond the body. Late swallows on the wires preening pointed wings.

1 October Opalescent western sky, west wind. I woke with the silently uttered words 'my soul has gone gallivanting', perhaps after reading Dodds on the 'Orphic beliefs' again.* But I thought in the blustery night this fine gallivanting meant (and until I hunted it out in the dictionary) something more like stravaiging. A letter from Will today and one from Rose also who says he has 'done in' his right foot again from too much Land Rovering. The sky grows more aetherially beautiful above the black elm tree, the rooks fly home. Stray swallows still flit by, shy now and hastening, the last slender V's one so longs to see in spring. Considering as I made gingerbread the shame-culture and the guilt-culture: must a culture be always nurtured under such desperate negative passions?

2 October 'A double portion of soul' is the cause, perhaps, for my doing everything I do as if it were a matter of life and death; for my intense seriousness over some matters, and unseemly laughter in other affairs whose worldly importance escapes between the 'souls'. A dream a few nights ago recurs now, a whole crop of that humble weed that grows on soil that has been disturbed but is often of the poorest, Shepherd's Purse namely, presented itself on a sudden upon a dark or black background thickset with silvery stars that were (I fancy) the purse-shaped seed vessels rather than the small cruciform white flowers; anyhow, a pretty spangle of stars on stalks.

9 October   Sunday, Trinity XVIII, was in its moods as moody as I. This morn is clean-washed 'with clear shining after rain', mist and robins, mellow as Keats's poem. My birthday was favourable this year with fine presents and an air letter in the post from Will himself, after one from Rose, writ in case he could not. So now I reassess my quietude, my agreement with the 'pagan' who wrote that 'philosophy consists exclusively in seeking to know God by habitual contemplation and holy piety', and immediately with my well-known greed that wants to be aware of everything 'good' altogether suffer a reaction to the *exclusively* as well as to the *holy piety*. Too much is done in the name of this same 'piety' in the name of religion, whether pagan or Christian, and I am tempted to say it has no part in philosophy which is more strenuous inwardly and cool outwardly.

10 October   'The wind goeth toward the south, and turneth about into the north; it whirleth about continually, and the wind returneth again according to his circuits.' Well, with north wind comes clear weather and at sunset the wind also rests, as the rhyme says, 'on the seabirds' rock in the gleaming west'. I have read at intervals today in Glen's book on the rural novel, finding most interest in the general analysis at the beginning and in the epilogue. I recognise myself in 'the emotional response to nature' which certainly is not enough to make a novel. Also in Iris Murdoch's study *The Fire and the Sun*, Plato's 'writing is a drug'.

11 October   'Each in its grave until'; my bulb planting this warm and dry weather continues, and there are still many more to have small graves prepared for them. Last evening in a high wind with despair at heart I cut off the sword leaves from strong iris clumps that spread from their corners into the open beds. No accounting for the woe, or this day's unharassed mood. But O dear, reading about T.F.P. in Glen's book, how little of himself emerged from this account of his writings which would all (by me) be willingly foregone for an hour's company and converse.

13 October   Firefinch's feather fled from the last page of my chronicle. I should stick them in, my pet feathers, but I like to discover their attitudes when I open the book as indexes of my mood, as signs whether another has opened it. Many mosquitoes drift about the room, my very eyelids are midge-bit, a pair of brimstone butterflies by a warm hedge fed on herb robert flowers.

19 October   Rainy unlit morning, St. Luke's summer ended with his Day, on which Gerard drove me into Somerset to see Mr. Madden at Chilthorne Domer. We stopped at Avalon Garage to ask for his house, and waited pleasantly in sunshine by an old butterfly-haunted wall, an old oak gate looking across the Vale. Sunshine soon caught gold among leaves on high, leaves strewn in green. As with my knees, my halt foot is caused by arthritis. I received in the ankle bone an injection of cortisone which caused a painful wakeful night but is eased now. It seems I must limp while I walk over the broad-wayed earth. I suppose Jacob had arthritis, too much walking and sleeping on the ground. I kept recalling in the night the words of the Cheshire man when the naturalist investigating the meres, 'flashes', or ancient salt-mining lakes, enquired the depth of two that were near – 'that one ain't got no bottom and t'other be deeper still'. Were I an African instead of a sceptic I should believe myself cured by the *shindano*.*

22 November   The earliest ray as the sun rose touched Mother's face as she came into the room for breakfast, and this morning sun shone till noon when November gray took over the sky. Now there is moonshine in thin vapour, and a fire burns in her room where she is with Francis and Sally who have come to wish her many happy returns of her eighty-seventh birthday – which is graced by a new painting of Mount Kenya by Will with flamingo tinted clouds, as even here appeared before sunrise. Gerard took her for an afternoon drive over Bulbarrow.

24 November   Wind month continues, with all but undeviating Boreas, keenly piercing yet without frost so that the leaves, denuded of colour, must be torn off, frayed and fluttered off; many remain whirled round on stalks the new buds thrust at. More letters from Will this morning. I continue to reflect on the I AM spoken by God, since I read (in Rist) to say 'I am' is a limitation; how then, if God is infinite? 'Be still and know that I am God.' Fear not: Ἐγώ εἰμι.* Never can I read those two Greeks words without an inward throb or shudder, an intellectual start, and with that: all is well.

30 November   Most gray gloom-laden finis to a sunny month, the November nature pressed together for St. Andrew's Day. Gerard departed for Sussex in the morning: for me a preparation for his flight to East Africa next week, Friday 9 December. Yes, this breathless day must be the one on which Theodore said you can feel the year die, and what an odd thing it is that our ears grow with our years. So deep a hush so obscure a tenth hour of light.

1 December   Day windless and warmer. Gerard will return tomorrow he told me last evening. I took Mother along the lane in soft sunshine. The afternoon post brought me a letter from Louise describing her apartment in the Rue St. Claude ... 'the bells for the first Advent service woke me this morning'. I retyped 'A Double Initiation' and wrote a second Maenad poem.

2 December   Ll.P. 1939. Wind, after so long a time, returns to the southeast, cold but not frosty, sunshine in the afternoon. I listened last night to discourses about Communist China with its 800,000,000 inhabitants. At 2 p.m. I took my loaf of bread from the oven and Gerard returned. His mother is restless again and urged him to take her away from the Home at once. This made it more difficult for him when he visited her. I am reading again Armstrong's *The Architecture of the Intelligible Universe*.

3 December   Darkest day, mere traces of red in the eastern cloud banks to mark sunrise; east wind strong and noisy all the sullen hours soon swallowed by night. I baked a good gingerbread to warm my spirits (or 'cockles') and typed a few poems for Christmas greetings. Read some lines from Charlie's *Republic*,* and looked at a catalogue of late Roman Art 300–700 AD. Somewhat shadowed by Gerard's leavetaking next Friday ... this day next week he'll be at his own better loved cottage.

4 December   Wicked wind from the east to shrivel flesh and spirit, fierce by day, somewhat mitigated after dark, as yesterday when after the overcast murky sky all the stars shone forth. Grieved by many things and with a turmoil in my breast I keep quiet and (as I am able) pray.

6 December   The hummingbird's feather has quitted my journal now, as the fire finch's, and it is more than half a year since I have heard from Cathy who sent it. This day is surely the darkest most drizzly the year has brought forth in its age, its dying age, but the wind has altogether died. Being so far down in the Powys tree and having no offspring gives me, as I age, a sense sometimes of both freedom and finality, a detachment not painless it is true, in ache and sudden stabs exceedingly painful, but at the level of consciousness without grief now, or regret. I marvel continually at the intense egoistical devotion Mother has to all her 'little things', to her still certain knowledge of each possession and its whereabouts: the tone of deep and quavering feeling with which she declares she has *decided to give away* 'when I was awake in the night' some precious book that she would 'dearly love to read'. It is an experience being companion to someone who has lived so many human years and retained so childlike a look, and a response so different from mine to the condition of being a living creature. This transitory world is as real to her as it was in the beginning.

9 December   Beneficent healing sunshine, from the very storm embossed rising until towards noon the sky became, with blue spaces, beclouded ... 2 p.m. with north-east wind rearing clouds thickening and travelling with firm outlines and smoky dull ones over-riding these. At 1.30 after we had walked together to the church and he'd shown me the lion's footprint* in a flagstone, Gerard went off with Mr. Clarke to Heathrow. Until Mother wakes I stay alone with a considerable sense of pleasant intercourse ended and that acute mingling in the pit of the stomach of tension and release that goes with partings.

20 December   Surely those who lead quiet lives, even without the 'quiet mind' prayed for in the collect, should be thankful for the enhancement of evanescence: otherwise the necessary routine that work calls for, or the very preservation of life (in those hobbled or confined by sickness) could become an intolerable monotony. The exquisite memories, enchantments, poetry in painfully sharpened responses, all depend on fleeting time *because* they 'contain' all the before and after. That *is* their poignancy.

21 December   Raw cold; becoming perpendicular rain in afternoon. First air mail from Gerard came yesterday. The holly tree down the road shining stilly with painted globes, so to take the eye when no stars appear. St. Thomas's Day who, as Homer says, must 'see with his eyes', or as Plotinus, 'touch'. As Rist says, Plotinus favours *presence*, and the living presence, the voice, put away Thomas's doubts. There is in the air a radiance that can be named goodwill, Hope.

Christmas Eve   Awesome gales all the night through, until I was certain the world-ship was blown off course, and raised my head to see the whirligig yew and cypress trees, for the new full moon kept an opaque illumination. Ships along our shores wrecked or aground, crews perishing in mountainous seas: Christmas supplies not to reach the lighthouse keepers, so ran the first news. Today there was living blue sky, coloured and shapely clouds; at last the wind jumped to north-west, before dusk was lost the moon shone forth beside Jupiter so the light altered, became more clear; there is no dark. More visitors in and out to see Mother through the day. We listened to singing and lessons from King's College.

25 December Strangely still and warm, bird song on either hand as Mother and I went to church for the Holy Communion service at 8 a.m. The weather is as it were overcome or subdued by its previous violence now and then as a ghost a thin wind passes. At mid-day I started a fire at my rubbish heap, and spent one hour later tending it with no extra clothing from what I was wearing indoors, so balmy the air is. The first news this day was the death of Charlie Chaplin, one of the greatest entertainers (surely) this world has seen. He was eighty-eight. I do so little, the days go so gently by, yet I am mostly weary and often impatient too. Unnecessary tribulation, and what Whitehead calls 'objective immortality' (for I returned to *Process and Reality* this afternoon) may be part cause; and today, the sacrifice of praise and thanksgiving.

29 December How can these things be, is what I mainly say when I look out; out of the inky window, for instance, at lit windows over the way, down the street at the toy Christmas tree with less shining coloured balls in the glass vestibule. The mystery of selection and pre-selection in each one can (I think, after reading the essay on Free Will) never be explained. It does seem to be decided for one: what in one's life is taken for granted, is too universal or too trivial to receive unconscious attention; what is accepted what regarded with horror or incredulity. How can the mind so swing between intensity and indifference? Be so determined to deal with its ingrained sense of guilt by all the life-saving equipment it can devise?

30 December Jupiter rules the night rising at dusk huge, luminous, cold; tremulous in the raging winds as the Holly Tree globes, and his intense lamp narrowing near the elm tree as the dayspring's white light leans across the zenith. Isobel returned from Yorkshire this evening with her small granddaughter; it pleased me to see this other brown-eyed Lucy kneeling at Mother's side to show the bird calendar she had made for a present. I saw logs and chop dead wood, too long left to decay, under the ash tree in the sunny wind-swept afternoons. I have glimpses of thrilling dreams that dissolve as I wake as hoar-frost in fire.

1978

16 February Snow fell in the night so we woke to a white world, four to six inches; so it chose to float secretly silently, to lighten our nocturnal darkness. Letters from W.E.P. and from Gertrude, who, after two successful exhibitions and sales of pictures, is going to Katmandu on the 25th. On the wall before me appears an infinitesimal gray moth, appears from where, below the Samuel Palmer August landscape – sheaves in moonlight and the evening star? The holly tree at the left side of my window is so Decemberly decorated with clots of snow, the yew opposite laden, Mother's myrtle bowed to the ground. Dorset (says the news) is the snowiest south county.

17 February Deeper snow after another fall at night; sparkling and blue in sunlight all day, neither thawing nor freezing. The snow-plough went up the road. Peggy Mahuzies brought Mother a branch of wattle in full flower and daffodils, so the little room is lit with yellow. The children pass with toboggans, in red jackets and round gay caps. Gerard saw them pelting a snowman with balls.

18 February Day most inimical to all life, no sun, no thaw, frozen snow on all the ground but, by a howling east wind, dislodged from the trees where yesterday it appeared to be an adornment. A most sinister mixture this evening light, between black and white, difficult to adjust the sight to, the customary mind-responses are distracted as the eerie radiance rises from below to a blank glowering heaven. I read today a review of a new book on brain and mind by a philosopher and neurophysicist. Of course thought and science must (as best they may) keep abreast; still I have a notion they do not thrive at such close quarters as this. The workings of brain and mind in these two hemispheres are unlike, except in Aristotle.

19 February Snowed in. All night the powdery snow flew and piled into mounds and mountains, dunes of snow higher than the windows, rarely and frighteningly sculptured, suspended over nothing, arched like sculptured or frozen waves, Henry Moore abstracts. Almost all day there is snow in the air whirled up in clouds from below, sifted down from the opacity above. The afternoon Gerard spent in baling snow out of the roofs of both cottages – 20 or 30 pailfuls I must have tipped out of the window. At tea-time the air thickened moment by moment until again it is stuffed with flakes turning every way, all agog again to fill our roof loft.

20 February   Months, one feels, one has been 'cut off' or 'snowed in'. However there is no great coldness, no freezing by day, no more falls after last night's session of freezing window-scraping rain, no violent wind or gusts. My heart misgives me for Mother, so weary now, frail and suffering and unable to see, and I know I am often rough, try as I will, impatient. Thousands of farm animals (they reckon) must have died, many more will follow. And there is the horror of throwing away hundreds of pounds worth of milk. A few villagers have walked to Hazelbury (3 miles) to buy bread.

21 February   Stillness and warmth; birds awoke to trill, coo, saw-sharpen before the ardours of food-hunting begin again. Early, while the village was still deserted, Gerard and I walked to see the snow dunes lifted above the hedges, perilously scaped, scooped in on themselves. Soon the sound of a multitude of shovels arose, blocks of weightless whiteness accumulate on either side of the road. The farmer from the Walnut Tree said as he passed he had two thousand gallons of milk waiting to be collected. A speckled missel-thrush perched on the holly tree among prickly leaves and snow clots yesterday afternoon, and after resting took the last withered berry and flew on.

22 February

> *There is fallen snow*
>
> snow has fallen
> and it's not the season
> someone throws balls at me
> my track is all snowed in
>
> my house has no gable-ends
> it's grown old about me
> the window-panes are broken
> my little room is cold
>
> ah love have pity on me
> that am so sorrowful
> and clasp me in your arms
> while winter goes its way

(From the German anon. 16th–18th Cent.)

Ever-spreading green in blocks and pools as I look from my vantage-point. Young and old red-cheeked red-nosed go down the road armed with spades and shovels. Up the road men on foot, the postman with heavy bag; our neighbour with a plastic sack full of white loaves of bread visible through its transparent side on his shoulder stepping stoutly; then an older man with a close-packed buckled-up workman's knapsack on his back more bowed and weary from his tramp to the grocers: all scenes and hues heightened in the unwonted flat upturned light. Snatches of bird song, one cutty wren doubling round the dark trunk of the warrior; stray peewits course the sky wanderingly, while starlings run over from a different quarter; the elm beautiful.

25 February Snow all but gone save the banks made by the snow-plough; snowdrops reappear and multiply in the mild rainy air. Birds begin anew, some new since the blizzard; chaffinch, blackbird, misselthrush, hesitant and infrequent trail strains. A certain dinginess in the light after dazzle and transfiguration; the Stour, mighty, sullen, foam-flecked, overflowing low-lying lands along the banks.

1 March All mad March should be: wind, soft rain, sun; tender new radiance upon trees and downlands; my singing birds ... On the lower road to Dorchester at one point snow was still being scooped up and transported on high in bright blocks. Penetrating rain at Chilthorne, a wait in the dark; Mother went with us. I saw the doctor was tired, kinder than last time. He suggested therapy at Sherborne Hospital when I refused an operation, to 'set' the ankle joint. Seagulls tumbling about the sky with pure mastery above the flooded Puddle.

2 March Within this cloud perfect stillness, round drops remain where they have formed on twigs, rain is inaudible, snowdrops are white pools in greenness; they are calm again, yesterday's warmer airs were not welcome; the narrow ellipses opened wide as though their hour ended. To live without 'spending' life is one mode of hidden inwardness, reducing the cost of the outer 'actor's life' that the force may be energy for intellect, consciousness. Letters came from Will in the twilight afternoon, well-timed as ever for us, and on the eve of his ninetieth birthday.

8 March Frost finished, wind west, sunshine in the afternoon when I started a bonfire and felt warm. The ivy crackled splendidly and sent leaves as black ash up into heaven, resembling the ash from burnt letters; the winter roosting-places, the nesting quarters of many birds, toppled over in the gales, disappeared as a trunkful of old letters. Yesterday I had my first treatment in the Yeatman Hospital 'gymnasium'.

9 March Severely gray, east wind. My ankle is more painful from trying to take off on the heel instead of the ball; left-handed left-footed

I cannot change to the right. A good strong letter arrived from Will describing his ninetieth-birthday guests, and the iced cake like a Merino ram which Rose had had made for him.

23 March 'I wield the flail of the lashing hail, and whiten the green plains under, and then again I dissolve it in rain, and laugh as I pass in thunder.' But this morn's storm, dense pea-size white stones, took long to dissolve so cold the wind so hail-cold the candid sunlight. Proud-spirited letters from W.E.P. in reply to mine. I wrote I'd decided that the only thing to deal with arthritis or joint-evil is will-power and that with him as godfather I *should* have a double share. The later day sun is bright but the hardy children go by proving the wintry blasts by their anorak hoods tied down and resembling small cowled monks.

24 March Good Friday. Daisies bask on a green bank a little while, clouds re-cover the sky, wind continues but less shrill by evening. I think of Sylvia, ill and much alone as day darkens, wonder whether she calls, Valentine answers. Words in mind from the appointed readings, 'a new and living way'; a recollection of the red flowers at the foot of El Khalil I praised in a poem one Good Friday long ago;* the words make clear all that wind, heat, landscape, yet now I reluct, revolt at the multitude of words, turn away from men's huge labour with words, become more silent in my need, but not less anxious, nor inwardly angry ...

1 May I woke at the window open to morning mist, to a cuckoo calling, began to think of spring. Rain soon came with the north-east wind, and ceased not through all the glooming daylight hours, never ceased, though all afternoon a blackbird sang – clear cajoling certain phrases with meaning drawn from the heart, direct from bird heart to my heart. The news came then that Sylvia Townsend Warner died last night, between April and May ceased to be Sylvia.

2 May Equally wet and dim and gray, and that obscure yesterday did not end without other sad news from Rosemary: that her mother now is lost in her head, does not know her, talks of the 'other Rosemary' or says 'I never had a child'. This losing of the other, the trusted response and life-long reciprocity before the bodily death is especially felt as a menace to all loving human relations which begin to assume a total unreality as though life were rendered vain throughout; we cannot tutor ourselves in advance for this dilemma.

4 May Ascension Day. Meek and subdued, moist with weak whistlings and twitterings after a sunny day when we all felt warm, growth surged; blackthorn so newly white at once begins to scatter; cherry blossom present in silence, mind lifts and sinks before the gates of inexorable Hades that open with spring-flowers to take in another. How the hair-splitting continues; matter is reckoned unendingly complex with always more named and invisible parts, and for philosophers language is the same. What is to hold after analysis ...

14 May Gerard is again afflicted with thrombosis, a particularly deep and painful one. After a bad night we drove to Cerne Abbas to collect medicine from the doctor there. A soft showery West of Ireland morning, banks lined with bluebells and one chalk steep above the road studded with small cowslips which gave my spirit a quick lift for now too rare, too rare are Cumnor cowslips. In the afternoon I baked a loaf of bread and read some essays in *Theology*, notably a writing on Auden, and on nuclear power, how this will, or will not, kill nature, for future generations or end men of human speech themselves. The blackbirds' voices are liquid as rain.

16 May Befogged heavenly. Theology is the sport, the athletics of religion, without this intellectual strenuousness the pleroma as experienced in worship and praise becomes rule, rite, sentiment, emotional release, self- or muscular-righteousness: sententious? Beflagged and bedewed earthly. Mist fills the atmosphere as if the illusory aether were just discernible to the glassy eye.

5 June 'Life is full of obstacles, Mrs., full of obstacles.' The bitumen painter eyed me in a way that was equally friendly and crafty. My heart assented completely after a difficult day ankle-wise and with a headache. 'You know that shed of yours I painted two or three years ago? I could do him again.' 'I think he's alright for a while,' I said. The painter accepted this with resignation. He had anyhow spent the day working on barns. 'Hard work,' I said. ''Tis,' he agreed with feeling. We parted in low spirits, pondering obstacles.

7 June Fine cool blowy morning, thrush on the tree pinnacle, eye running up the green incline lifts this fresh hue to the dead elm instinctively tinging it with life. The word of the prophet Ezekiel goes well with June's high sunlight as I read my mind still imbued with the afternoon's study, which was the concluding section of the *Republic*, the soul's bliss. Charlie's copy with his marginalia to sustain me; I shall read again the tenth book, and Taylor's Commentary. Considering Mr. Trundle's sermon two evenings ago on the theme of not having time to converse with God, all life being busy and bustling, over-filled with activities which however necessary and 'virtuous' are designed to leave no energy for prayer and meditation, and where (it may be) the remnants of the Christian guilt sense are used to keep up the rush, I observe now to myself he said nothing of preparing a space for prayer or quiet thought by that most ancient practice, most Stoic and Christian, curtailing sleep.

8 June   An especial penance for a poet is a lame foot, perpetual painful reminder, verses limp also. I won a faint wintry smile from Margaret last evening; soft summer rain fell, streets and Abbey empty, only in some recess boys practising familiar hymns on a piano touched the dim vaulting as from another epoch. I visited Wyat in the Horsey chapel, and also the one of the Holy Sepulchre. Gerard and I both felt desolate in mood. Cuckoo this windy morn in the now thin-leafed ash tree.

10 June   Gerard saw an aged man being guided down the church path by a woman who asked whether he could show her Theodore's grave. This was Jack Clemo,* the Cornish poet, deaf and dumb and later become blind also. Jack felt the tombstone with his fingertips and said, according to his wife and interpreter, Ruth, 'It does not say he was an author.' She communicates things to him by writing words, letter by letter, in the palm of his hand with her index finger. They are staying with Ruth's sister at Rodwell above Weymouth, quite close to Thornloe school where, half a century ago, I spent two years. Today Gerard brought Jack Clemo and the two women here and he is now, I hope, on his way home from Weymouth. Francis was with Mother so the poet who had such an admiration for T.F.P. was able to have an encounter with his son. Clemo can read Braille and he types his poems key by key on a typewriter. He has to be reassured by constant contact with Ruth who appears to be full of energy, but she admitted she was glad of her one day 'off' a fortnight when a foster-sister of Jack's takes charge. North wind, the dryness grows unfriendly but well-rooted plants flourish in the deep down moisture.

15 June   Seagulls return to inland arable, I saw many on the green convex roof of a Dutch barn. The chaffinch, like Tweedledum, is losing his rattle. I bought *Frequencies* in Dorchester, by R. S. Thomas, a new collection. I read the bleak little poems under the honeysuckle, short lines that break off to make a mark, to startle, several do hit the mark; one man's mind within the perennial theme. Gray day by day and not warm, dry and dewless. Frequencies Intensities ...

2 July Most gray day, blowy with wind shifting from east to west. After two days I leave off leaf-cutting, read Nicoll, copy three Κίρκος poems* for Peter ... Κίρκος – a kind of hawk or falcon, which flies in wheels or circles: a circle, ring. They begin with the kestrel picture for June, continuing with the hosts of migrant kestrels from Siberia and northern Asia in Kenya, and conclude with a kestrel that crossed my window space and a fox below, quitting the aftermath at the field's far corner.

22 July A long long sunset-twilight I looked upon last evening from the foot-end of my bed; presently in the opposite quarter with a fire-glow rose the moon, one day past the full, huge behind the regimented row of beech trees upon Bulbarrow ridge. The top arc appeared as a mushroom, a yellow fairy toadstool rather above the meagre wind-thinned tree summits. Mary Magdalene, Mappowder fête, scarlet swing-boats, thumping music a loudspeaker voice across the meadow.

3 September Trinity xv. And this morning I entered for the first time Holy Trinity church, Bothenhampton, of which I've heard all my life from my father, for John Hounsell,* Nellie's father, gave the ground, a steep southward sea-ward facing slope, on which this strong structure was built in 1888. So like Will it is ninety years old this year. New dwellings in shimmering shoals have rushed upon it, but as it happens the view from the porch contains a stone barn wall on a green hillside; and in the peak of the roof a swallows' nest – even thine altars O Lord of Hosts. All grave-stones have been swept away, only a pair of brass plates neat and modest on the inside south wall of the church give the names of John Hounsell, for 30 years church warden, and Pamela Mary, his wife. 'His word was his bond' they said of this miller. Mother recalled he acted as pall-bearer to a near kinsman and strained himself in this labour of love and never recovered from this injury. The new Pope blesses ...

13 September Complete cloud cap all day, north-east wind. Gerard is attacked again by phlebitis, two days before the long anticipated Powys Conference weekend in Weymouth. He is busy the last few days preparing a writing for it, as two lecturers have announced they will not give their talks. I picked plums climbing into the tree, reaching out, drawing the pliant laden branches towards me. I made jam and then picked more to stew and give away; and the while I pondered on Thomas à Becket. Under the willow tree with blue tits overhead and a softly singing willow-wren I read some chapters of David Knowles's biography. What an inexhaustible theme for drama the course of this archbishop's life is; he is even now most powerfully animate.

15 September   Warm sunny afternoon when I rested between two willows and read the final chapters of *Becket*; later the summary of his life in the Encyclopaedia. The more I read of his story the sadder it grows: a man so alive the plain scholarly biography quivers to the hand with the archbishop's energy. At the end there is nothing in the way of judgement to be said because he is touched with reality. Gerard went off this afternoon to Weymouth for the Powys Society Conference.

21 September   On this day not impossible to say, 'Be still and know', so calm the air, such a benedicite the benevolent sun stranding the misty atmosphere; all life, one has the sense, has slowed upon the brink of fulfilment, and for an amber spell looks not before or after. A letter came from Rose this morn writ in part by her father, some of his wavering lines clear, some not to be deciphered, the meaning unsure.

2 October   One of those days of distresses in calm, with morning mists and dim recurrent sunshine ... A delayed letter from Rose – writ on 18th of last month – tells of Will sleeping his life away painlessly. Naturally each letter on this theme lowers Mother's vitality, the bright flashes of her old self are more brief and at longer intervals, brave as she is. The Italian people and papers are questioning the Pope's death, talking of poison – as in far-off days of the papacy, and demanding an autopsy. I wonder whether from loneliness he took his own life. Then Callaghan the Prime Minister here has been outvoted more than 2 to 1 by his own party and the Trade Unions on his 5 per cent pay policy. I refrain from continuing with other minor disturbances. On the right side Kath worked steadily and hard in the garden.

4 October   Night. We saw the sun set far in the west over the sea. Rose telephoned at 9 o'clock to say Will had just died; she was with him, and wanted Gerard to ring the school in Scotland for the boys to know. He spoke to the wife of the headmaster who had stayed at Kisima, and seen W.E.P. 'She sounded quite upset' he said. I shall tell Mother tomorrow, with a memory of Marian's words, 'what a thing to be the last Powys'.

> The loud wind never reached the ship,
> Yet now the ship moved on!
> Beneath the lightning and the Moon
> The dead men gave a groan.
>
> Sometimes a-dropping from the sky
> I heard the sky-lark sing;

> Sometimes all little birds that are,
> How they seemed to fill the sea and air
> With their sweet jargoning!
>
> And now 'twas like all instruments,
> Now like a lonely flute;
> And now it is an angel's song,
> That makes the heavens be mute.

5 October   Calm and gray with fiery banner in the west as day fades out, and in the other quarter in the garden a single poppy, a single small rose, both salmon pink. Gerard drove us to Montacute this evening, a pilgrimage to the Tower with a golden cock on the top facing west. Mother went to the graves, and Bertie's stone. Presently the tenor bell began to toll, a passing bell for Will; the full peal is to be rung later. Gilfrid telephoned this morning to remind us of this; his father had written about 2 years ago to the head ringer to make his request. I was glad to hear Gilfrid's voice perfectly clear. Gerard enters, leans his stick in the corner.

6 October   Honeyed sunny autumn day, G.M.P.'s birthday, Will's burial. We all went to Sherborne in the evening; for a little while Mother was glad to be inside the Abbey walls, after sitting in the nave and asking me to repeat Wyat's epitaph – Wyat rests here that quick did never rest – she also went on to the chapel of the Holy Sepulchre which is dedicated to Silence. Outside again we sat on two small stone niches on either side of the porch, still warmed by the sun, as the mainly used door is on the south side of the building: as if we were two lions, as she said. So dry is it I see the whistling 'lion' across the way watering his garden with an infinitely tender sunset beyond.

7 October   Stars at dawn, sunshine, but the east wind is more in evidence than the north-west was. Chiff-chaffs still haunt the garden, even whisper their name. Gnats and mosquitoes in plenty sing and whine, perform their dances, ascending descending as the angels by Jacob but never going too far on the way up and the way down, which is the same, we are told. Gerard began to gather Mother's bramleys in the pleasant afternoon sunshine. My spirits are low, whether from reaction delayed, or from the experience of my first birthday without my godfather.

8 October   New risen sun shone on Mother's face as she came to the breakfast table, was hid then in cloud and mist for two hours, but most of the day proved pleasantly warm and sunbathed. Gerard devised a birthday present for me and drove us to West Bay between the hills covered with sheep. The wind was strong from the south-east, the painted craft rocked in the harbour and Mother seemed much refreshed by this excursion to the edge of the misty deep. Kath gave me a card (as well as tulip bulbs) with a line upon it by Coleridge: 'joy rises in my heart as the summer sun'.

10 October   Golden weather, turning trees in Sherborne breathtakingly lovely. Chiff-chaffs still in the apple trees and swallows overhead. We all three at certain times find it not easy to be brave ... unlike Haydn with his irrepressible cheerfulness whenever he thought of God. My green and blue hummingbirds on cards please my eye whenever they catch it, and the sunshine is a blessing.

11 October   To Dorchester under a golden canopy, a glory, where the tall beech trees tower by the wayside, a triumphal arch. Warm sun all day so I could stay between the willows for an hour or two. Apple-picking, and the high pile of bush I call Will's pyre twice relit is low now in ash and red incandescence after crackle and sheets of flame. I read aloud to Mother the letters from friends, beginning with Rose's writ the day before her father's burial, saying how fine he looked, and she would not want to part with him as he lay on the bed 'on which I think you all were born'. She told of the cedar wood coffin Will had had made fifteen years before, which they had lined with prize fleeces just back from the Nairobi show. And she added they would lay Joey, his faithful dog, at his feet; a Homeric tale to be followed by a funeral feast?

7 November   Sun from rising till early afternoon, most delicate yellow paling into cloud white; November dullness followed dissolving with darkness into a scattering of rain. East wind all day blowing. Gerard went off to South Wales by train. I read *Sursum Corda*, introduction and epigrams, and rediscovered the Loeb volume of the Greek Anthology given me by Uncle Jack, where he wrote $\dot{\alpha}\lambda\lambda\dot{\alpha}\ \varkappa\alpha\grave{\iota}\ \H{\epsilon}\mu\pi\eta\varsigma$.* Well, I started life with ten uncles and now I am left with one; who would have guessed Uncle Ernest* would have out-lasted them all? His head when I first remember him was perfectly bald. Measures to conserve water in the west of England being announced today.

11 November   Fog and mist until moonrise. New every morning is the love, life perhaps, for a journal; for a poem 'one of those rare black swans': is this why it is so hard to turn my hand to one, to turn one?

We met Gerard at Pen Mill Station yesterday at 2, he was content with his visit to South Wales.

16 November   Nights limpid in moonlight give way now to thumping winds, rain scuds, grim darkness. The last weather-stained apples crash, some split in half. Today we hear that the Sherborne clock-mender, who dwelt in his small ancient stone-built shop as a long ago craftsman, has died suddenly. Mother and I heard Walton's anthem 'Set me as a seal on thy heart'.

17 November   Friday. Tonight, this wild windy night, the Montacute bells are to ring out their peal for W.E.P. at 7 p.m. Friday night, Mother recalls, was always the one when the ringers practised. All autumn, you might say, is hung upon this troubled darkness. I have been reading again the valuable introduction to the Select Epigrams – *Sursum Corda* – by J. W. Mackail: 'behind the feeling there is now thought, the power which makes and unmakes all things.' May the bells ring upon the mountain, the seal, the signature.

22 November   Wondrous warm, gentle airs, the close together outgoings of morning and evening rejoice in long horizon bands in unshining gold. Mother is taking pleasure in presents and guests on her eighty-eighth birthday, at certain moments her face is radiant – the shocks and cares of so long a beholding the light of the sun gone in delicate emotion. The childlike qualities in the old are enhanced as her height grows less, a figure, one could fancy, beginning life. A small, silver-fronted, earth-brown-backed bird was shown me today, so long unseen, all but gone from mind. A tree-creeper suddenly flitted to the base of an apple tree and worked its way upwards with many turns and alert observances.

26 November   Sunday before Advent: first, for this autumn, ice and fields white (but not unto harvest); splendour of lights at daybreak, Venus a lamp on cypress point, crescent moon, Jupiter, Mars, Saturn. A good day for me, dare I boast, for general well-being, even a bit less 'foot-capped'. A fine missel-thrush at the window to peck coral-red berries; a blackbird puffed out on the wall with orange tawny beak waiting to take his feast.

18 December   Frost and fog, but presently weak sunshine upon the cold ground, the twiggy trees. More increases in oil prices to start New Year's Day. Gerard read aloud a page or two to me from one of my journals writ in the 1950s; not even a ghostly Mary seemed to come from the words – to me – another life, another writer. Curious to be so untouched by something into which I must have poured my then-reality.

1979

12 February Wake to white downiness over all, especially caressing twigs and 'tressy yew'. Haunted snow stillness over all the earth with slow diminishing as the day wanes of the mystic whiteness under the heavily charged unmoved heaven. A new drama, were there an Aeschylus to compose it, another *Persae*, is surely present in the desperate state of Iran. *Nothing* else could give meaning to anything so anarchic and laden with horrors past and to come.

16 February R.G.H.P. The desire for new being, for new modes of being, leads to the birth of a child, but, I have lately thought, what is most needed is new Being, some change, shift or transformation in the Nature of Being. Yet, would, or could, mankind conditioned as it is by time ἐξ ἀρχῆς* be aware, be able to recognise a hitherto unknown, unexperienced Being? A minister for Snow, or Snowman, has been appointed since the whole island is now snowed over more or less deeply from a few inches to 18 foot drifts; villages and whole areas are cut off, roads impassable in some parts ... The break with instinctive inherited apprehensions – instead immediacy or pure intellectual vision.

17 February A lifetime reading the Bible causes me to ask now at this late date in my pilgrimage 'here below' as they say, whether there is any room in all the many and varied Books for the concept of happiness, εὐδαιμονία* even. Perhaps this is a kind of reality for which there is no place in the Hebrew consciousness, because it is unattainable. Woe and lamentation, praise and thanksgiving, hatred of enemies, worship of God, between which the Psalmist sways, can be acted, and no doubt the hatred of enemies was spontaneous and, as we would have it, genuine emotion. Indeed the mental attitudes enjoined by St. Paul, as well as the obedience to the Law, can be recognised, respected, to some small degree assumed or practised. The 'joy' permitted to be experienced at certain events is not the fulfilment of the inmost soul's longing for happiness: even that response of the whole being to be good, that Aristotle speaks of, that activity directed to the Good, is not happiness. Nor is it pure contemplation, could that be, for a living soul. Perhaps addiction to Bible reading for me, apart from inherited instincts and a feeling for the deep and sometimes overpowering poetry is a way of escape from the trivial by preordained unoriginal uncritical concentration.

24 February The solitariness of every human soul, known to Coleridge according to Mary Moorman – the alone to the alone – tinged my nocturnal or sleep-waking meditation last night. You rouse with something like a 'visionary word' which continues presenting itself in a clear sense that is neither seen nor heard, presented with strong but colourless meaning upon the dark of the mind partaking with nature's night: something like the perfect separateness of each human being in sleep: subjectivity is happiness, kept being insisted.

6 April Frost fog, smoky sunlight at intervals through the obscure hours; no celandines have caught my eye in the hedges as I pass them in the car but they shine among primroses in the small bowls in Mother's room. Charles Lock called yesterday afternoon, he is a member of the Powys Society and a post-graduate research student at Oxford. He lately visited Athos, and told of the monks and the 10 monasteries. Among all the Greek-speaking religious he met only one English man who, curiously, came from Dorset, or had visited this part with his father who was an admirer of J.C.P. Charles Lock himself is preparing a thesis on Uncle Jack: he lives at Moreton not far from our dear Charlie Smith. The thoughts that present themselves in words at night, often quite clearly, and which I purpose to record here are always gone when I come to write yet leave a flavour that consoles my mind.

12 April All impulses destroyed by observation – no more to be said to myself or another – total dryness, bitterness, emptiness, what could be hatred, but this is gently, with all else, repressed. Real spring weather, strong wind, sun, too white, too harsh, undoing life.

2 May Coldest start to May on record, fierce north wind, several mini snowstorms with large flakes, hail and rain in scuds. But sun is more generous in light and clear rays if not in heat than yesterday. We passed gypsies on the move this morning with two vans, one painted ox-blood red, piebald horse, lurcher dog running by the wheel, several goats on board, standing and wearing coats. Election eve, signs, as usual in these last half dozen or so polls, of a close finish. Chaffinch calls me early for oats to keep his bright breast in the pink, but no dawn chorus at all. 'Have no fear O have no fear the flowers will bloom another year.'

3 May At last a gold crown to gild the icy-breathing winds. Yellow-tipped willows flick and sway, ash buds enlarge, I deal with dandelions, wonder, pray, unsay the thought that so was dear in other days it too seemed a gold irradiant defence against cold and cruelty.

4–5 May The small wails of a missel-thrush in the Warrior had something approaching a human note in them. I looked up at the gray bird with splendid speckled breast and knew grief in its heart and the cause. Again and again it swooped down on the marauding jackdaws, the outcries and threatening wings were of no avail. The sorrowing one returned again to its piteous lament on a gray bough of the ancient tree. I also felt smitten as I heard, and saw on the ground a daw with the bright orange egg yolk in its beak: and I remembered the birds described in Homer wailing for their pillaged young ones. Cuckoo's call from afar has at last reached my ears. Snow and rain alternate with sunshine; the sun rose and set with hue and light beams as of a liquid ruby, rich and crimson, staining with red shower that fell as the lower rim touched the ridge. I have been typing Tony's writing on Will and feel his life is still living, this very now.

16 May Sudden sunless utter change in the nature May shows, bestows upon earth, upon us who name the fickle month after Mary. A ten degrees drop in temperature proves this. 'However' my spirits are raised by reading an essay in *Theology* by a man, Stephen Platten, much influenced by Whitehead: even before the philosopher's name was mentioned a sense of strength came to me; later the paradoxical definitions that so oddly elate and liberate were introduced. Preparing an apple-cake for the first time and finding it baked successfully, a Cornish dish, causes the lord to sit lightly on his throne.

17 May A blustering May day, the wind so violent the clouds so swift the light changes with every breath, sky-scape and earth surface with each flick of those eyelids that in an hour or two after death will have their delicate hard-worked muscles set.

7 June Exceeding greenery. Curious awareness as orientation arranges cerebral sensation. When I have travelled in a certain direction from the centre, and returned, the preparation for this with its mild sense of exploration, the harvest, the ensemble, leave this mode and no other: a reformation to an inward and mental liberation for a little while, from the comparisons, the ego's calculations, by means of which we are adjusted and mostly find it inevitable to live our day by day nature ... 'new horizons of thought affect everything which comes after ...'

8 June All day grizzling and gray, drizzling and *damped down*. I always find a childish satisfaction in seeking for the Lectionary readings in a week, as this Whit one, when each day the appointed verses are in different, sometimes out-of-the-way, Books. There is an element of being an explorer and also of being led by the spirit in unknown ways, or wildernesses where no way is ... Strange how desirable the boundless can be to the soul while it is in a body supported by the concrete, near, familiar world: weather, apparel, furniture, birds that sing and wing upon rainy air; how terrifying a void when these 'buffers' are withdrawn, life is alone, left in one, known naked an instant ... give us this day our daily bread.

10 June Barnaby Bright's eve but no sunlight; the dragging gray day, sultry and chilly, dissolves in soundless rain. I saw the full moon rise last evening and heard a distant cuckoo, after re-reading 'The Scholar Gypsy' and 'Thyrsis'. Dyspepsia or something akin to it has plagued me for a week. The pain begins with sinister regularity an hour or two after each meal in the pit of the stomach, spreads slowly to the whole abdomen and continues until the next time for eating: an unwelcome harassing disorder which I've not suffered before, except briefly and accountably. Starlings again reassemble in flocks, my cock chaffinch sings as if he would not soon close his steel-gray bill. The late whitethorn bloom is at its height but there is no warmth to loose the heady scent. Whitsun past it is all Trinity to autumn.

17 June The only event in which to live unspied on is the quiet mind which keeps invisible record neither in place, as a diary page, nor in time, as measured by dial hand or gnomon: and that act in process is only while consciousness and control remain. Then, no doubt, all that is deliberately not communicated will be cried from the housetops and there will be none to hear, heed or care. The dyspepsia (if so it is) is renewed regularly and daily, although at night there is usually only a brief spell. The day's routine pain begins about 10 a.m., is at its worst from about 5 to 7 in the evening. The chaffinch continues to sing all day, often from the roof ridge a perch excellent for sound. I see no other chaffinch near.

21 June To write this how I wait all the twelve months the three hundred and how many days: hot hay-making weather, the early daylight hours before the world wakes are hid in the secret of his presence, birds slip through green arcades, pause in caves built by leaf darkness. The silent flycatchers are there, vanish at an eyebeam into the unvisited shed, pass across the grove as though to Africa. A swift that has stooped to the eaves flickers up and out.

23 June The longest day began with a cuckoo duet in changed tune, one in the top of the many-keyed ash tree fled on a broken note with a small dark bird, a speck, in hot pursuit mocked with that wanton chuckle, all duties plucked. Every day for me is Valentine's, lyric lark high up invisible in the garden air space, the gray whispering dove (my eye falls on now) parading on pink toes the metalled road, and from the tail catches a silent swift quitting its chink wide-winged.

9 July Grace in the flycatchers' farewell to their nesting roof so poignant to my spirit. I read Wyat's poems in an utter and most penetrating anguish pierced by the flight first one then the second with dip and silver turn from my clothes line to take an insect before the black wall below the slit by which they had entered hourly for half a century of days. Now the sky is slaty, drizzle chills the hills, the greenery is solid. A seagull returns to inland pastures, rooks with gaps in tail and wing caw overhead.

13 July Danger is 'in' the new and in beauty according to the Greek poets: danger is what life is about, shouts Marian to her grandson Christopher. For this my mind is too negative, oppressed by the summer foliage, a weight on the murky atmosphere, black absolutely as the Africans have it when green is rich and strong. Still, thought makes leaps in many directions, may enjoy the sensation in mid nought with no support, the being surprised, the rush of 'undifferentiated energy'; even the painful *reculer pour sauter mieux*. A pilgrimage last evening in dim old sunlight to the Stour by the seventeenth-century mill with still a lingering smell of meal at the chained-up wooden door; the weirs' revivifying airs on the cheek, arrowheads.

15 July Perfectly dry hot and sun-warmed all through – African; cars and motor-cycles stream and roar by, consuming the oil from the earth's bowels: 'when birds are faint with the hot sun and hide in cooling trees'. Distance mystic blue. In reading Wyat's poems from the Devon collection I am aware of the difference on my palette; more variety as it were and the arid love exchange I feel in reading the so artificial authentic verses is absent. For my second book for afternoon meditation I have returned to Pindar, perhaps for his Orphic strain.

17 July So slumbrous a morning the gray cloudbank rests on the rise, the far side of the Vale, in the likeness of a mountain; land and cloud equally insubstantial and dreamy, and the mind abstracted the eye is lifted upon them. The idea of being strangers and pilgrims is a difficult one; to have meaning there must be people and places 'in one stay', a stable inhabited earth over which pilgrims and the homeless stray: yet in reality nothing is 'in one stay'. Transitoriness in the nature of being is meaningless without what is taken-to-be lasting. It is partly a matter of the different pace of objects in process, gauged by the subject in its own way: or relativity.

19 July   Thursday. A mark on the silent flow, nights and days in patient passage, so long unarrested so always about to end. In comparatively secure regular lives conflict begins with desire for surprise and dread lest the pattern, the received harmony, be broken. The two mental poles – within time, without time – play and byplay between them; or the moment in and out of time. The clay vessel overbrimming and all but drained and dry. Seven swifts swirl across the muffling gray from the ether above eternally clear, leave all bare, one redescends, edges into the hole. Again nothing, no event. How are the young birds fed when entrance and departure from the crevice is so rare? Yet droppings build up below.

2 August   Cool gray-gold blowy morning; with a shriek the wild swifts dash out of the ether, winged beings not of this cosmos for all they share their holes with sparrows. Why, I ask myself, as I pounce on my Bible each morning to read the appointed passages, does this sense of austere satisfaction spread over my mind? And the immediate answer, before more considered analysis, is magic. The whole lordly volume is an incantation worked out on an instrument of many strings, or many stringed instruments. The reading is a ceremony. The metaphors liberate, there is certainty, concrete reality, each footstep taken on the firmset earth which does not become empty in the rush of transcendence.

4 August   Lovely summer sky. Somewhat (although I hope not obviously) oppressed by the terror by night mentioned by the Psalmist for the last three nights. Partly the scaffolding darkening the window, and all the word scaffold suggests, may have started this hitherto not often lived-through horror. First night ultimate black black horror; nothingness. Next night loss of individuality, no person, or as I once heard in a dream long years ago, 'you are returning to the anonymity of the skeleton'. Not returning now though, rather never having been anything else. Last night while my body lay quietly at rest the threat, the terror, was entirely mental; mind emptiness that appeared close to madness. Madness maybe as escape, for there was not the dread of such a state as used to on occasion beset me. May this evil be exorcised by expression here, by the recollection of Beethoven's sonata for horn and piano and the *Winter Reise* I listened to for a whole hour afterwards, sung by Peter Pears. His singing meant much to Sylvia in her last years and I thought as I listened under the buddleia, that she may have heard this same recording. Meanwhile the tiles are piled up in the sky on the scaffold planks; the workmen were chased off the roof by cold rain yesterday. Mother's staircase, passage and spare room ceiling are in danger of collapsing, and her treasured scrubbed staircase is pronounced unsafe, from dry rot, and the roof rafters to be unsafe, from worms' borings.

6 August   Our jobbing builder, 'one of God's unfortunates', as a woman in the village dubbed him, arrived early, knocked down the chimney and departed till late afternoon when he returned to nail a piece of ceiling board on part of Mother's passage and began in the rain to rebuild the chimney, pausing over a cup of tea to describe his whiskey drinking feats to Gerard. Neo-platonists, idealists, have the illusion that the one safe, that is controllable, 'position' in life is the mind. The Christian doctrine of the resurrection seeks to overcome the body/soul dualism. The immortality of the soul *on its own* will not do. Transfiguration. The rain descends on our unroofed dwelling –

> The soul's dark cottage, battered and decayed,
> Lets in new light through chinks that Time has made:
> Stronger by weakness, wiser men become
> As they draw near to their eternal home.
> Leaving the old, both worlds at once they view
> That stand upon the threshold of the new.   (Edmund Waller)

The philosophers declare all time is equidistant from eternity ... so what of pilgrimage?

9 August   Boisterous west wind all day making a scattering in the garden; apples and pears pelting down, plants twirled all ways. Tremendous discussions concerning scaffolding with brief spells of violent hammering overhead. Now, very now at the seventh hour, warm sun spreads among the vaporous clouds. Quiescence and quintessence sum up in age the heart's desire; but how to define the human personality, that mystery which in the occident seems to be the value, the reality in relativity?

14 August   Chronicle continues with a return of the gales. In the night the ceiling descended in Mother's bedroom, all but upon her. She did not even call us to her aid after the startling crash but moved into the next room. So now follows another work for the builders who do not work. Disaster also (as I've just heard) for the Fastnet yacht race, the largest rescue operation since the war, on the south coast. Ouspensky's *Fourth Way* has steadied me many times over the years in *Sturm und Drang* in my backward-looking life.

16 August   Yachts are still being sought over the wide surface of the sea. Meanwhile gale warnings for tonight again all along the south coast. The roof further opened today by the workmen is causing, in this streaming rain, considerable flooding in the cottage. I write to a dripping drumming constant but irregular water music and keep turning my head as new tappings promise new unwanted entrances.

18 August   Amethystine sunshine to make gentle the breath from the north-west that causes a somewhat steely white light. A sense of a return to sanity after the indoor deluge but the dilatory workmen achieve small advance. Charles Lock was here yesterday afternoon and appeared happy and more at ease than on his previous visit. When you write you see with the mind first, in reading, with the eyes.

23 August   Storms, rain with a thunderclap, floors and ceilings gone in Mother's house; both were a kind of honeycomb in wormy ancient woodwork although this she still does not quite believe. She has moved into my house while the men demolish, and soon we trust, begin to rebuild.

31 August   So with a wholly dull day this plastic-coloured month concludes. Hammers and saw next door this evening; water gone for three hours. Gerard gone to Weymouth for the Powys Conference. Glen had tea with Mother under the acacia in the warmth yesterday, and where now are the many butterflies? There was a letter from Peter by the afternoon post which cheered us. He sent an ancient air mail writ by Katie, Gertrude and Lucy to Marian in 1949 describing L.A.P.'s* return from Africa to Chydyok. Katie at Chydyok lit a candle in the window. Gertrude went to London and saw the ship steaming up the Thames. Mother wrote of smelling the flowers in that April long ago.

18 September   Sun gone out of my world; wind, drizzle, grayness instead; this only today. Kathleen dug all her potatoes, a fine crop, sound and clean. Gerard and I went to Sherborne for my 'day out'. Afterwards to Nether Cerne for our cheese and biscuits under a mighty horse-chestnut in the avenue. Seagulls endlessly gliding over the river, the swift clear current. Hills blank with burnt stubble; a flock of sheep rounded by a pair of collies. Young soldiers with maps walking up into the downland that looked African. The dismantled church lonely with broken or loose windows; a haunted place. Chiff-chaffs at play in the garden, calling faintly in the willow tree.

21 September St. Matthew – his eve marked by the arrival in Mappowder of Gilfrid and Anne,* blue-eyed *ravissante*; his day by a clear sweet-breathing sunny daybreak. Sirius autumn's herald glittering in dark cherry leaves. Gilfrid's voice as he talked with Mother below so memory-rousing with its own tone and familiar Will undernotes: his face haggard in some lights and pain-ingrained, then again all but unchanged from the boy's on those Uaso Nyiro safaris when he built high-towering fires and fished the river's murky pools for whiskery catfish. In between entrances and exits I listened to *Coriolanus* the proud, and still this morn feel exhilarated by echoes, strong utterances, arrogances, and the fun of the Cockney- or Sussex-voiced Romans. This season and mellow September is full of rewards heaped upon inward and 'Oedipodian' woes. Pain, it struck me, as I moved first today, is 'totally silent in itself'.

26 September Storm winds, soft airs drift in from the sea, rain drips in from the unfinished roof; the strangle-hold the builders keep upon us while they suggest ever more inside necessary repairs and milk us weekly and promise weekly that the work will be completed in two days, tomorrow or the day after ... Gilfrid gone, his visit a most happy one for us all. He and Mother had an afternoon and evening in Montacute in bland early-autumn sunshine and brooding stillness. Together they visited the tombstone which resisted all the masons' efforts to take it from the ground, which they'd intended to do in order to restore it in their workshop. They had to do what they could to the slab of Ham Hill where it stood, firm-set, as L.A.P. exulted, by A.R.P. She saw her own name also carved upon the stone's rear below Will's, by her own wish, so that this worn memorial need not be disturbed again; until, shall I dare to say, the last trump. And in her bath that evening as she lay in the warm water she said aloud to herself, 'I'm a happy Lucy.' 'Our passions are ourselves.'

19 October Today I have been at home for a whole week after my stay in hospital and sudden operation. An internal experience somewhat akin to Judas Iscariot's when his bowels gushed out, overtook me on the evening of 2 October, with great agony, in spite of the doctor's attention, continued all that night. The ambulance took me away at about mid-day and soon afterwards I was put out of sense and feeling for four hours. A week of drip and water followed in the public ward with noisy nights, wild animal nightmares and perpetual thirst. The kindness of the nurses redeemed all, and the wide sunny south-facing window. The fellow patients, a cross-section of the local inhabitants, provided a kind of entertainment in those days without books or liveliness of mind. A woman dying of lung cancer was in the bed directly facing me, her face remains imprinted on my mind, prepared for it by some half forgotten illustration in a Victorian children's storybook. One night in the dimly lit ward a staff sister with difficulty removed her rings; I heard the whispers ... engagement, valuable ... Two nights later, when I had been moved to the convalescent bay, she died. Gerard visited me most faithfully, driving over 20 miles to Weymouth and back, and bringing Mother on my birthday and on the day before I left hospital. Privately in my curtained cell I received Holy Communion in thankfulness for my swift recovery. Almost every day this month has had its meed of sunshine; sweet-tempered weather. Yesterday, St. Luke's Day, each hour was sunny, warm and healing. Now all recedes; my long limbs feel less like those of a helpless cranefly or daddy-long-legs, although energy remains low voltage as they say. Below, surprise visitors, all but unknown Norfolk cousins talk to Mother and Gerard. Mother said she was eight years old when she saw the lady last.

20 October   Day by day customs resumed: bread-making, prayers; watching, after my Orphic nature, dawn and early touches of colour over Bulbarrow's ancient sky. A low arc from hill outline to church tower barred with short cloudlets to resemble rungs of a ladder; a smudge of smoky vapour in the clearness below; hoot owl and one that shrieked composed this daybreak. Jupiter high in the east adorns the heavens. A few nights ago we all three listened to George Steiner's first Hannah Arendt lecture on *Antigone* and the Book of Job. The constant Jewish or Biblical theme: 'we are strangers and pilgrims'. Steiner's conclusion – man is not wanted on earth. Or 'is not a very welcome guest in the house of being.'

2 November   All Souls. A perfect calm sun-blessed day with a golden dawn, a gray nightfall. I recollect moments of my marriage day and in the autumn days after, before Gerard went back to Africa; how he would set my back to a tree trunk so that I stood as though ingrown to some tall tree in the wood behind the house at Shootash, and on the path that went up the steep to Cae Coed.

4 November   Blowy, gray with rare transparent spaces in the cloudscape, tinted towards sundown with vague hues, as I watched from the rush mat. One flock of seagulls moved southwards into the not cold wind. My thoughts have been somewhat haunted since that solitary communion by the sop with the strong association that word has with the betrayal, the exit into night of the one who received it. Also there are those pink pinks with crimson blotches, sops-in-wine, the flowers of paramours, as Llewelyn likes to remind his readers. A point where the bread and wine of remembrance are received in the form of a sop.

13 November   How wealthy modern states would be were weapons of war not essential; the whole world now is interlocked in a merciless struggle concerned with food, arms and trade in which the space for manoeuvring is fractional as well as being infinitely complex.

1 December   Translucent twilight sky when the clouds touched with colour dissolved, the great moon rose to shine over all; a mysterious mild soft-breathing beginning to the first winter month so that world news recedes to the mind's fringes, where however, it clings and grimly hovers. In the last two days Mother has crept into her cottage again to explore its newness and regret what's been cleared away, lost, gone astray in the upheaval. For all the careful plans to make the staircase easier for her the steps prove to be both steeper and narrow; more difficult for her to negotiate. The work of moving in again and replacing the innumerable objects of so many years will be slow.

2 December   'At the round earth's imagined corners blow/Your trumpets, Angels, and arise, arise/From death, you numberless infinities/Of souls and to your scattered bodies go', so John Donne in his second 'Holy Sonnet'; so all this dark day blow the trumpet winds in strong blasts; and beside this my mind sets 'John Donne arriving in heaven', the title of Stanley Spencer's painting. 'Here on this lowly ground teach me ...'

3 December   The thin red line from waist to mons veneris, as I see it in my bath, reminds me of Waterloo, and surely my life depended on this cut as Europe's did on Wellington's. The full moon that shone on me early today is risen far to the north and the sun from sanguine bannered rise shone in each brief daylight hour. Each afternoon Mother continues to re-enter her rooms and seems to grow more used to the changes.

4 December   Gusty, with no touch of sharpness, rather softness, soughing, receding as wind music to fringe silence, reaching in again with deep troughs, reverberant. Winter drive to Sherborne; trees quite bare, pricked out on the return drive on a torn yellowish banner in the west. Kath brought Mother blue violets, most sweet, with three tiny primroses among them. Letter from Gertrude with some words about

Timothy Hyman's exhibition at the I.C.A. In the evening Gerard played *The Bird* for me, that most perfect witty quartet to my ear; peerless Haydn. Woke a night or two past to a wondering what is the soul? The very question eternal. Later I decided: Desire. With desire I have desired ...

10 December Wind and rain, wild tempestuous weather since I last wrote; electricity gone last evening for three hours when the wind made a sudden swing from the south-east to north-west, swept the starry heaven clear of cloud and cast a tree upon the wires. The Piddle is so low nevertheless, a series of puddles; two moorhens near Alton were running about the road in search of food. Green fields with grazing sheep and dazzling gulls among them, or floating above like sailboat flotillas. Gerard and I went to Dorchester; I felt the town to be sad, if not drab, people looking shabby; yet the 'spending spree' is said to be greater than ever. A kind of faster faster madness possesses the land. Louise sent me a particularly fine carving from Chartres, haunting, a left-handed Pythagoras.

11 December Night bombarded with the year's fiercest gale. Gerard and I saw this morn, on our way to Hazelbury, the huge half-hollow willow stump left of the ivy-hung tree that fell on the electric wires. Even then less than half the road had been cleared for traffic. The holly opposite has its coloured lights; for three nights now they have winked in the wind. Jupiter, Mars and Moon kept tryst in the Warrior at daybreak. Today, with a gentling wind, sunshine, wide blue sky, Mother returned to her beloved cottage. Her decision to do this was clear and firm although we wished her to stay with us for the winter. The two Kathleens helped gallantly, one in the forenoon, the other from 2 to 4; no easy task for either.

14 December So violent a squall at 5.30 I cowered under my blanket in terror not daring to rise; yet the morning bred faint sunshine among gusts and the rain that returned in mid-afternoon was soft if persistent and vastly darkening. Adventous weather according to my Lectionary readings, if not Apocalyptic. Gerard and I sped into Sherborne in the gloaming. I bought a red torch as I broke my other old friend, also red, last evening; and for a few minutes after, in the warm library, looked at *Country Life* as I like to do to remember my father and Horsebridge; this periodical is unchanged in set-up except for the coloured cover photograph while most of the other papers he would buy are no more. I read last night 'St. Lucy's Nocturne' which is unfailing in giving me cause for awe and praise. How can such poetry be? We listened later to a Mozart flute quartet and a modern one, also thrilling – 'mere breath of flutes at eve, mere seaweed on the shore'. Pensive elegiac mood, wind stirring.

16 December   Sullen sky after the frenzy the elements indulged in; sulky, hangdog, dampish. In the last moment of sleep before rising I saw a pair of yellow furry animals lying along what I took to be branches, apparently legless although they moved about, turned, looked on me – they were at a higher level – and at one another. 'I don't know these animals' I said as I woke. During the morning I took down an already opened packet of tea and saw yellow on a card in it, a card in size like the cigarette cards I collected in childhood. After tipping the tea into a cannister I took the card to examine: Vanishing Wild Life. The two pictures on its face were of monk seals which in colour and shape seemed so closely to resemble my dream creatures. The close-up of the head, dark-eyed and cowled with brown over the yellowish coat, was curiously moving, the expression almost human. I read on the reverse these seals, now reduced in numbers to about 500, lived in the eastern Mediterranean and were first identified by Aristotle. It said as other perils, they were killed by vine-growers who believed they ate their grapes; surely more likely that the vine-dressers wanted to eat the seals?

27 December   St. John's bright beams beaten by gales and torrents unrelenting all the dark daylight hours. Certainly the worst day this year – worst in Wales for twenty years we hear. A weariness upon the spirit at elemental and international violence. It is inclined to be a feature of English weather, this oscillation between stillness that can be oppressive so that one longs for a fresh breath, a stir in the blocked atmosphere, and strong winds, gales, gusts, a thunderous alarming uproar; Zephyrs, I am tempted to say, are the rarest, the most desired visitors. However, the boisterous weather has for some reason set me after five songless months to write two backward-facing poems for creatures. So near year's end there should be another to look to the future, but the only notion that summons is the wind-whirled yew tree I see from my bed.

28 December   The 'demonic' day over and done with, floods and all; this one followed in tenderness with sun, silver seagulls, anchor clouds and grass mossy in richness and hue. The little sparrow without a foot and white feather in her wing, which for the past two years has always been first to take the scattered bread crumbs, is a casualty of the storm. I saw her early on Mother's window-sill puffed out and sick, later on the ground near the kitchen door when she took a brown bread crumb and tried to search for others. Soon after she was dead, lying on her side eyes closed. I took the warm feathery body to the end of the garden and placed it in the hedge near the willow tree. The small enduring creature must have had a narrow escape when first we noticed her, footless and with a bare hurt place in her neck.

29 December Storms, bright white sky, then again blue-black with the shining gulls adrift upon it as souls; spaces for sunshine. Snow in perforated patches by the roadside, on the coarse graveyard grass, remained from the previous week when Gerard and I went to Plush for the memorial service for Anne Jackson. All, however, had gone from the hills and their contours swept the eye from earth to sky in satisfying lines, shaped (one could fancy) by free-breathing winds. But two days left in the last year of the Seventies decade, and I seem to write more daily in this mode of *recueillement* – self-communion. I heard last night a reading, introduced by C. H. Sisson, of poems inspired by Africa by David Wright, kindred visual impressions.

31 December Decades pass as years as one grows old. The year to end the Seventies for ever gave a serene day with sun filtered through thin cloud; moon and Venus faint in mist. The earth rests after floods and whirlwinds in green-ness; cattle appear in the fields, sheep safely graze. The news continues to be all of the Russian invasion in Afghanistan, 30,000 troops are now said to be there. Picture cards of camels from Gilfrid at his International Camel Conference in Khartoum arrived today, posted however in England. He says, 'I have a desire to purchase camels here and walk them to Kenya, a distance of a thousand miles or more'. So in a cloud of memories, farewell.*

these latter days of December. Mother also heard today of the death of an old girlhood friend from the farm called Windmill near Mortimer. The north-wind day is clear and luminous, a robin sang freely at dawn, and now there is a (gibbous) gibbous moon bright and Venus in splendour. The news of Russian troops in thousands being flown into Afghanistan, and Carter's warnings, is alarming; the U.S.A. actions regarding the hostages in Iran remains internationally irreproachable.

31 December 1979. Decades pass as years as one grows old: the year to end the seventies for ever gave a serene day with sun filtered through thin cloud: moon and Venus faint in mist. The earth rests after floods and whirlwinds in green-ness, cattle appear in the fields, sheep safely graze. The news continues to be all of the Russian invasion of Afghanistan, 30,000 troops are now said to be there. Picture cards of camels from Gilpin at his International Camel Conference in Khartoum arrived today, posted however in England. He says "I have a desire to purchase camels here and walk them to Kenya, a distance of a thousand miles or more." So in a cloud of memories — farewell

A page from the Journal for 1979 (reduced)

Notes

1963

3 Jan	Part of the lower farm at Ndere.
16 Jan	Catharine Edith Philippa Powys: aunt of MC.
17 Jan	Theodore Francis Powys (died 1953): uncle of MC.
21 Jan	Retired postwoman.
21 Jan	Francis Powys: son of T. F. Powys.
21 Jan	Isobel Powys Marks: daughter of A. R. Powys, uncle of MC.
21 Jan	Kathleen Ryall: neighbour and friend of Katie Powys.
2 Feb	Rowland George Hounsell Penny (born 16.2.1882, died 2.2.1945).
2 Feb	'night is an everlasting sleep' (Catullus, *Carmina* v).
18 Feb	John Redwood Anderson, the poet.
21 Feb	T. F. Powys.
26 Feb	Rose Dyer: daughter of William Ernest Powys, uncle of MC.
26 Feb	William Ernest Powys: uncle and godfather of MC.
26 Feb	Theodore Powys: son of T. F. Powys. Died in Africa in 1931.
26 Feb	Elizabeth Powys: wife of W. E. Powys.
26 Feb	Charles Powys: son of W. E. Powys.
2 Apr	Gilfrid Powys: son of W. E. Powys.
6 Apr	*The Powys Brothers* [John Cowper Powys, Theodore Francis Powys, and Llewelyn Powys] (1962).
18 May	Phyllis Playter: for over 40 years the companion of J. C. Powys.
18 May	John Cowper Powys: uncle of MC.
18 May	Worked for many years on the Caseys' farm.
8 June	The dogs.
15 June	J. C. Powys.
18 June	Kathleen Vallence: helped MC's mother in the house.
19 June	Gamel Woolsey, the poet and writer: friend of the Powys family.
19 June	Home of J. C. Powys and Phyllis Playter in Blaenau Ffestiniog.
26 June	'Forth he went in silence along the shore of the loud resounding sea' (*Iliad* 1.34).
27 June	Louis Wilkinson, the writer: friend of the Powys family.
27 June	Violet Powys: wife of T. F. Powys.
6 July	Marion Linton: at one time engaged to be married to MC's uncle Llewelyn Powys.
17 July	Valentine Ackland, the poet: friend of the Powys family.
6 Aug	R. Bosworth Smith: author of *Bird Life and Bird Lore* (1905). Lived in Dorset.

Notes 1963–64

13 Aug	Llewelyn Powys (born 13.8.1884, died 2.12.1939): uncle of MC.
13 Aug	Wife of John Redwood Anderson.
21 Aug	Anthony Dyer: husband of Rose, W. E. Powys's daughter.
22 Aug	W. E. Powys's driver.
23 Aug	Gertrude Mary Powys (died 1952): aunt of MC.
29 Aug	David Craig: husband of Delia, Elizabeth Powys's daughter by her first husband.
29 Aug	Farmer and lay reader.
29 Aug	Dorothy Carles: friend of the Powys family. See MC's poem 'For D.F.C.' (*The Clear Shadow*, p. 50). Mother of Richard Carles.
29 Aug	Wife of Charles Powys.
29 Aug	The first farm W. E. Powys acquired in Kenya after World War I.
29 Aug	Frederick Davies: friend of J. C. Powys and Phyllis Playter.
4 Sept	Alyse Gregory: wife of Llewelyn Powys.
4 Sept	John Baring: farm assistant at Ndere.
2 Dec	A study by V. Lossky (1957).
6 Dec	'patience', 'endurance'.

1964

27 Jan	Gertrude [Judith] Shackleton (née Jefferies), the artist. She and Mary became friends when they were in their teens.
2 Feb	'I am a Meru.'
12 Feb	Worked for many years on the Caseys' farm.
12 Feb	'scientist'.
27 Feb	An Arthurian romance by Chrétien de Troyes (12th cent.).
3 Mar	Wife of Gilfrid Powys.
3 Mar	Michael and Francis Dyer: the two eldest sons of Tony and Rose Dyer.
13 Apr	St. Teresa of Avila, the Spanish mystic.
14 Apr	MC always writes 'Wyat' as his name is spelled on his memorial tablet in Sherborne Abbey: 'Wyat resteth here, that quick could never rest.'
14 Apr	'in him was life' (John 1.4).
18 May	Albert Reginald Powys (died 16 July 1936): uncle of MC.
5 June	Christopher Gibson: leased part of The Beale farm in 1964, first with his partner, Martin Becker, then alone. In 1969 he leased the whole Beale farm.
22 June	Vera Wainwright: artist and poet. She came to live in Mappowder to be near her friend T. F. Powys.
28 June	Dr. Samuel Jackson: last Rector of Mappowder.
6 July	Yvonne Mahuzies: friend of the Powys family.
15 July	C. A. Johns, *Flowers of the Field* (1925).
2 Aug	Gerard Casey's eldest sister.
13 Aug	Llewelyn Powys.
31 Aug	Neighbouring farmer: had bought a part of The Beale farm.
4 Oct	Neighbouring farmer.

14 Dec	Third son of Tony and Rose Dyer.
18 Dec	Catharine Donne (née Johnson): one of MC's great-aunts.
22 Dec	Nickname for Mbui Manyara, meaning 'the long one'.
22 Dec	R. G. Collingwood, *The New Leviathan* (1942).
22 Dec	'constraint', 'necessity'.
24 Dec	'blameless', 'noble', 'honourable'.
26 Dec	Family name for Llewelyn Powys.

1965

7 Jan	David Craig.
10 Mar	C. M. Doughty, *Travels in Arabia Deserta* (1888).
12 Mar	One of the horses.
20 Mar	St. John of the Cross, *Ascent of Mount Carmel*.
31 July	Translated J. C. Powys's *Autobiography* into French.
3 Aug	MC's historical novel about the Crusades. Unpublished.
5 Aug	Prehistoric site, thought to have been a hunting-ground of *homo erectus*.
23 Aug	Gerard Casey's mother.
25 Nov	Son and daughter of Canon Theophilus, Rector of King's Somborne near Horsebridge in MC's childhood. Mary, David and Angela did lessons together under the Canon's tutorship.
26 Nov	Rosemary Davidson: daughter of R. A. (Reggie) and Edith Penny, uncle and aunt of MC.
20 Dec	Cattle traders.
29 Dec	Wife of Canon Theophilus.

1966

14 Jan	Littleton Charles Powys (died 1955): uncle of MC. Headmaster of Sherborne Preparatory School from 1905 to 1923.
7 Apr	Isobel Powys Marks had moved to Mappowder in 1967.
8 Apr	J. C. Powys's house in up-state New York.
2 May	Kathleen Ryall.
2 May	An isolated farmhouse on the downs near East Chaldon: one half was for many years the home of Gertrude and Katie Powys, the other of Llewelyn Powys and his wife Alyse Gregory.
2 May	Wife of the local farmer James Cobb.
16 May	Collared doves first came into southern England around this time.
18 May	Francis Powys owned a bookshop in Hastings.
3 June	Cousin of Rose Dyer.
7 June	Sylvia Townsend Warner, the writer and poet. She and Valentine Ackland were living at Maiden Newton, Dorset.
11 June	*Sir Gawain and the Green Knight* (14th cent.).
14 June	Kathleen Vallence.
19 June	Oliver Wilkinson.
30 June	Plotinus: *Enneads*, translated by Stephen Mackenna, with an Introduction by Paul Henry, S.J.

Notes 1966–69 226

7 July	'Eden' (*The Clear Shadow* p. 36).
28 Aug	The little church of St. Andrew at Winterbourne Tomson had been restored by Isobel's father, the architect A. R. Powys. He was buried there in 1936.
28 Aug	Gertrude Shackleton.
9 Dec	Eleanor Walton: daughter of A. R. Powys by his second wife.
21 Dec	Sally Jones (née Cornish): a friend. See MC's poem 'Sally's Dream' (*The Clear Shadow*, p. 153).

1967

14 Feb	Low thorn bush scrub.
18 Aug	*A Notebook on William Shakespeare* (1948).
19 Aug	'I am'.
2 Sept	Tony Dyer.
7 Oct	A farm assistant.
4. Dec	'for we have the mind of Christ' (1Cor.II.16).

1968

11 Jan	Francis Powys had become the new owner of the cottage.
12 Jan	A collection of poems selected by Walter de la Mare (1939).
13 Jan	Edith Penny: wife of R. A. Penny, brother of MC's father.
4 July	Katey Pagerey-Grey (née Grey): daughter of Peter Powys Grey.
4 July	Peter Powys Grey: son of Emily Marian Powys, aunt of MC.
31 Aug	Florida Scott-Maxwell.
17 Sept	'excellence', 'nobility'.
2 Oct	MC was herself left-handed.
6 Nov	A volume of poetry by T. S. Eliot (1943).
11 Nov	Gertrude M. Powys.
12 Nov	Woodbrooke College: Quaker Adult Education Centre.

1969

28 Jan	John XIII–XIX.
9 Apr	MC's historical novel based on the life of Plotinus.
20 Apr	When MC first went out to Kenya she was suffering from tuberculosis: the illness was brought under control, but remained a health problem throughout her life.
20 Apr	The fourth and last child of Tony and Rose Dyer.
21 Apr	Provincial Commissioner.
24 Apr	The Revd Austin Johnson: cousin of MC's mother.
28 June	See MC's poem 'T.F.P.' (*The Clear Shadow*, p. 174).
28 June	See note to 26 June 1963.
12 July	One of Plato's *Socratic Dialogues*.
19 July	B. Russell, *A History of Western Philosophy* (1946).
21 Oct	G. S. Kirk and J. E. Raven, *The Presocratic Philosophers* (1957).
28 Nov	The Caseys' accountant.
5 Dec	A. E. Taylor, *Commentary on Plato's Timaeus* (1928).

5 Dec	Huw Menai, *The Simple Vision* (1945).
18 Dec	'On Well-Being' (Plotinus: *Ennead* 1.4).
26 Dec	A novel by Louis Marlow [Wilkinson] published in 1930.

1970

3 Jan	Gertrude Mary Powys.
3 Jan	Francis Dyer: godson of Gerard and Mary Casey.
15 Jan	Friend of the Powys family.
12 Feb	Sir James George Frazer, *The Golden Bough* (1890).
23 Feb	J. C. Powys.
4 Mar	See Mary Casey, *The Clear Shadow*, p. 74.
11 Mar	'soul'.
18 Mar	Emily Marian Powys: aunt of MC.
21 Apr	A tragedy by Euripides.
13 May	Llewelyn Powys, *The Twelve Months* (1936).
5 June	Tomb in Mappowder churchyard, which carries the inscription: 'Robert Davis, son of Robert and Mary Davis, died August 1726, aged 19'.
21 June	Giles Davidson: godson of Gerard and Mary Casey.
29 June	Dr. Charles Smith: friend of T. F. Powys.
25 July	W. E. Powys's last dog.
7 Oct	Dorothy Carles.
8 Oct	Rembrandt's 'Titus'.

1971

6 Jan	W. H. Blake: headmaster of Sherborne Preparatory School, when W. E. Powys was a pupil there.
23 Feb	'Full Circle' (*The Clear Shadow* p. 29).
28 May	Mabel Powys: wife of L. C. Powys.
28 May	Littleton Charles Powys.
9 July	'mighty, mysterious Love'.
9 July	Daughter of the scientist Sir Francis Galton.
17 July	R. A. Penny.
23 July	Barbara Kerr, the writer: friend of MC's mother.
4 Aug	'spectacle', 'speculation', 'theorem'.
4 Aug	Mary Barham Johnson: cousin of Lucy Amelia Penny.
25 Aug	Peg Manisty: cousin of Valentine Ackland.
19 Sept	Old apple tree in MC's garden.
2 Oct	Poem by Robert Frost.

1972

11 Jan	Cathy Lentz: a friend. See MC's poem 'Upanishad' *(The Clear Shadow*, p. 46).
2 Feb	Margaret Casey.
10 Mar	Son of David Craig.
7 June	Theodora Johnson: sister of MC's maternal grandmother.

Notes 1972–75

14 June	The house where the Revd Charles Francis Powys, grandfather of MC, had lived with his eldest daughter Gertrude after his retirement.
24 June	*The Cambridge History of Later Greek and Early Medieval Philosophy*, edited by A. H. Armstrong (1967).
16 July	A. N. Whitehead, *Process and Reality* (1929).

1973

25 Jan	John Donne and Jonathan Swift.
1 Feb	A Mountain in the Northern Frontier District of Kenya.
14 Feb	The house in Somerset where MC's godmother Monica Blake used to live.
10 Mar	Wife of Francis Powys.
5 May	Daughter of Yvonne Mahuzies.
12 May	J. C. Powys.
23 June	A play by Sophocles.
1 July	Johann Wolfgang von Goethe, *Poetry and Truth*.
26 Dec	Gertrude Mary Powys.
28 Dec	Wife of Dr. Samuel Jackson.
31 Dec	Karl Barth, *Commentary on the Epistle to the Romans* (1919).

1974

29 July	G. Wilson Knight: scholar, writer and Shakespeare performer.
29 July	The Powys Society annual Conference.
10 Sept	Founder of Enitharmon Press: published a selection of MC's poems in two volumes, *Full Circle* and *Christophorus* (1981).

1975

14 Jan	Littleton Alfred Powys: only son of J. C. Powys. Died in 1954.
9 June	Edward Davies: a friend. First met the Caseys in Africa.
20 July	'[Our days] that perish and are scored to our account' (Martial, *Epigrammata* v 20).
28 July	Dr. Charles Smith.
28 July	E. Bréhier, *Plotin: Ennéades* (1936).
28 July	Timothy Hyman, painter and writer on art: friend of Gerard Casey.
28 July	'swifts'; literally: 'without feet'.
6 Aug	'truth', 'sincerity', but literally: 'unforgetfulness'.
13 Aug	Louise de Bruin: a friend. First met Gerard Casey in Africa.
1 Sept	The T. F. Powys Centenary Conference, held by The Powys Society.
19 Oct	Captain Littleton Albert Powys: brother of the Revd Charles Francis Powys.
1 Nov	'This then is our end and our rest' (Plotinus, *Ennead* VI.9.8, line 43).
11 Nov	Christopher Grey: son of Peter Powys Grey.

13 Dec	'unceasingly'.

1976

12 Feb	Literally: 'doorway'; the arch formed by a group of yellow fever trees behind Spring Cottage.
3 May	A work by Plato.
5 July	'Water is best' (cf. Pindar, ἄριστον μὲν ὕδωρ).
6 Aug	Memorial stone of Llewelyn Powys on the downs near East Chaldon.
6 Aug	House of Dr. Charles Smith.
10 Aug	Jeremy Taylor, *The Rule and Exercises of Holy Living* (1650) and *The Rule and Exercises of Holy Dying* (1651).
10 Aug	Mary Barham Johnson.
25 Dec	R. Hooker, *Treatise on the Laws of Ecclesiastical Polity* (1594).

1977

31 May	'great farewell'.
5 Sept	Glen Cavaliero, *The Rural Tradition in the English Novel 1900–1939* (1977).
1 Oct	E. R. Dodds, *The Greeks and the Irrational* (1950).
19 Oct	'hypodermic syringe'.
24 Nov	'I am'.
3 Dec	Copy of Plato's *Republic*, which had belonged to Dr. Charles Smith.
9 Dec	A natural mark in a flagstone at the west end of the aisle that resembles a lion's footprint.

1978

24 Mar	'El Khalil' (*The Clear Shadow*, p. 87), written on 4 April 1969.
10 June	Jack Clemo, poet and writer. See his poem 'Mappowder Revisited' in *A Different Summer* (Tabb House, 1986).
2 July	See 'Wanderers', 'Windhover', and 'Jessed', *The Clear Shadow*, pp. 180-82.
3 Sept	Sea captain: cousin of MC's father.
7 Nov	'but all the same for that': a favourite expression of J. C. Powys.
7 Nov	Brother of MC's father.

1979

16 Feb	'from the first'.
17 Feb	'well-being'.
31 Aug	Lucy Amelia Penny.
21 Sept	Gilfrid Powys's elder daughter.
31 Dec	Mary Casey died at midnight 30/31 January 1980.